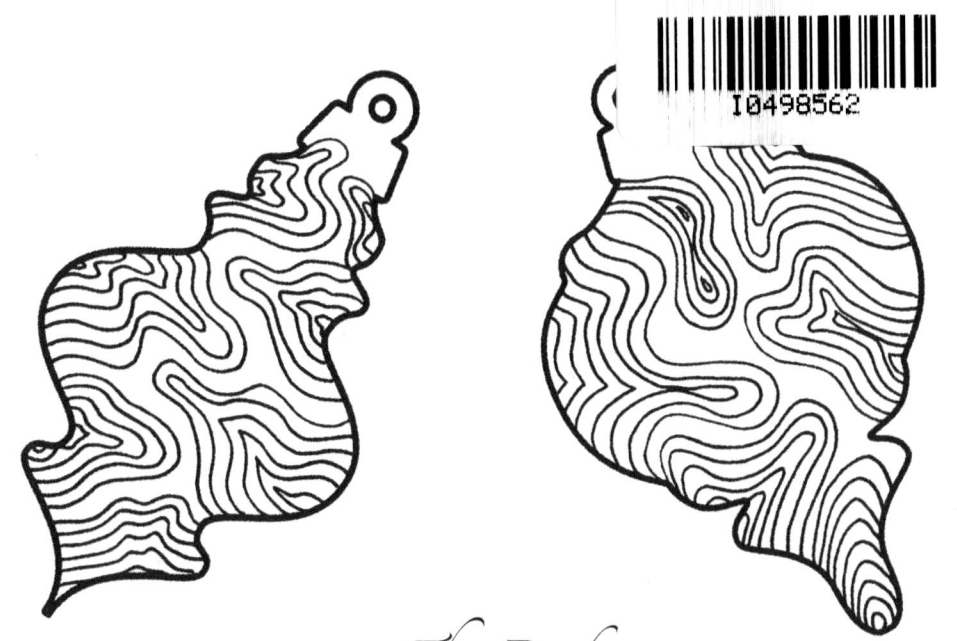

This Book
Belongs to the collection
of

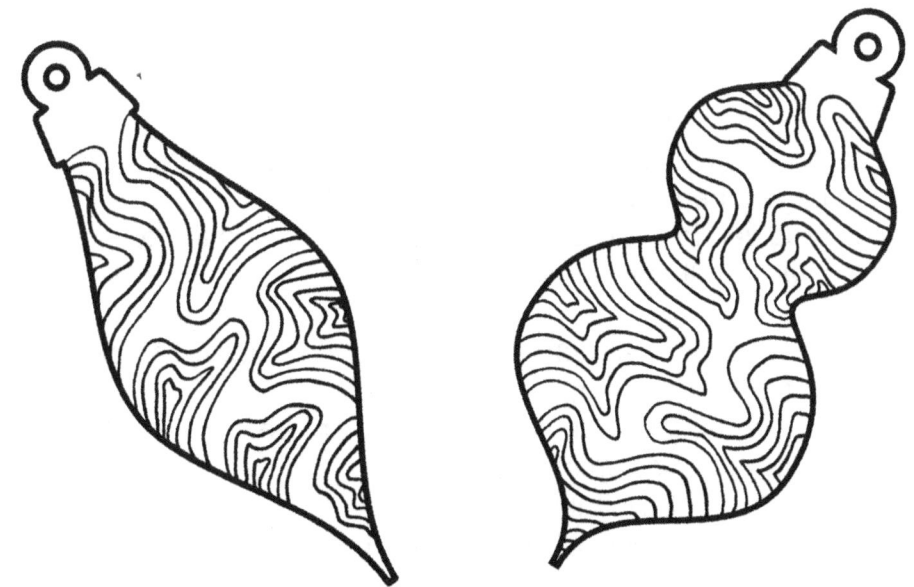

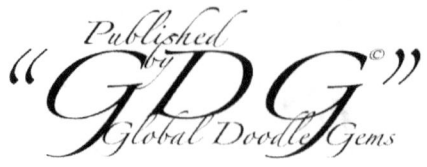

Share your colored versions with us! We love seeing your results and hearing from you we are social!

The Official FB book page, stay on top of what we have in the works!
www.facebook.com/globaldoodlegems
The Community group, share your colored pages, meet the artists, enjoy exclusive freebies, take
part in community Charity books and so much more......
www.facebook.com/groups/globaldoodlegems/
Follow us on Twitter.... @GlobalDoodlegem
We are on Instagram too
@globaldoodlegems for instagram
...and if you are not social like that we have a blog
globaldoodlegems.wordpress.com

Copyright © 2016 Global Doodle Gems
All rights are reserved by Global Doodle Gems.
Duplication of pages for personal use are allowed. You are invited to color the pages then scan/post
your coloured versions to social networks, mentioning the book title and author/artist (Global Doodle
Gems).
All artwork and images are protected by copyright laws. This book or any portion thereof may not,
otherwise, be reproduced and/or distributed or transmitted without the express written permission of
the artist/publisher of Global Doodle Gems.
All of us from the Global Doodle Gems wish you a colortastic time and look forward to seeing your
wonderful color results online!

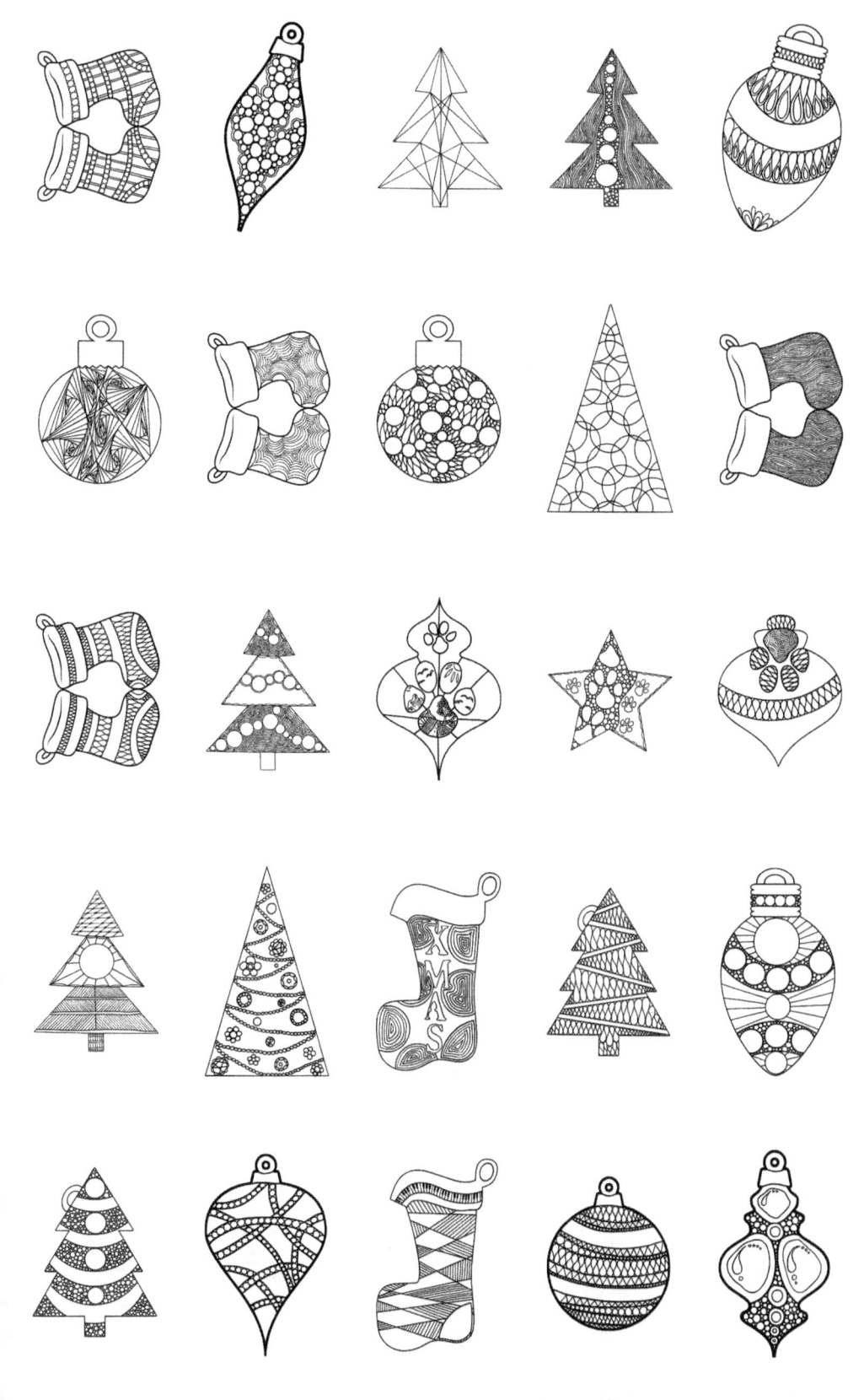

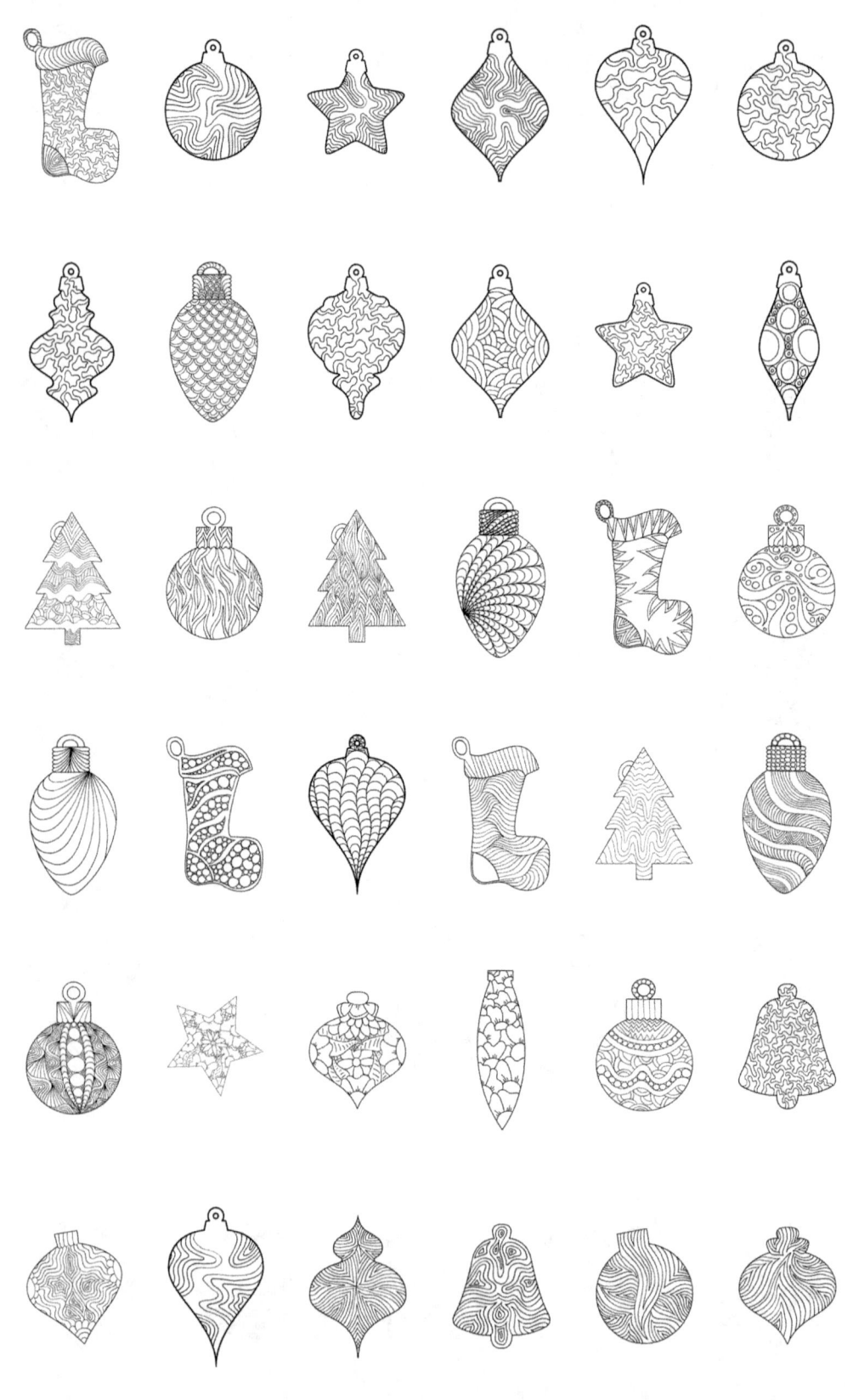

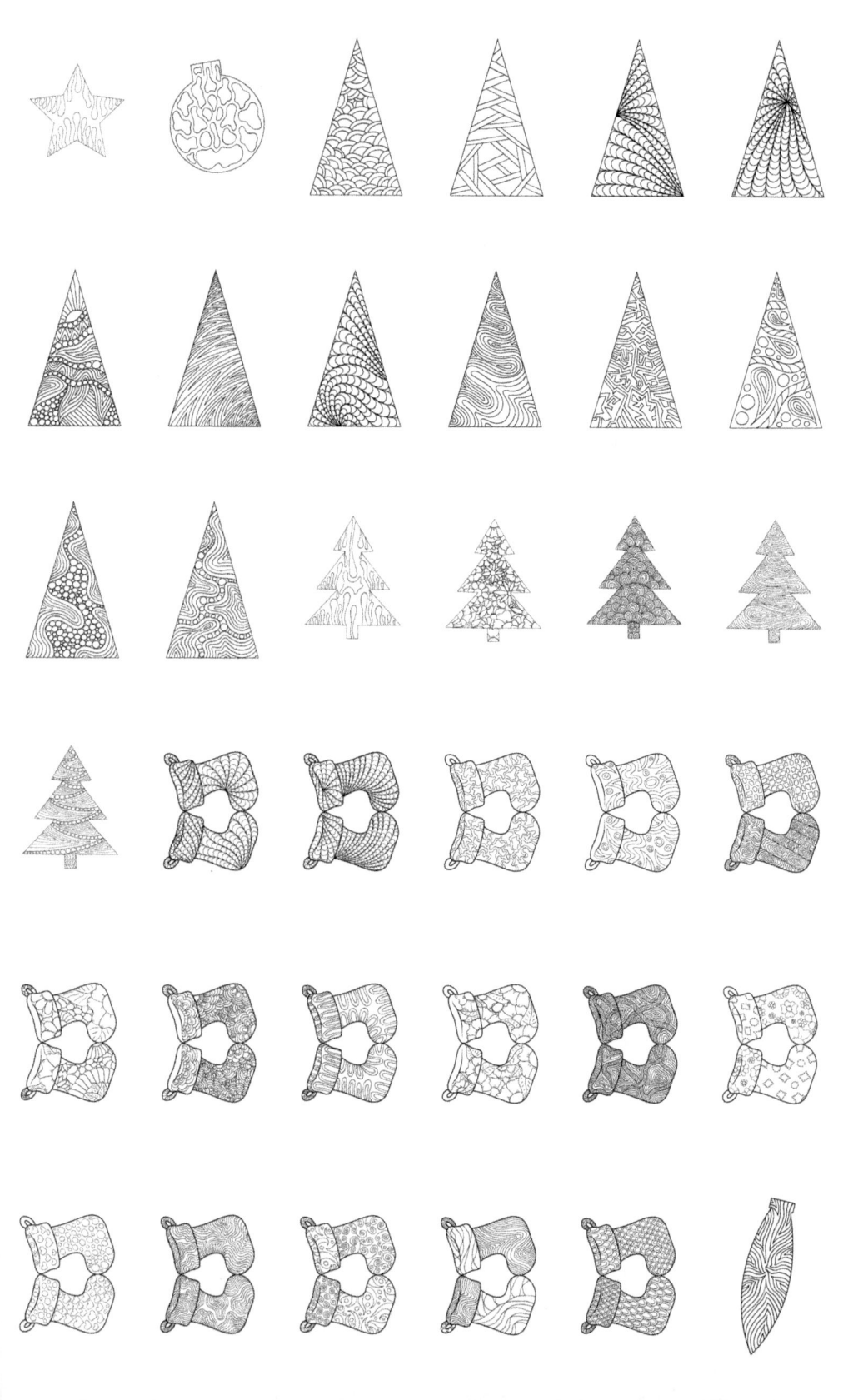

76 Designs from Maria Wedel

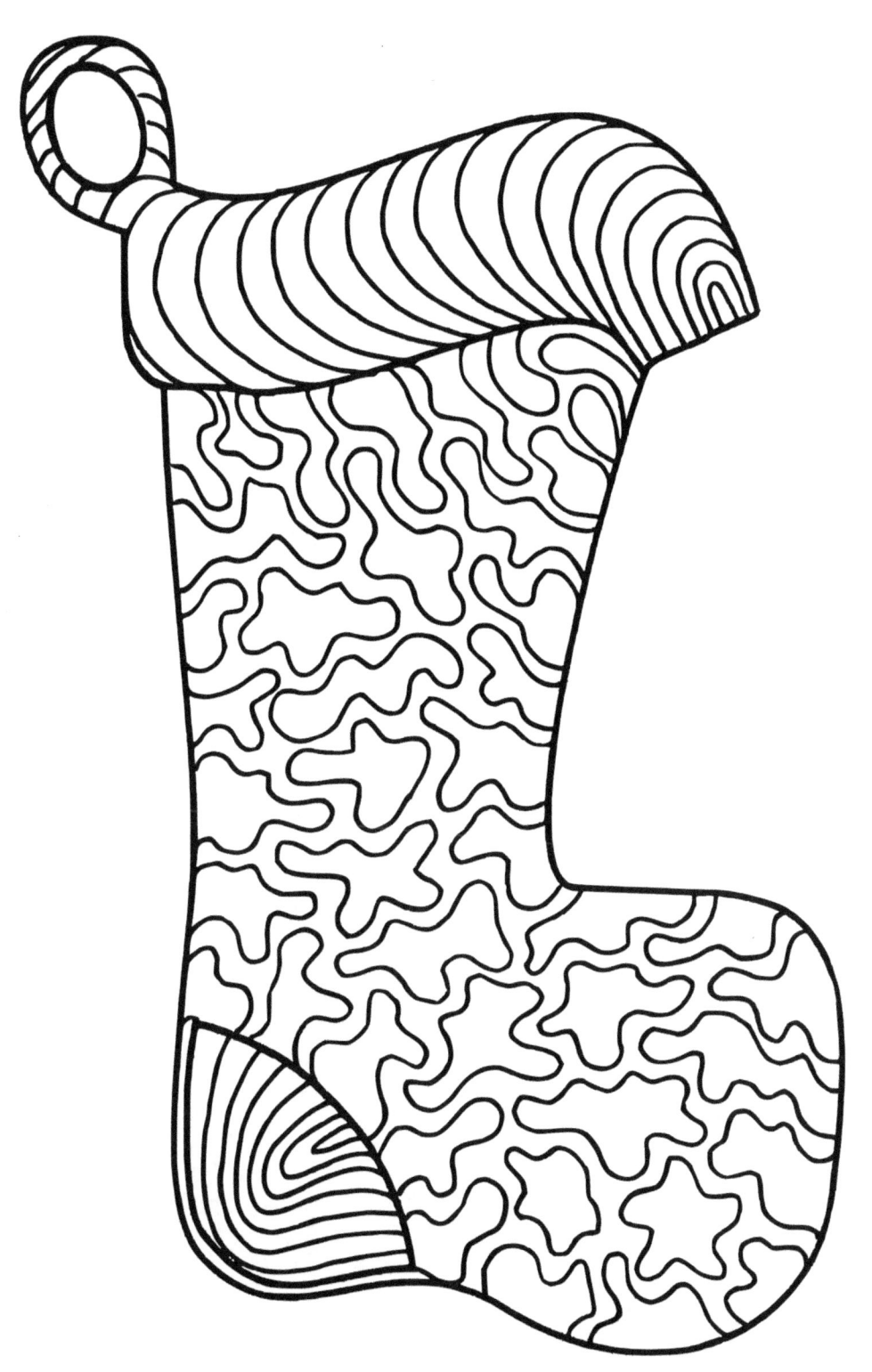

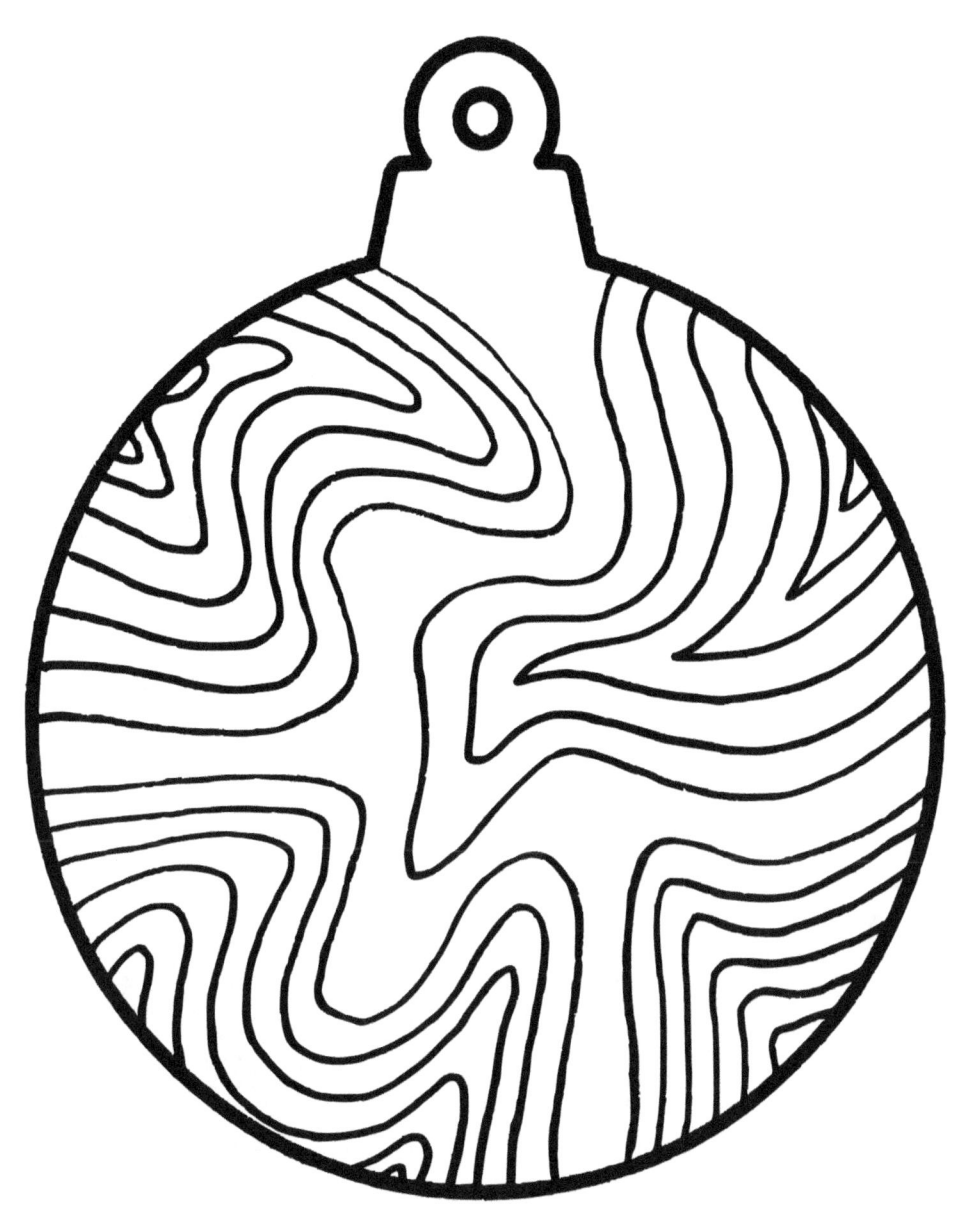

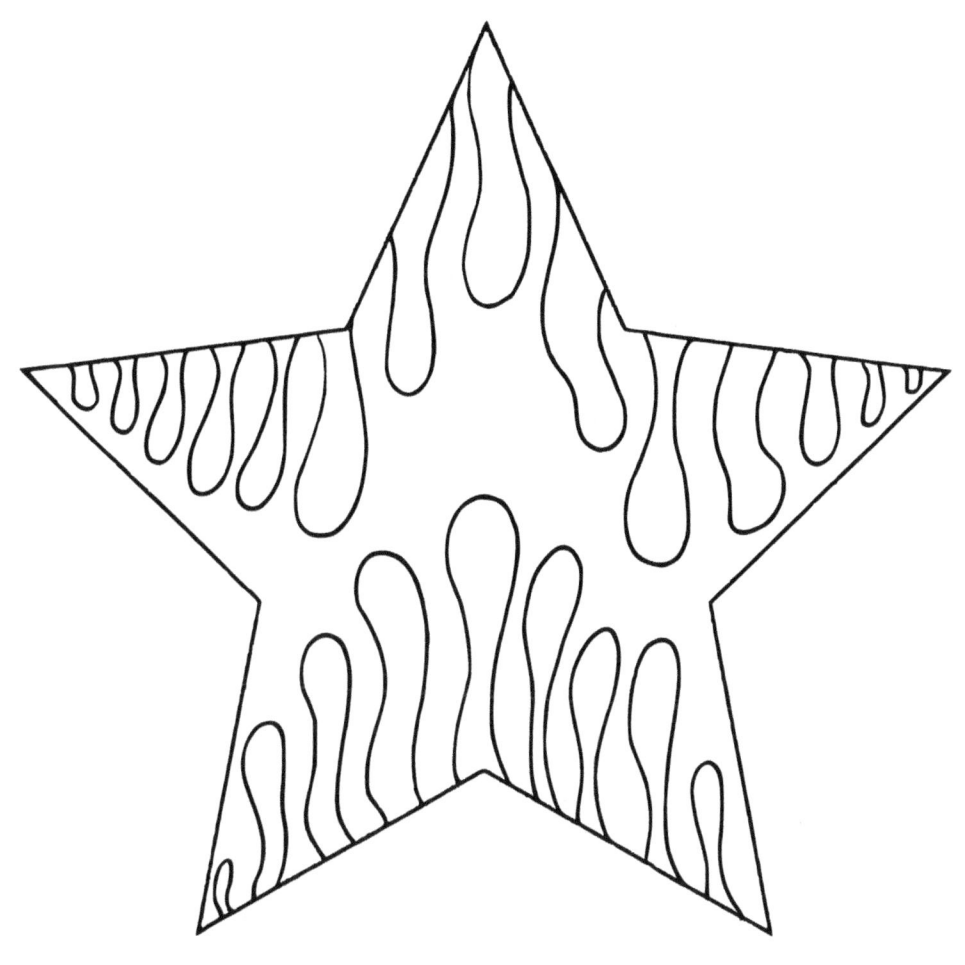

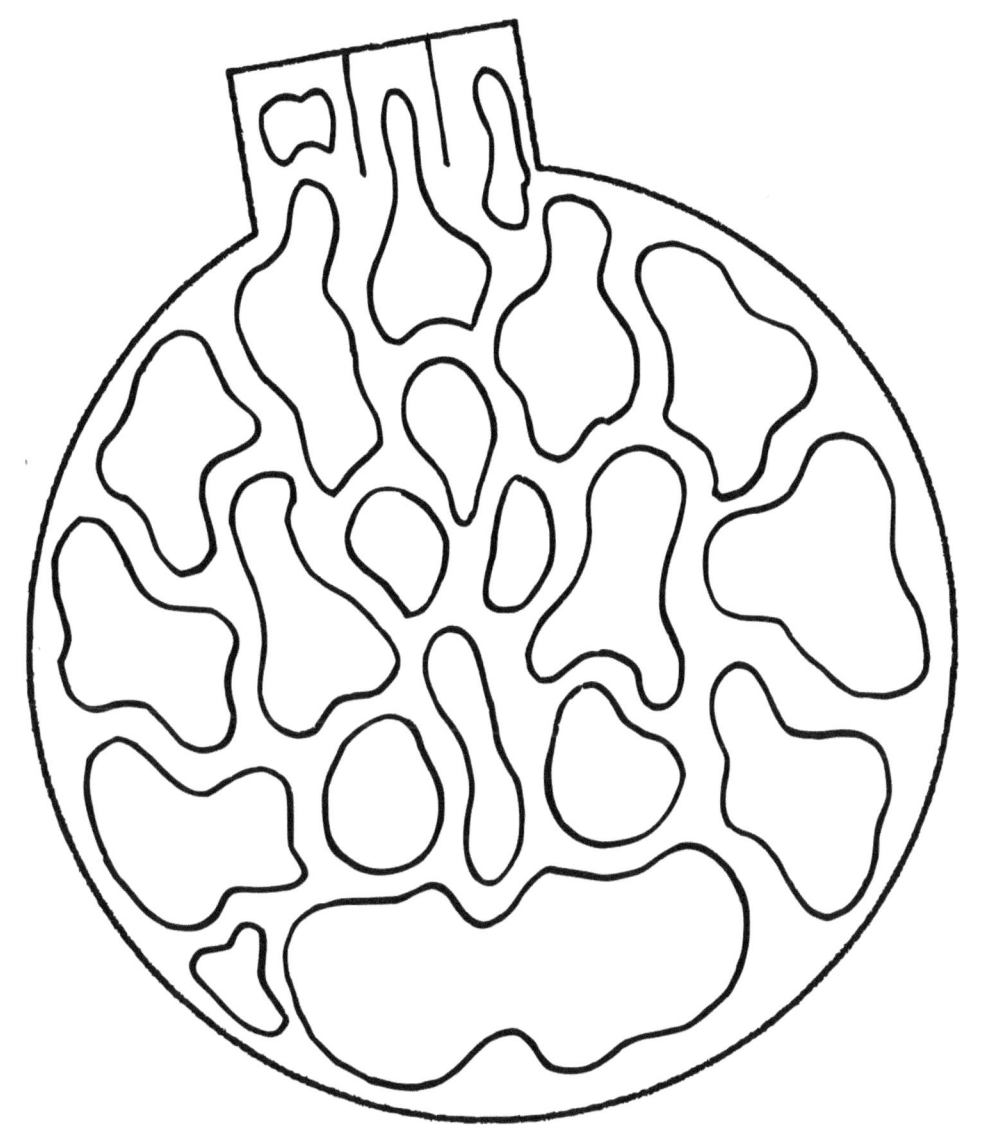

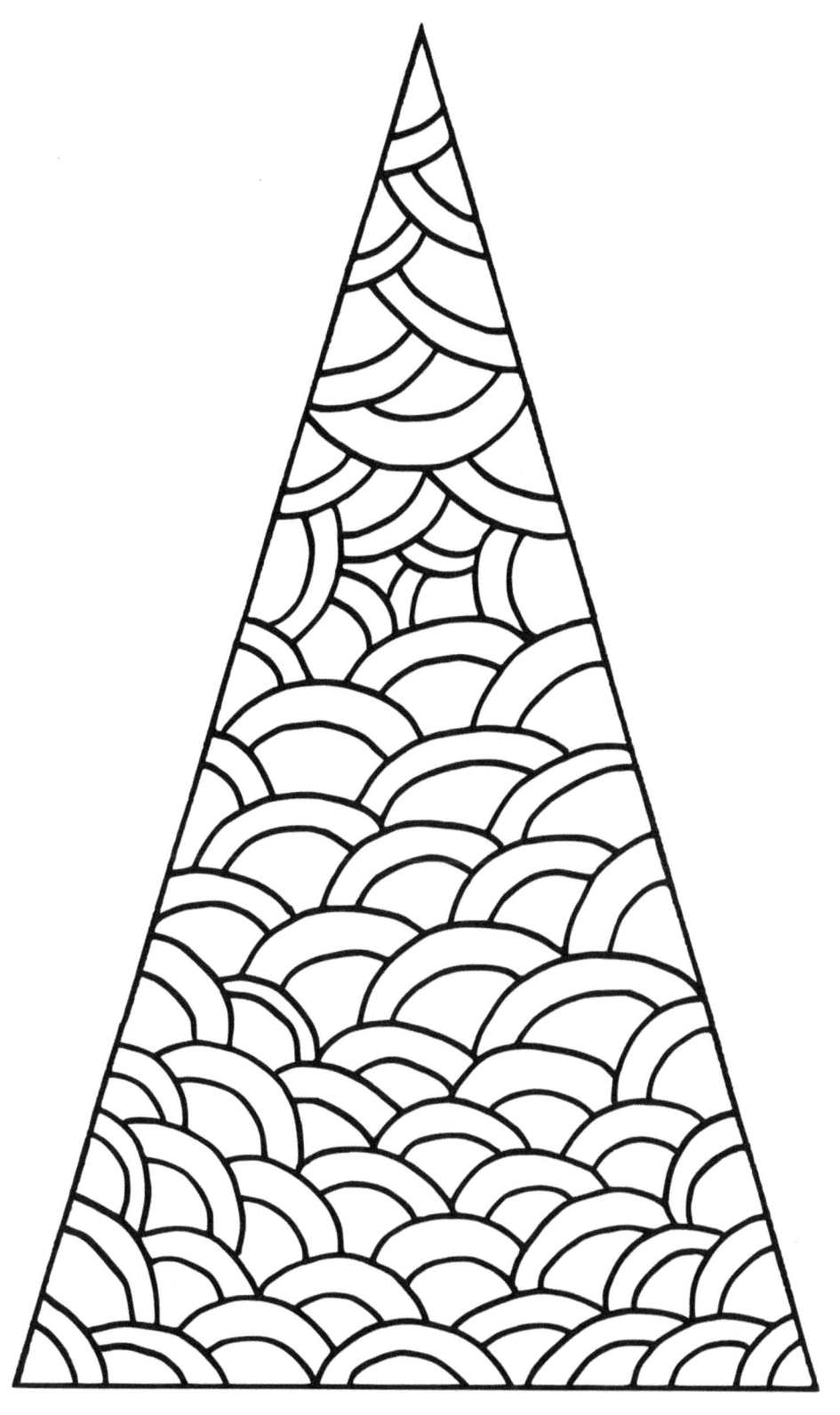

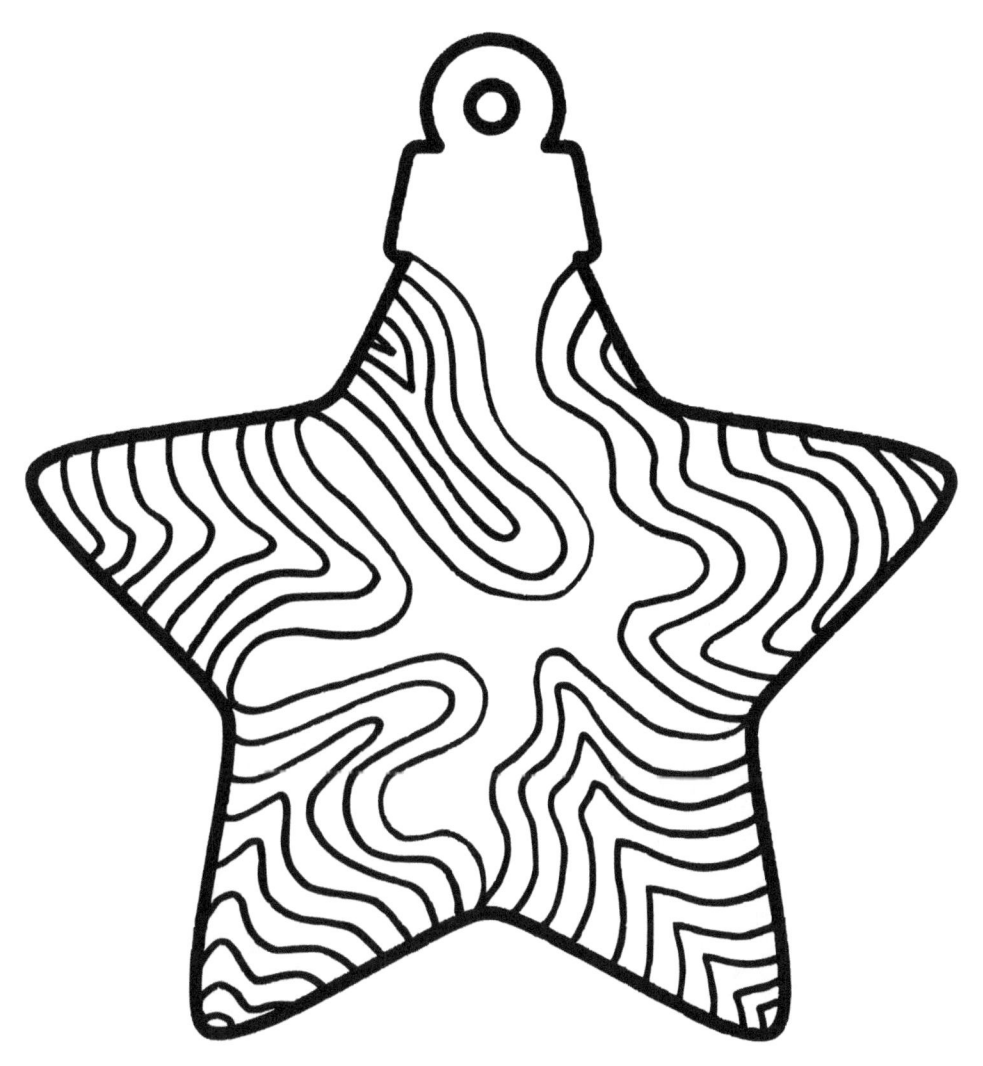

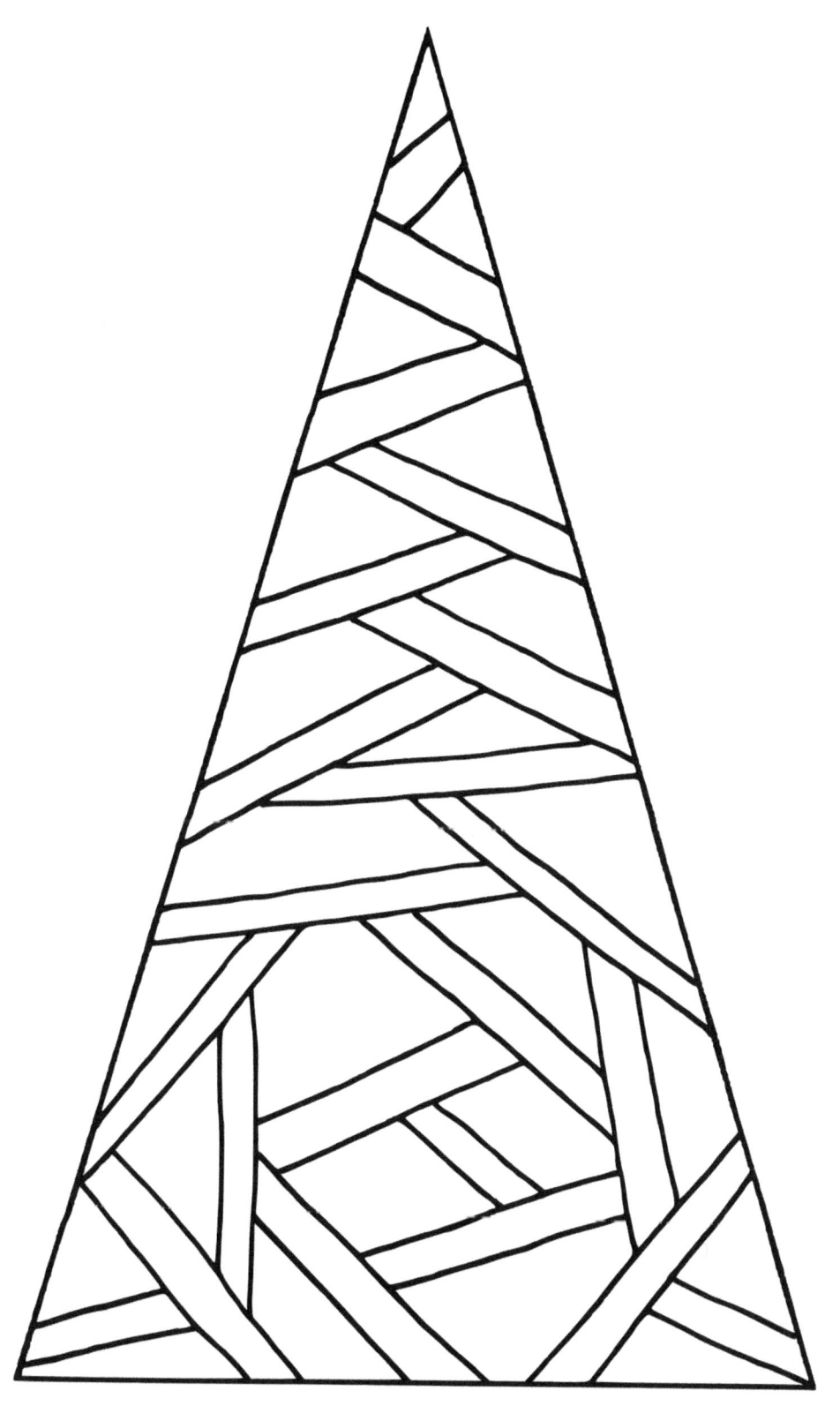

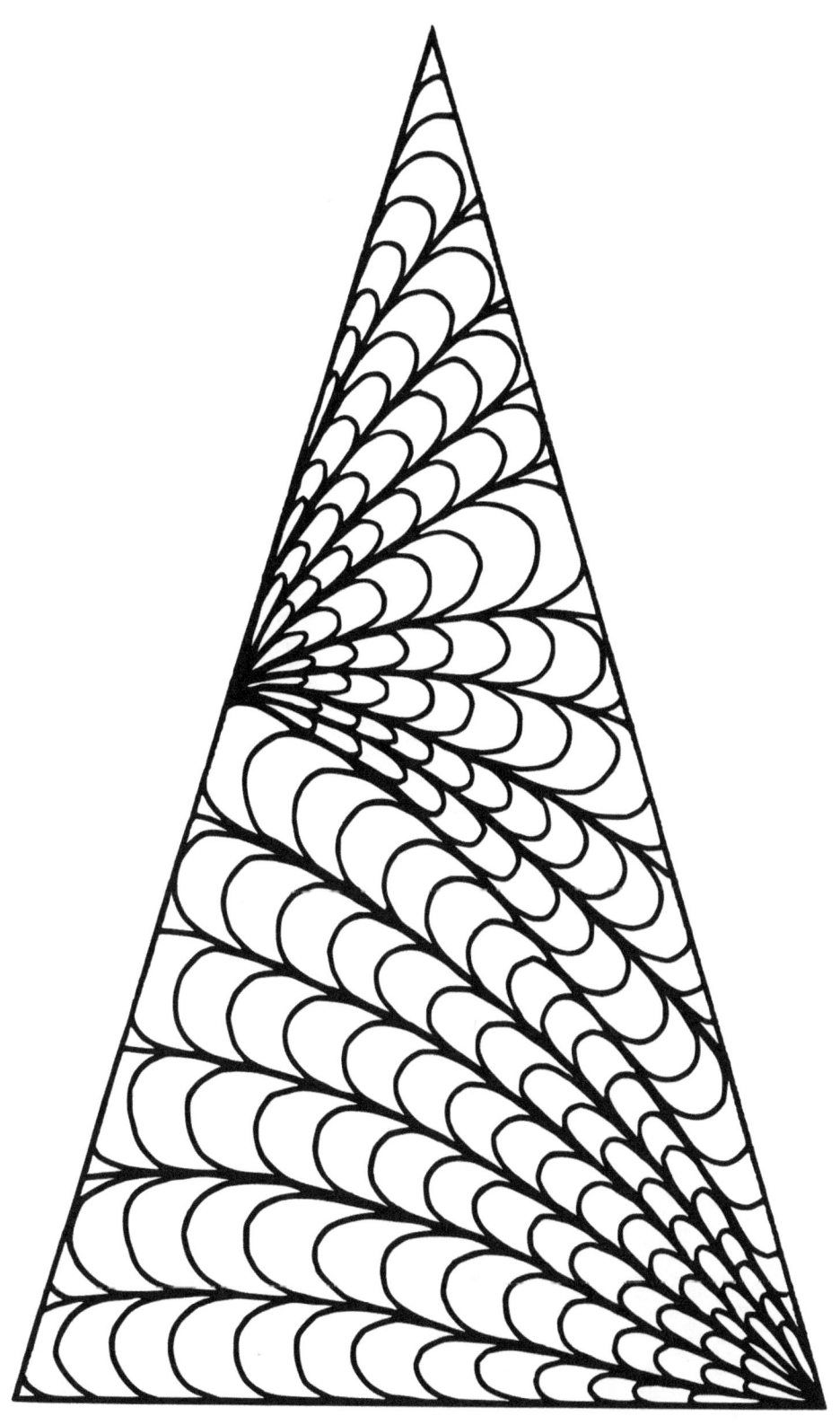

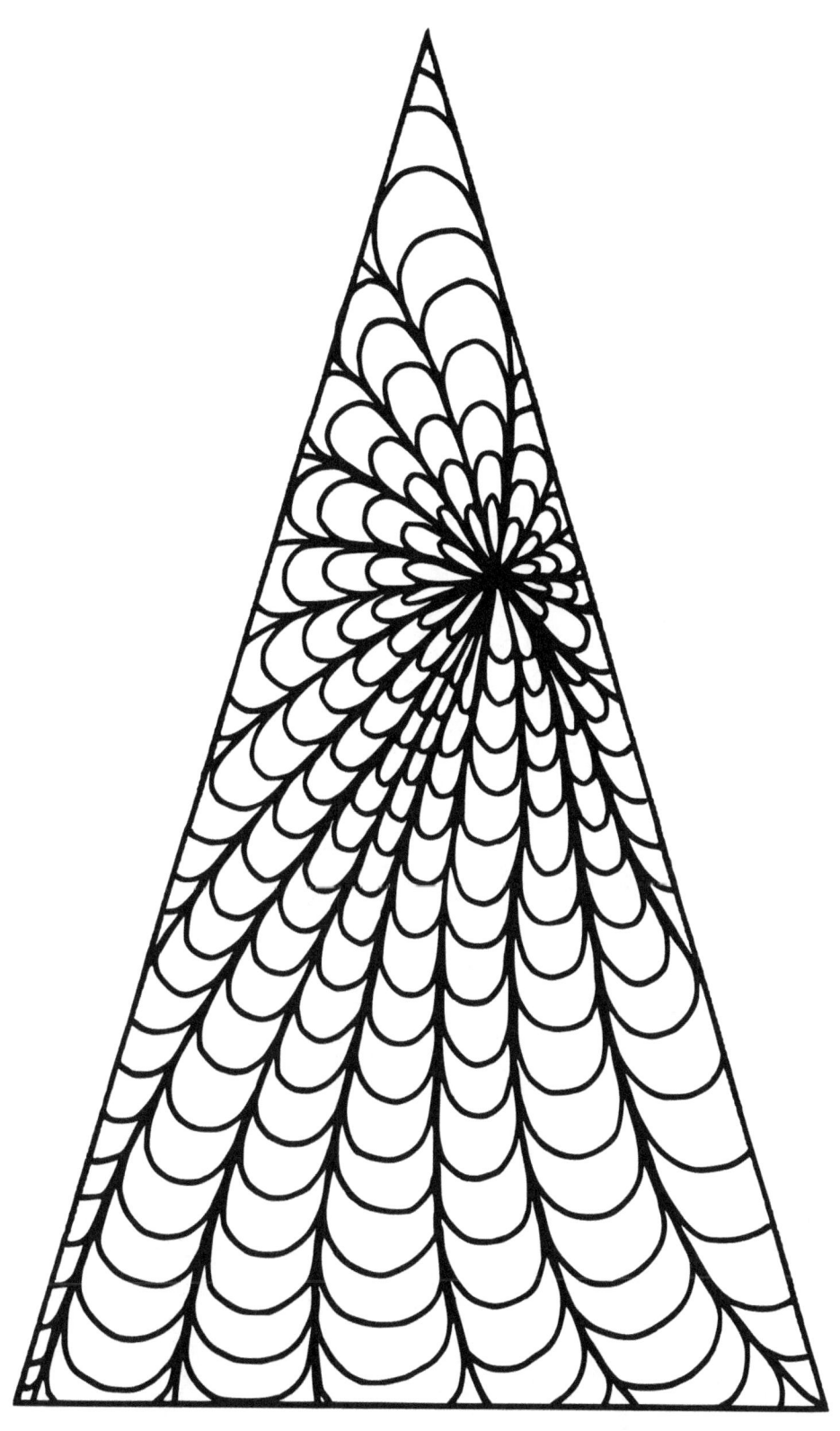

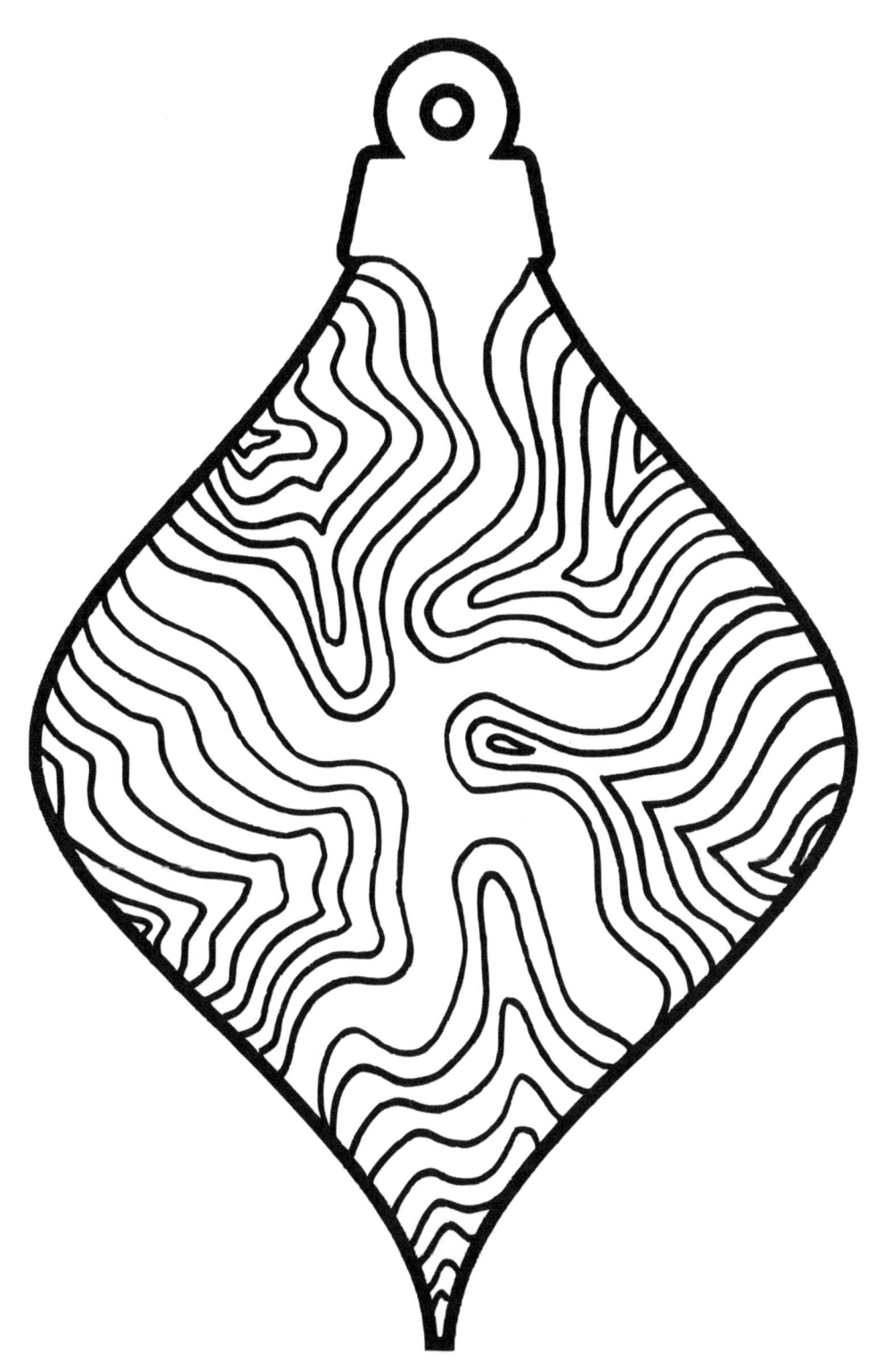

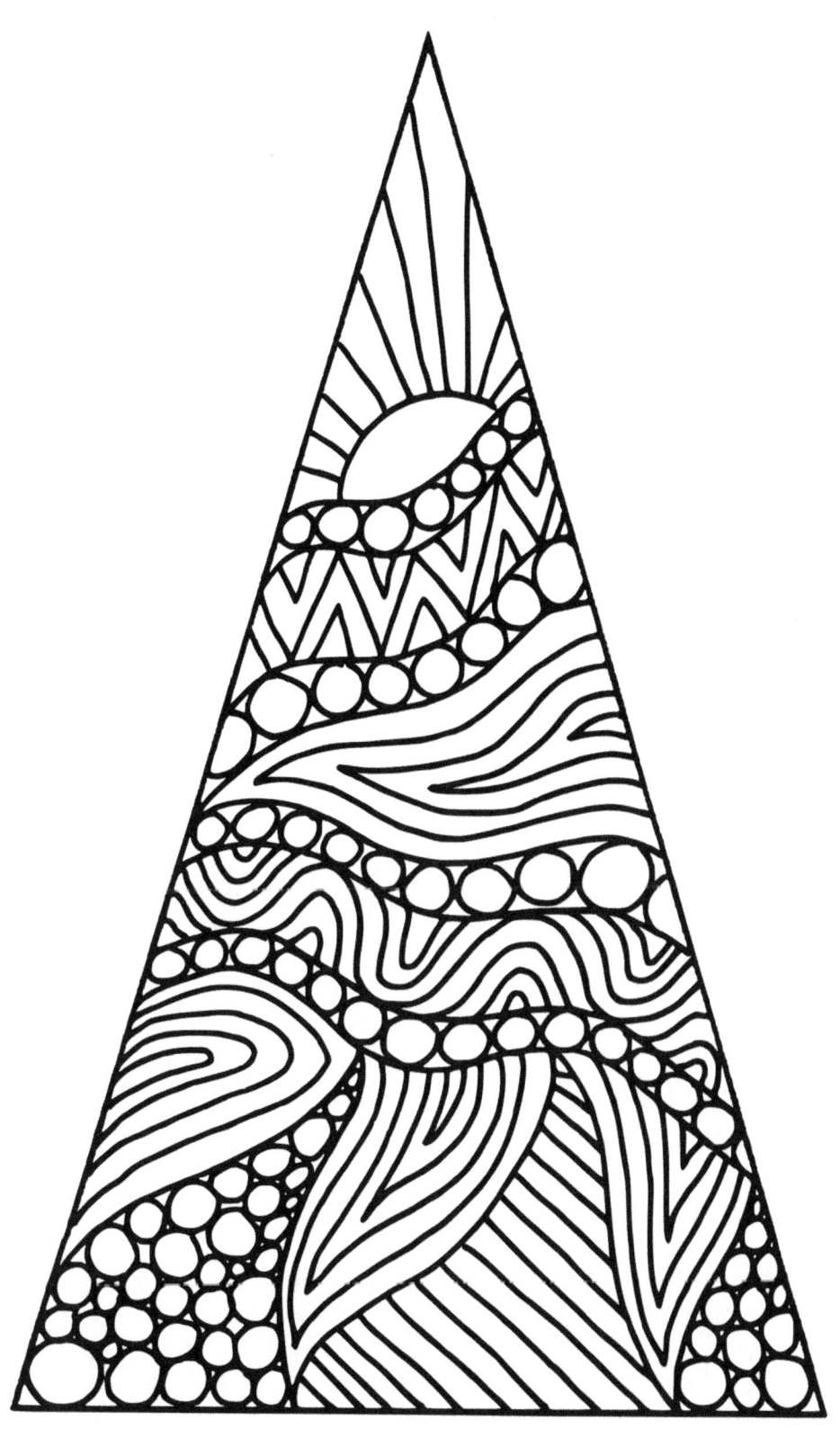

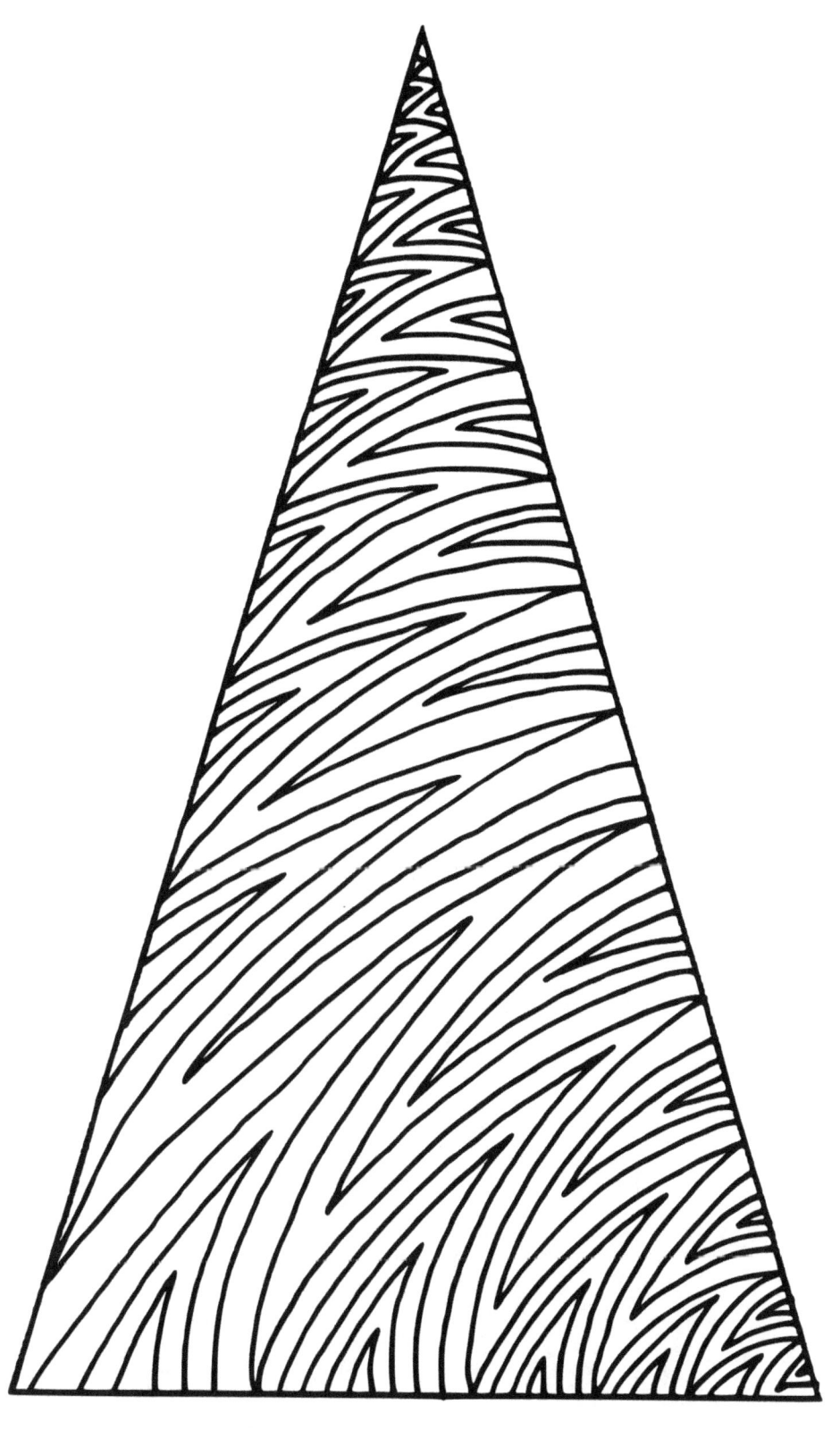

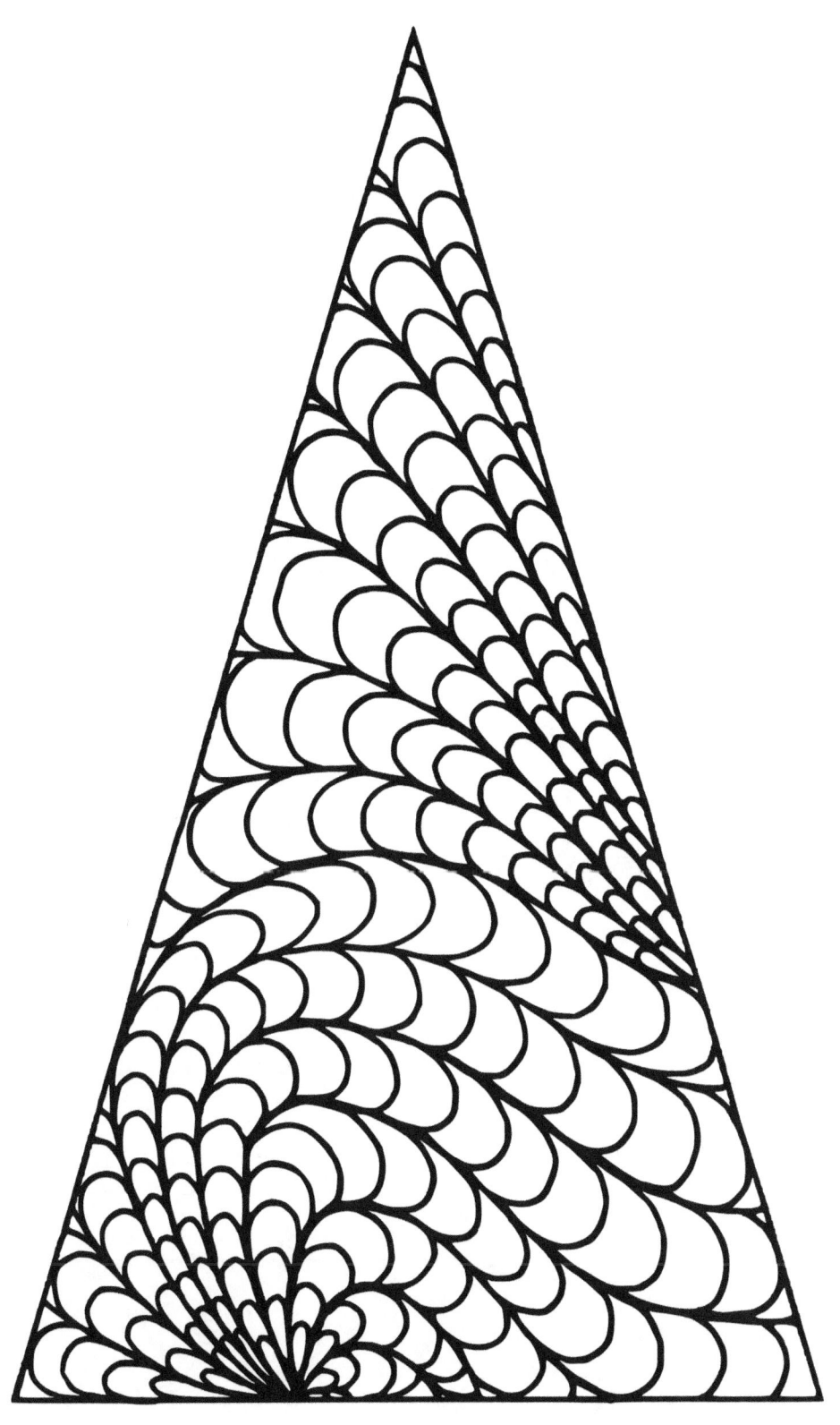

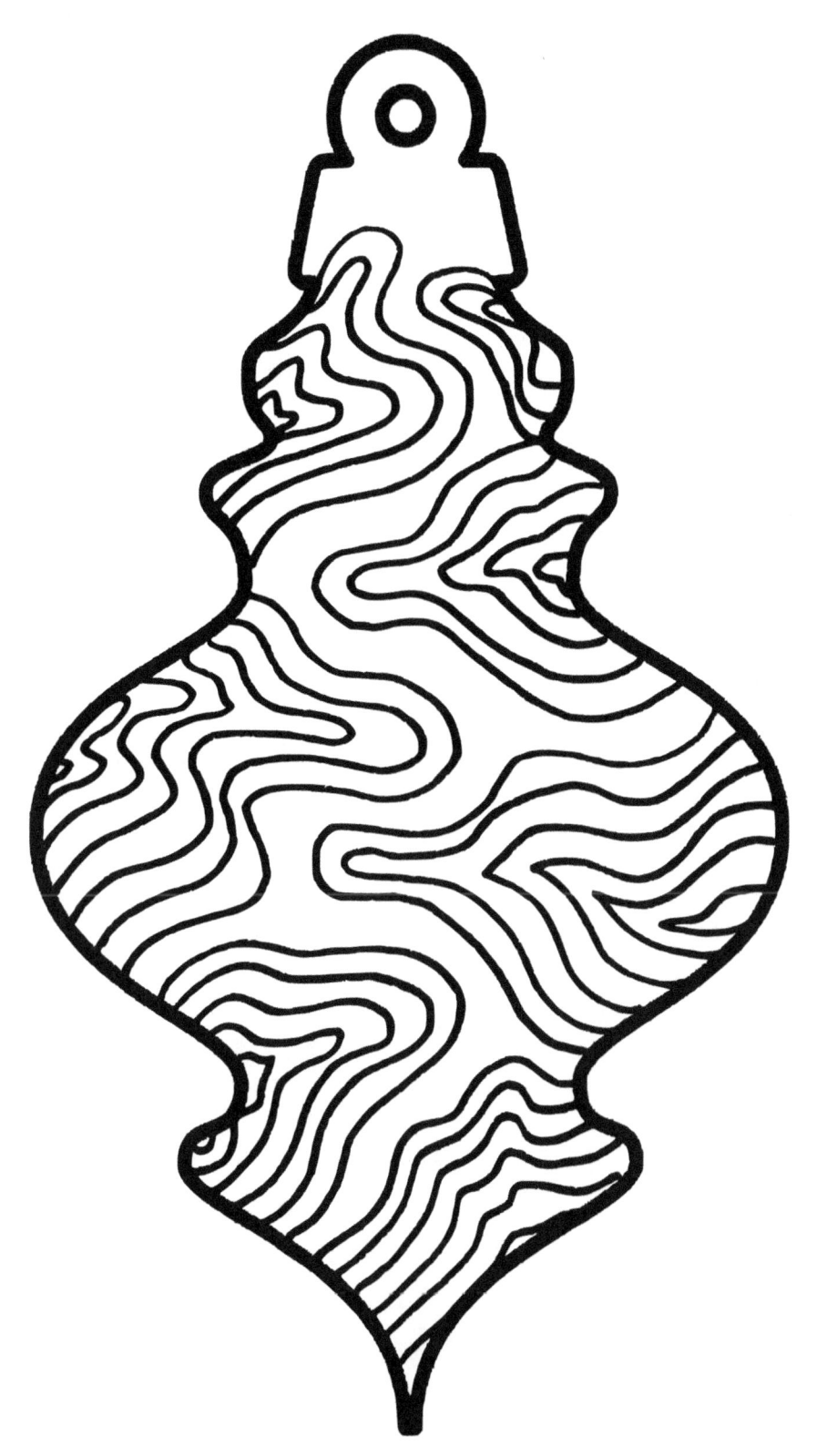

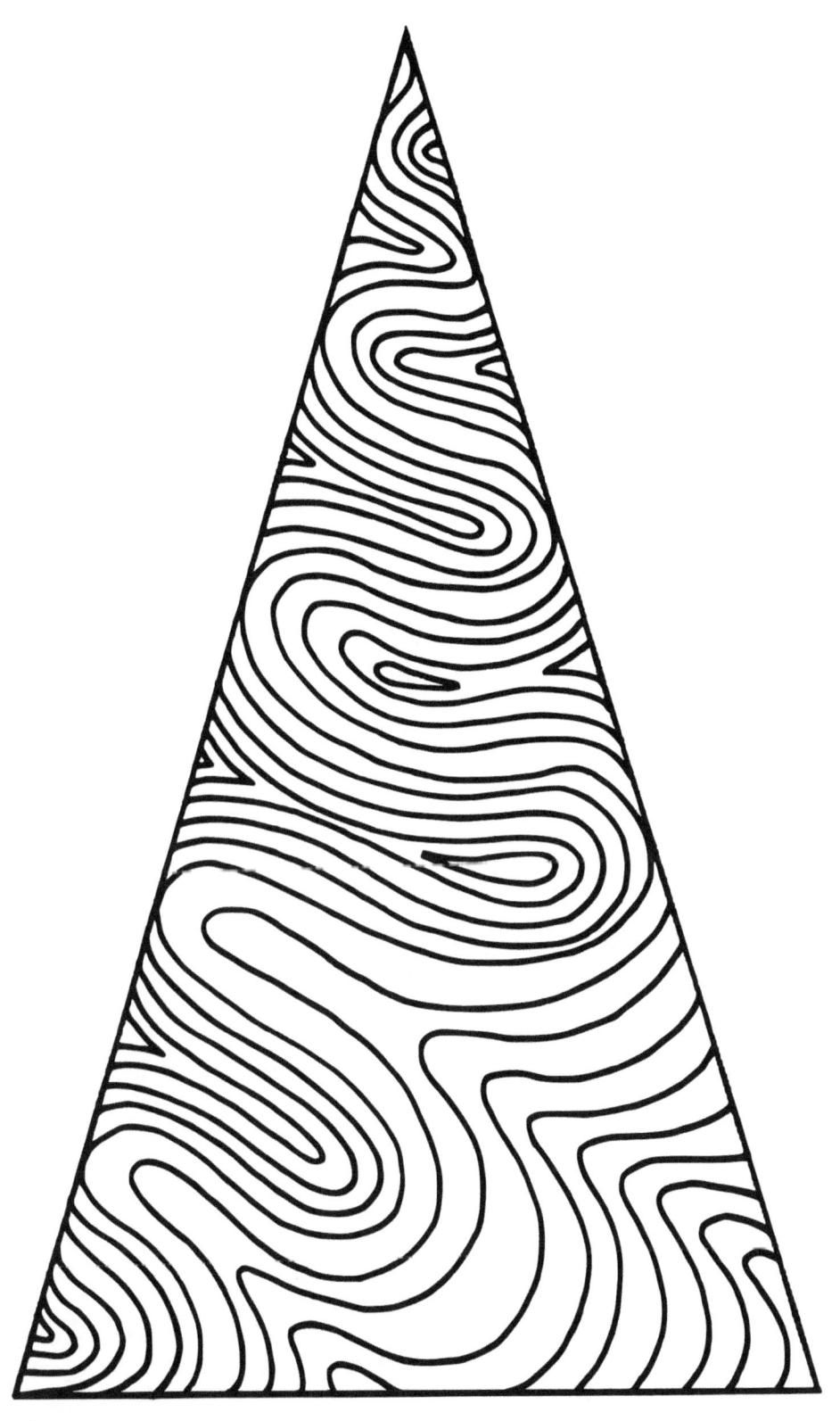

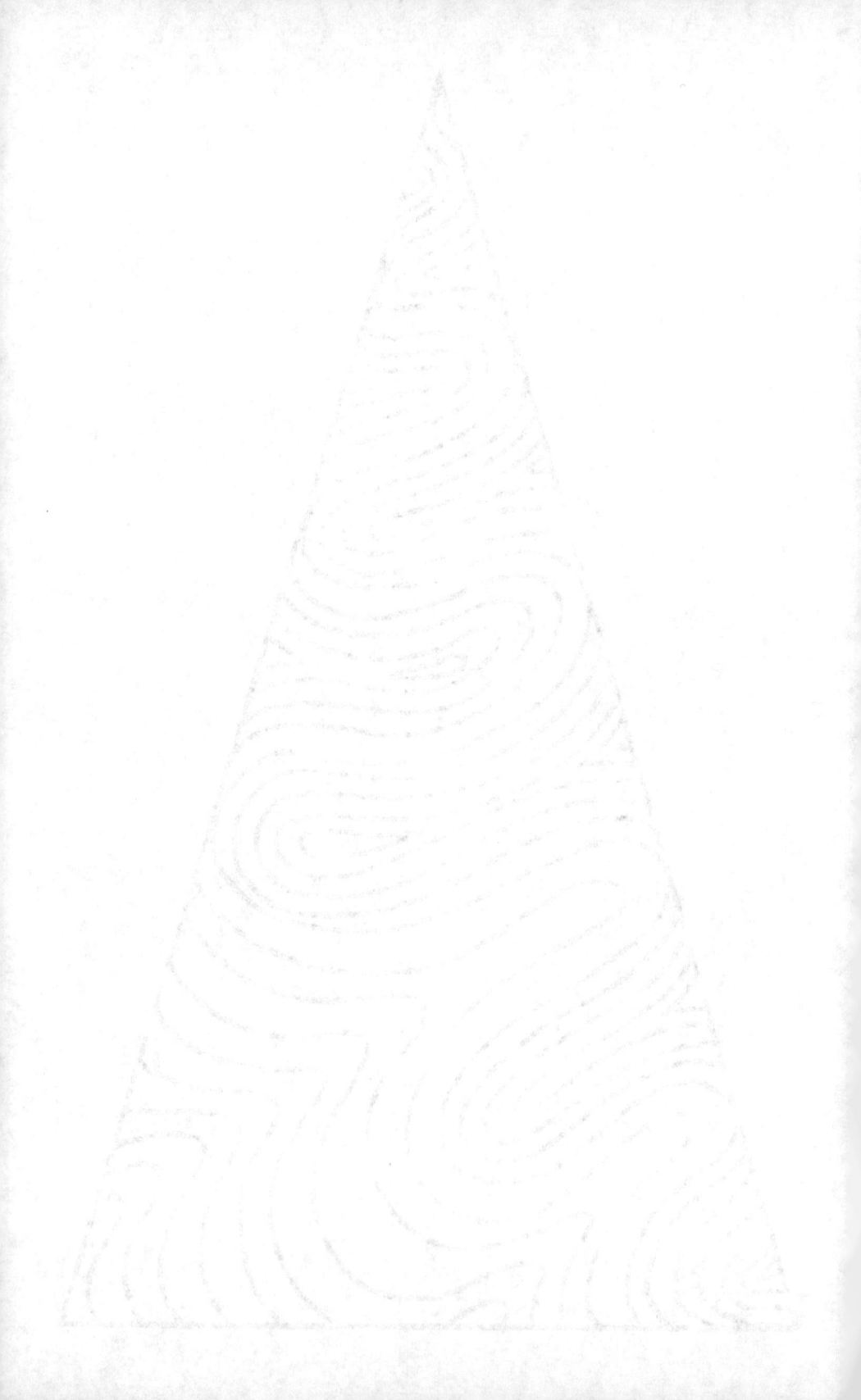

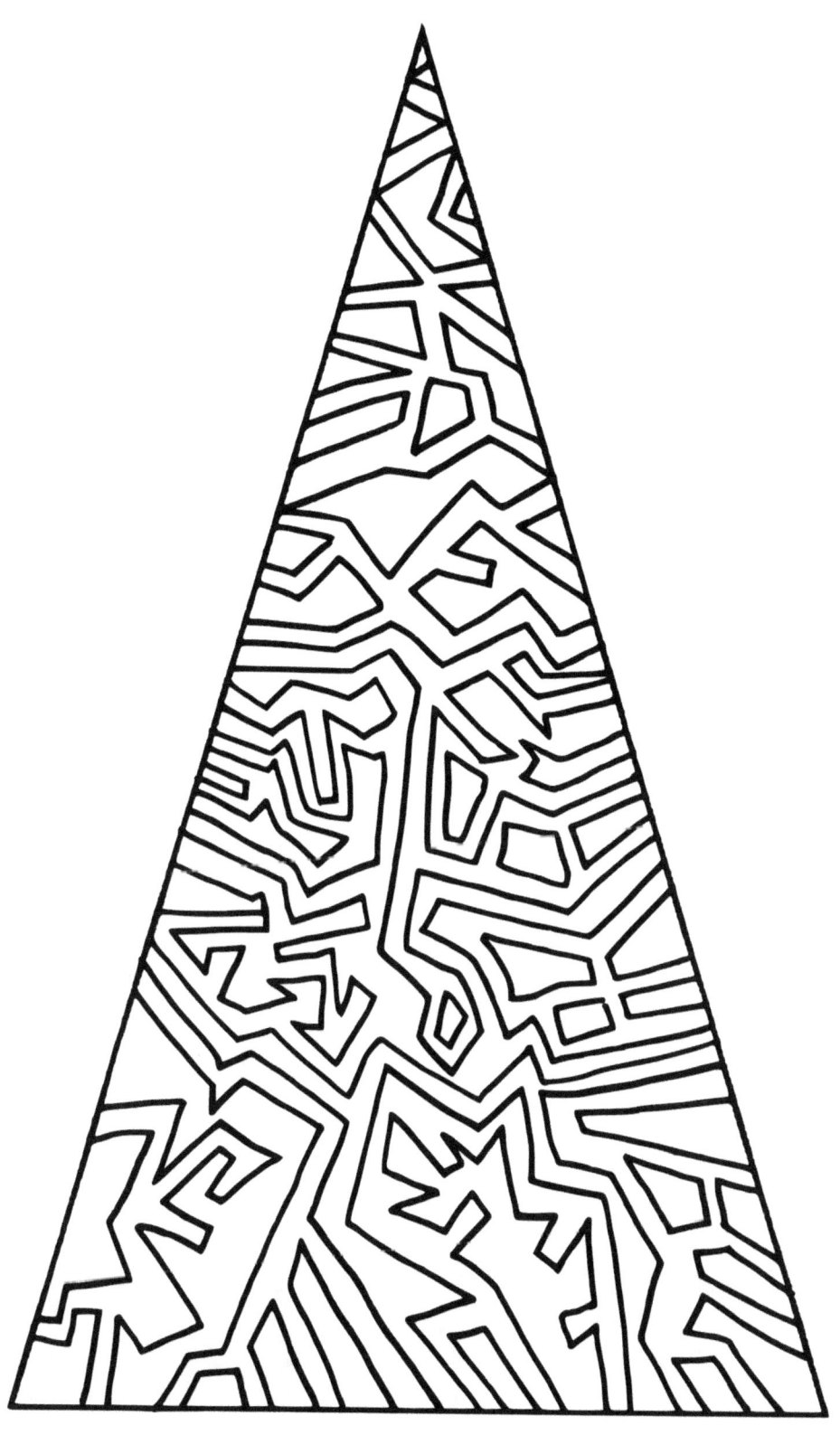

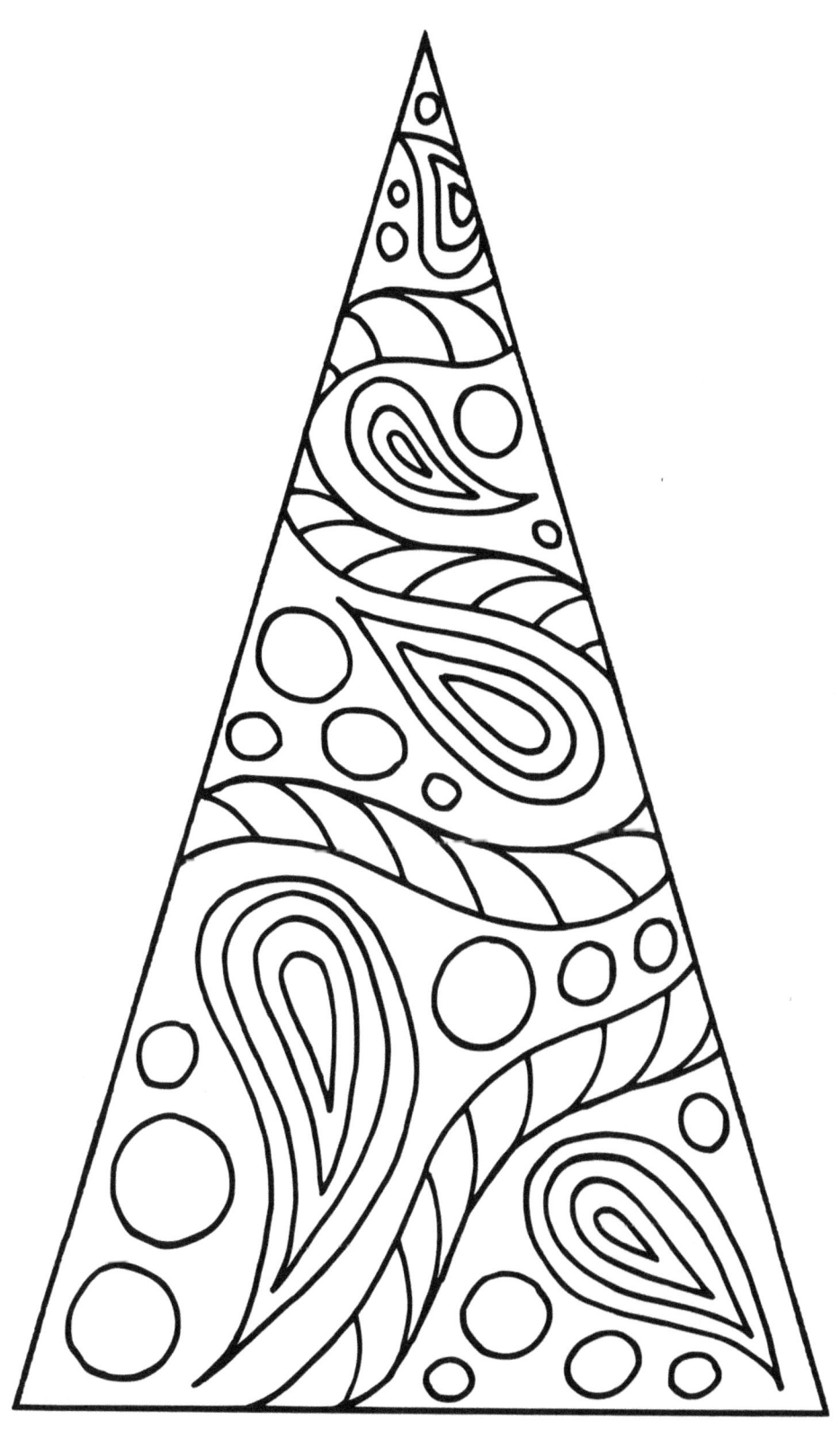

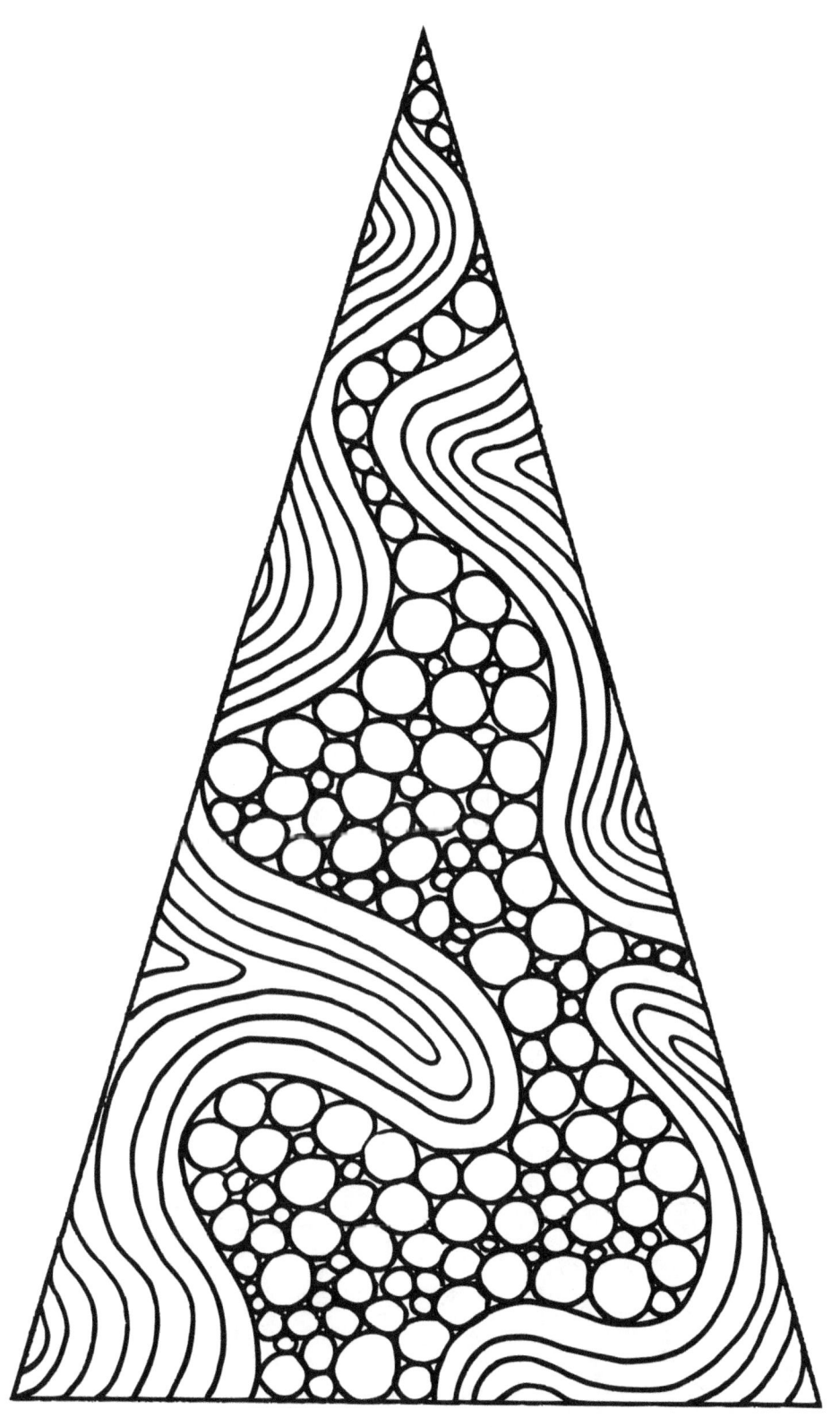

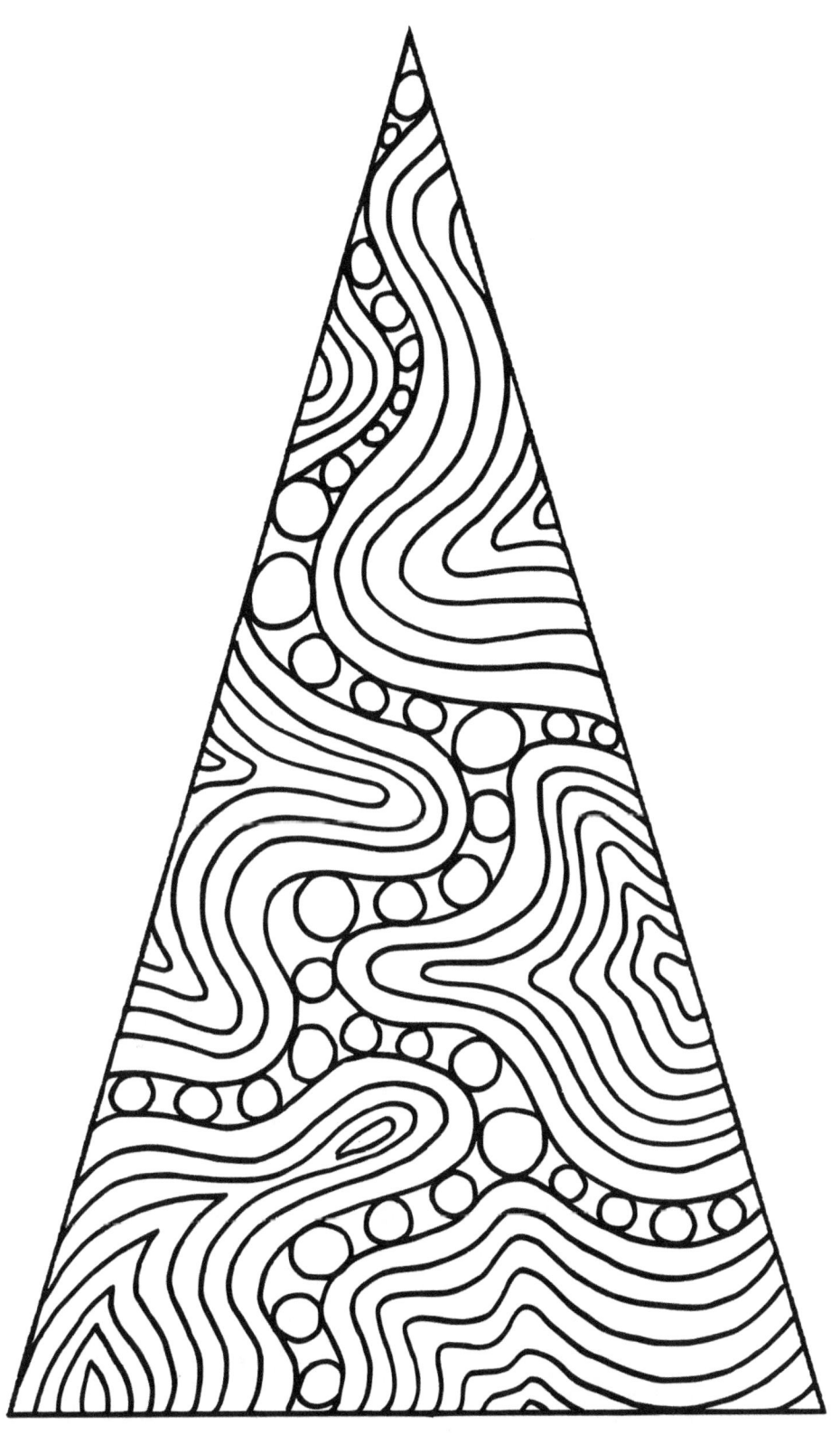

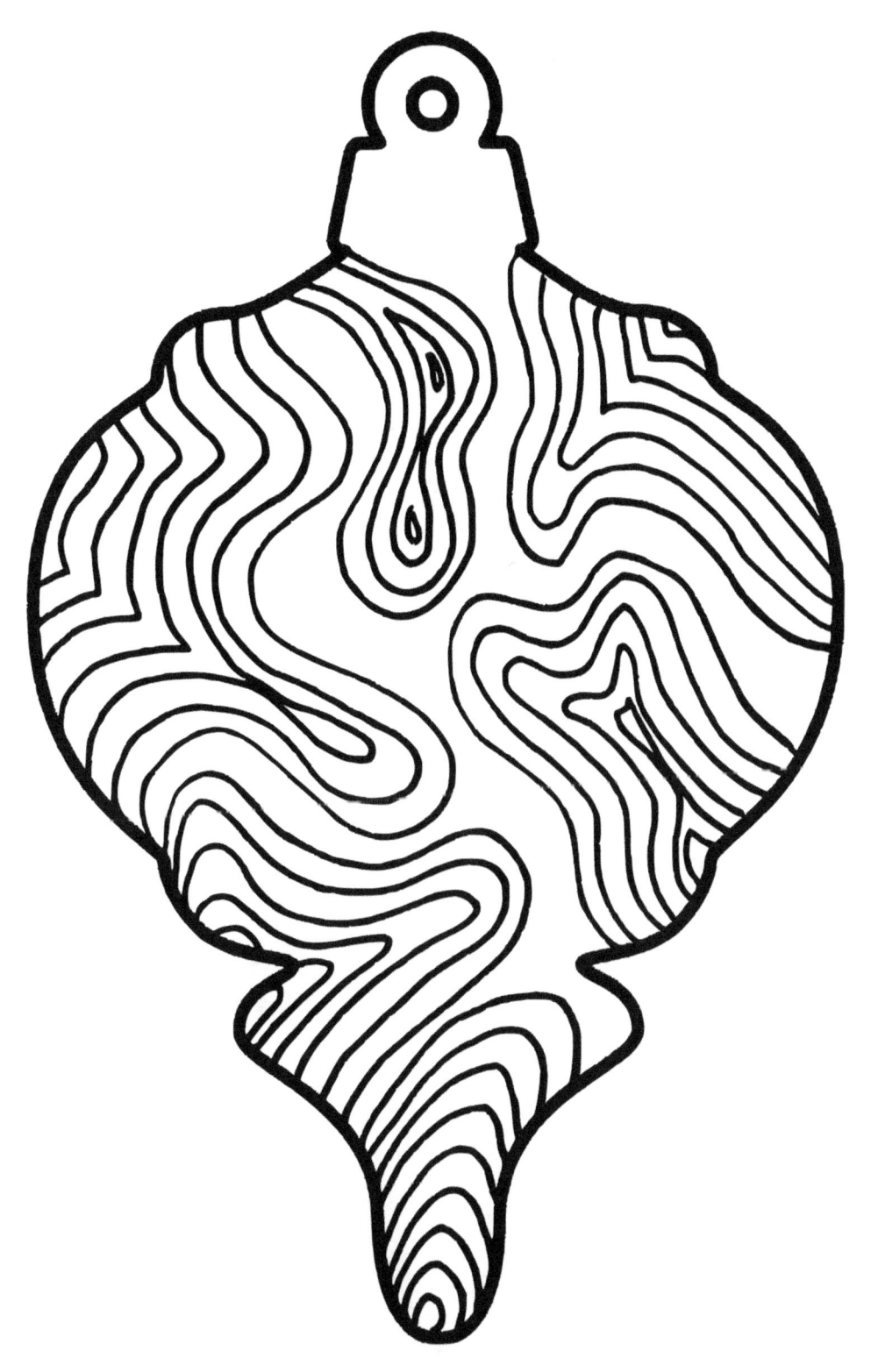

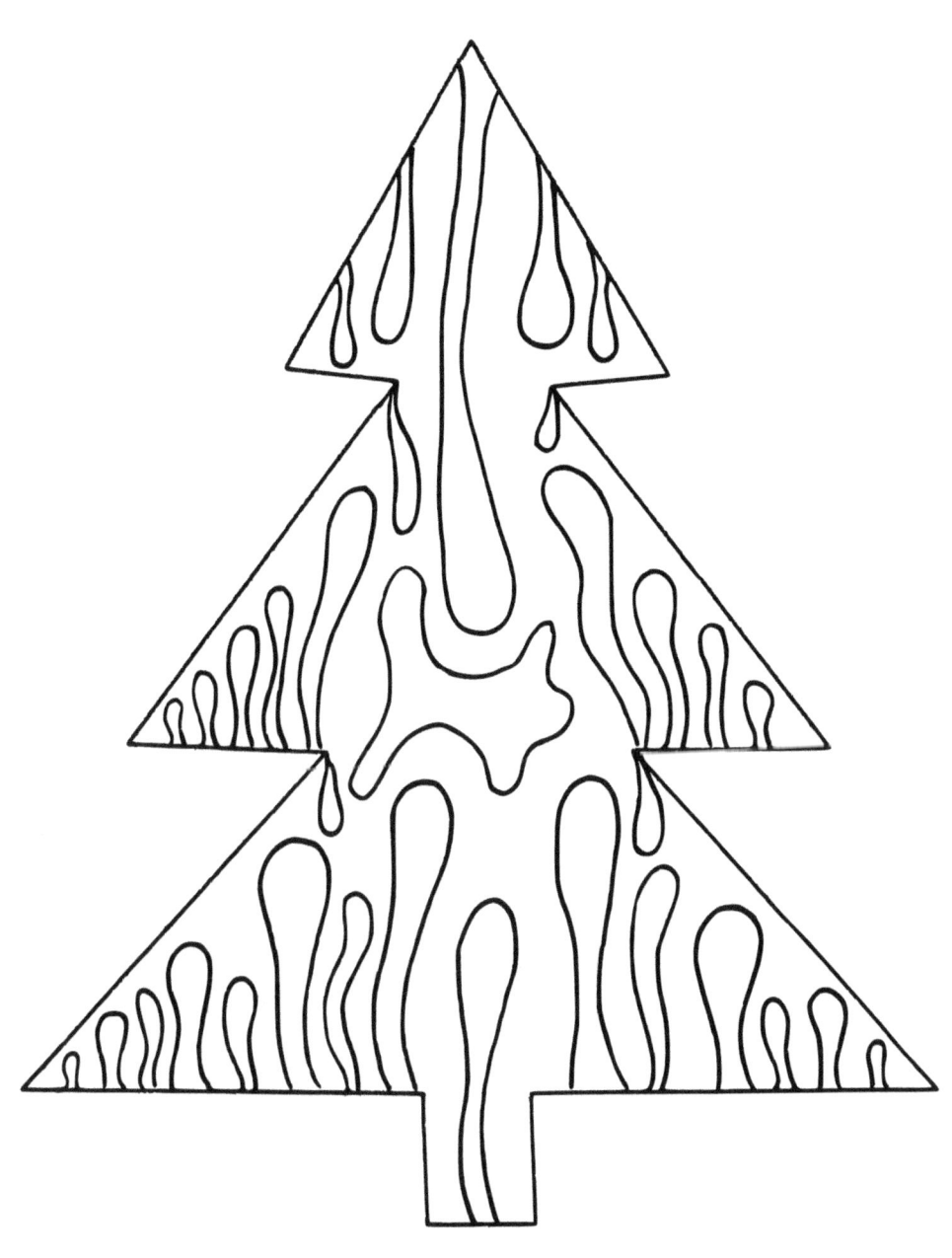

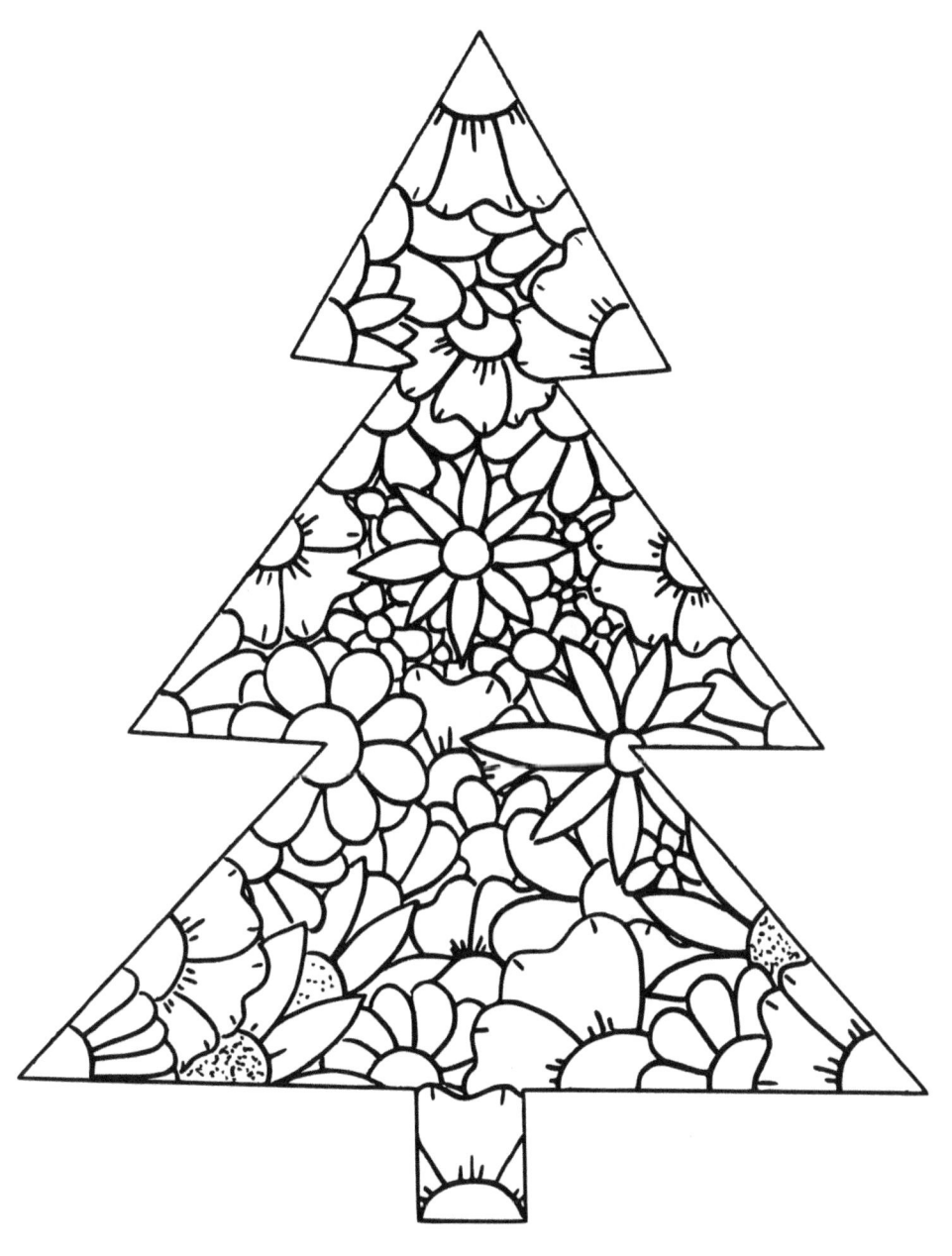

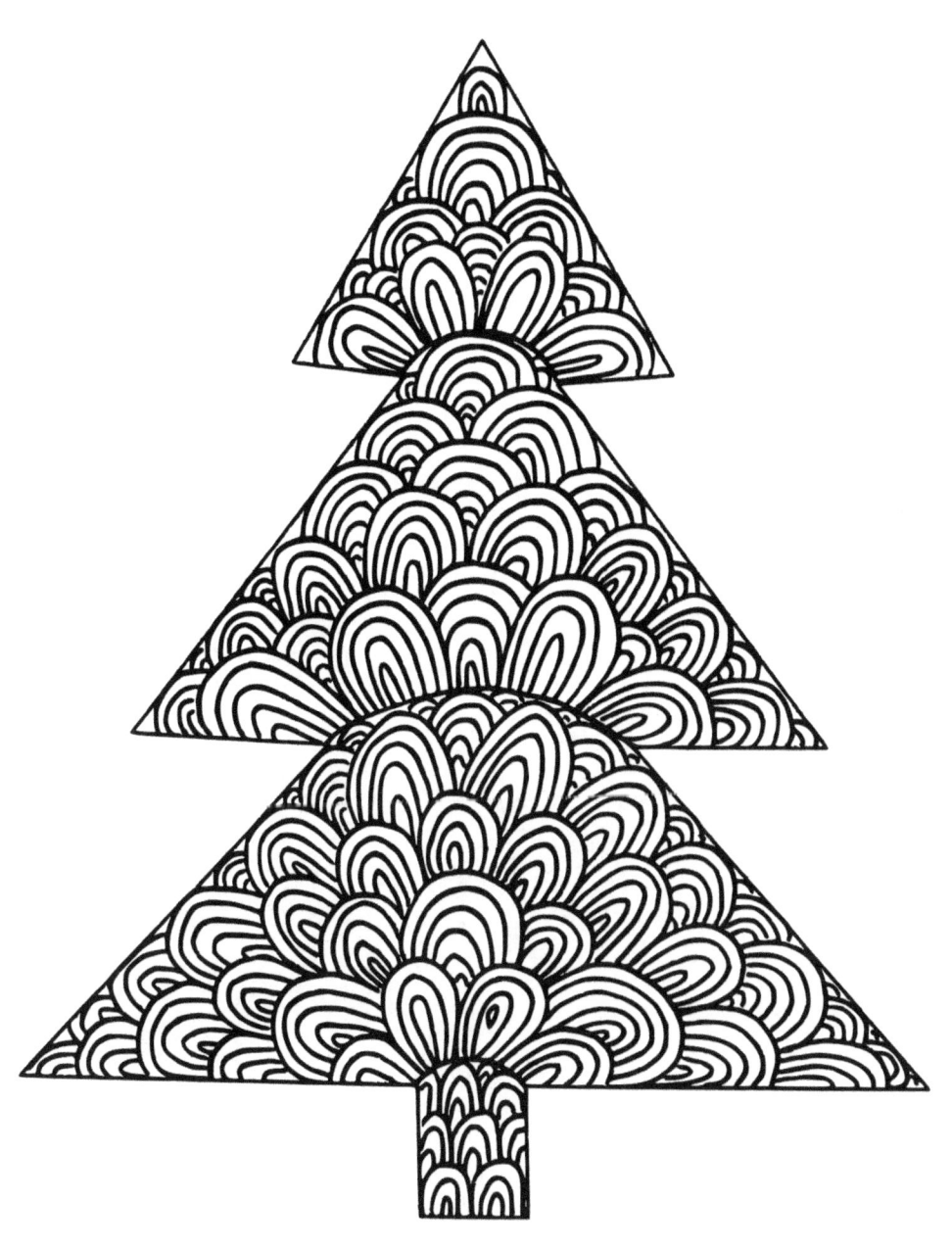

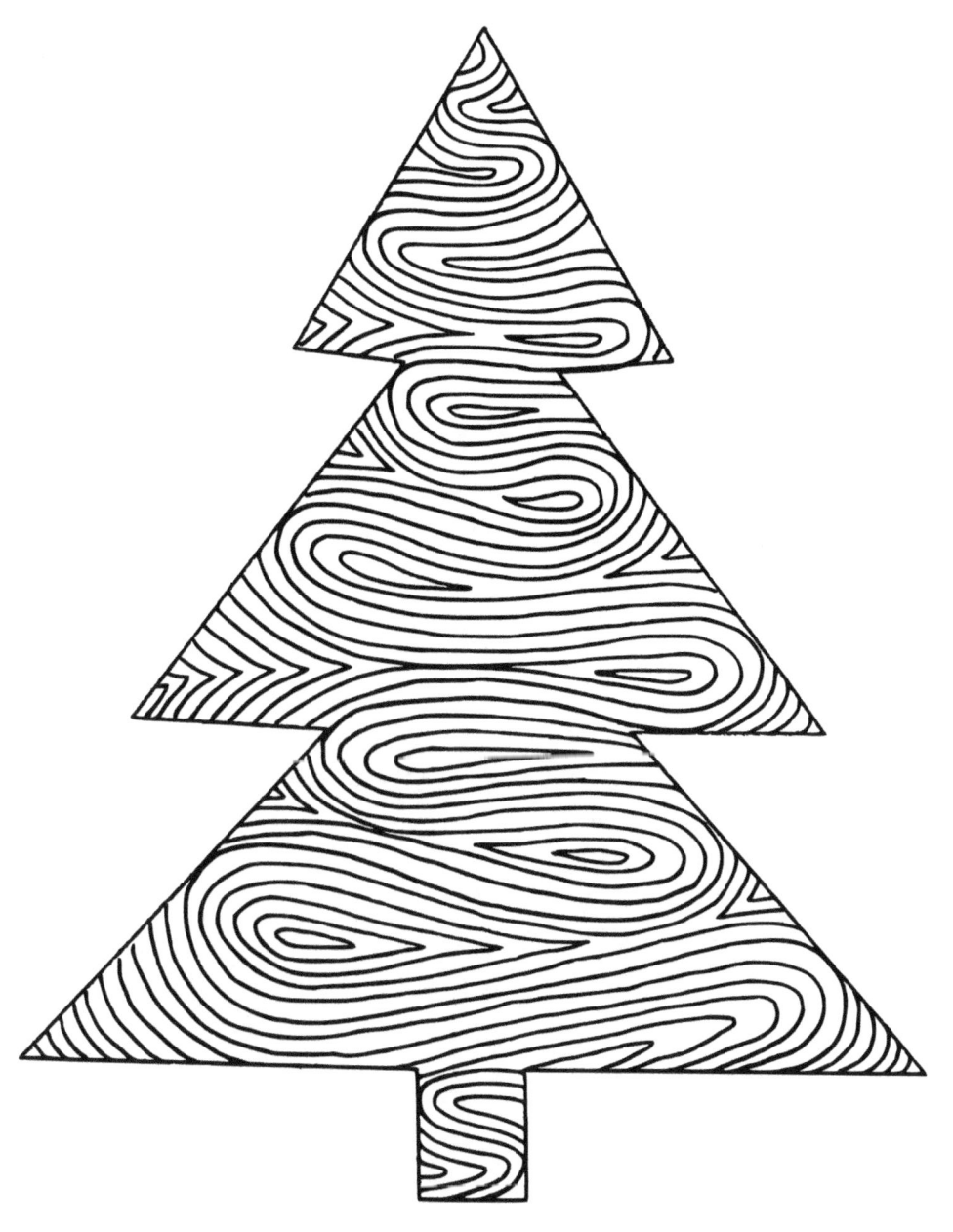

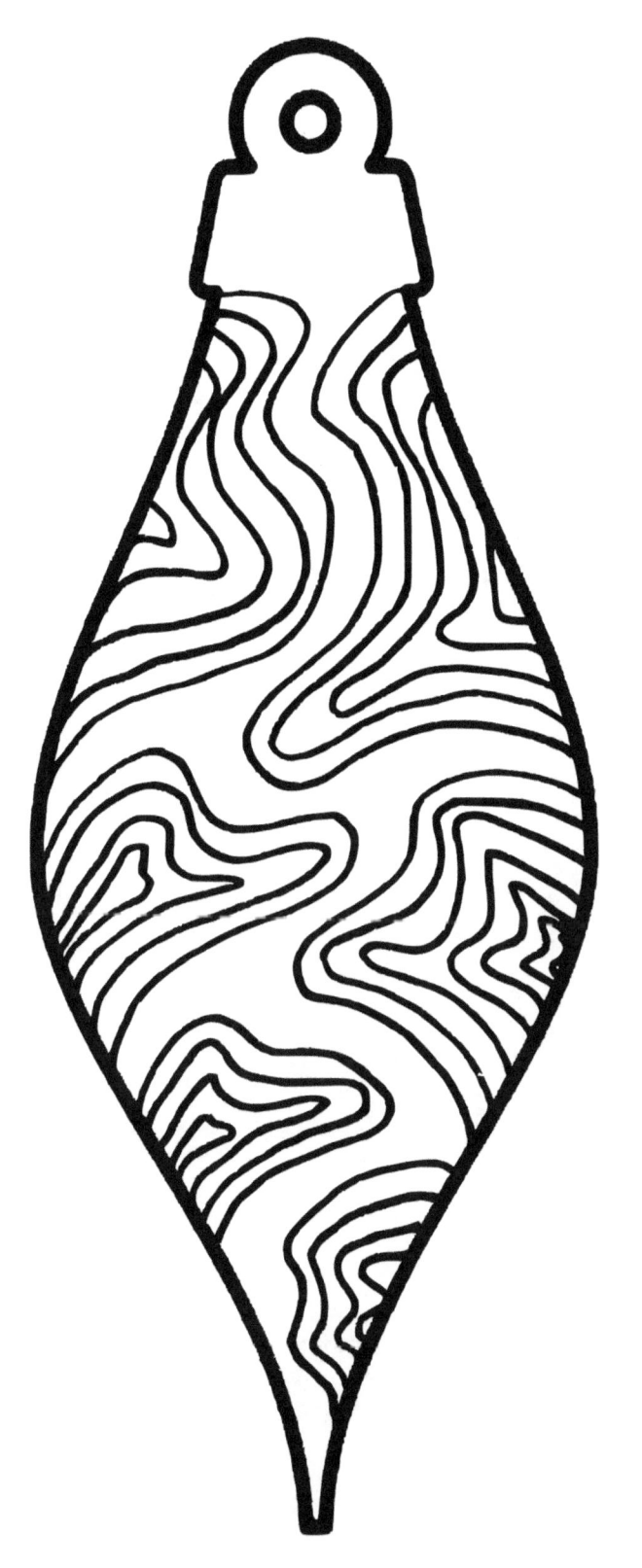

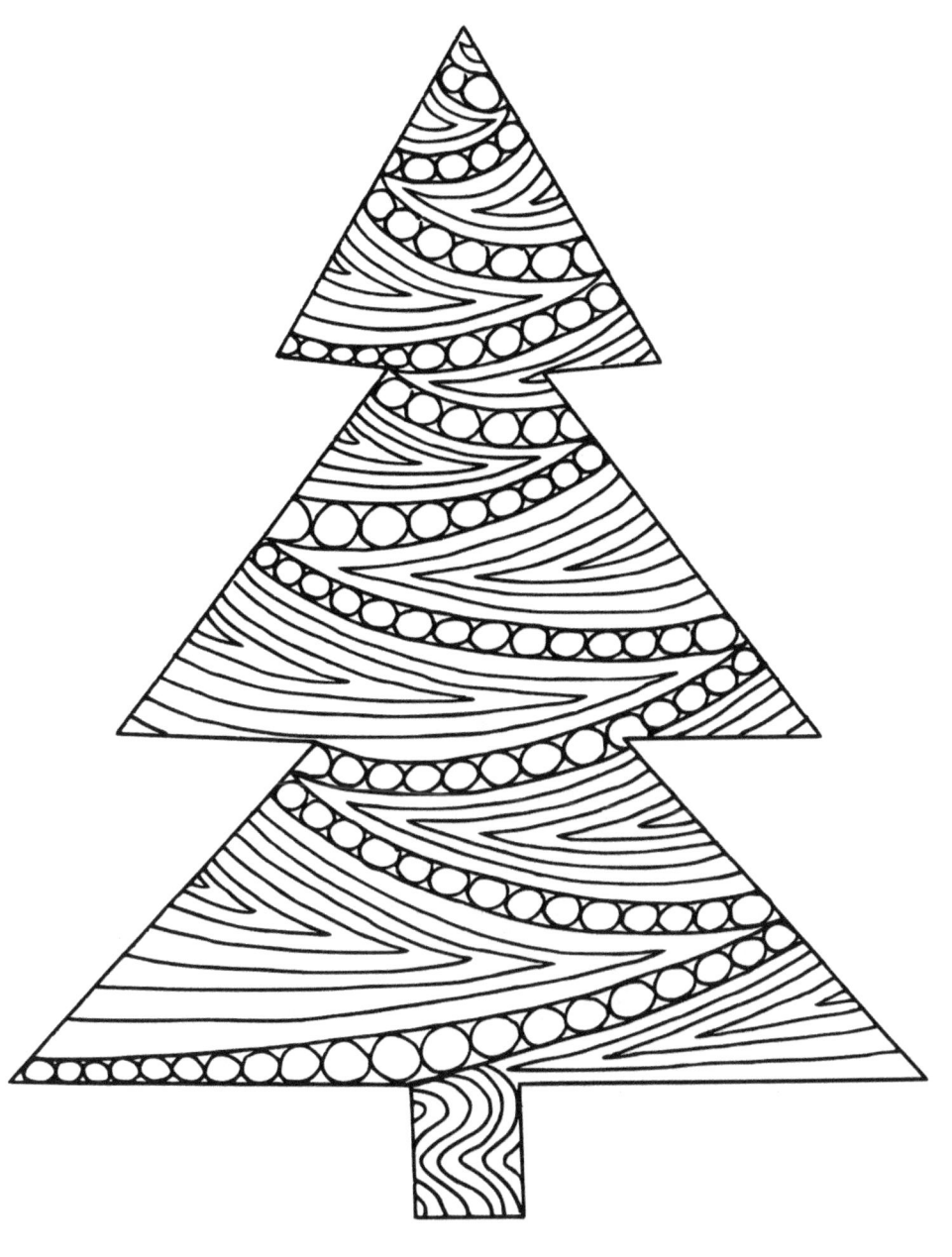

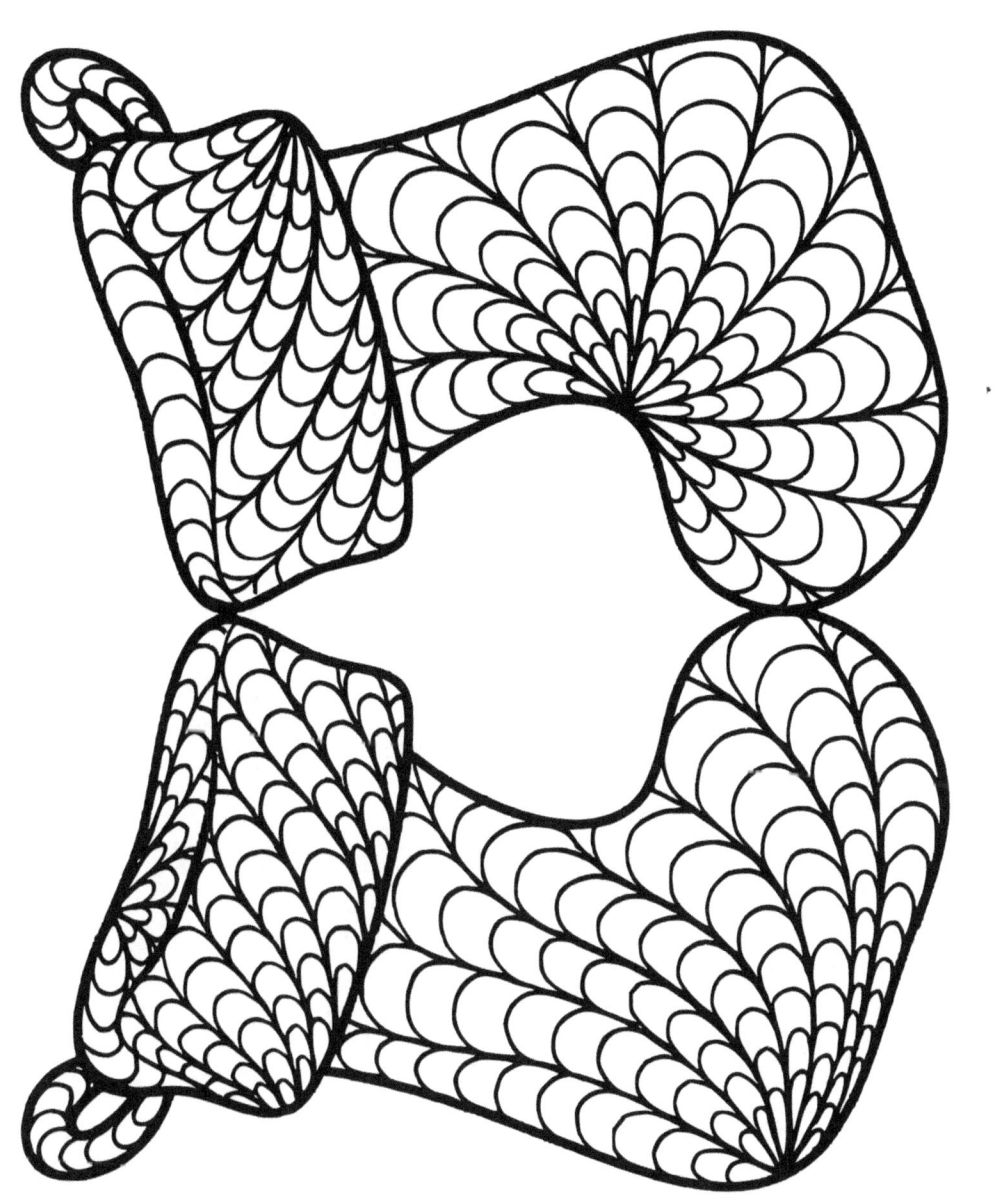

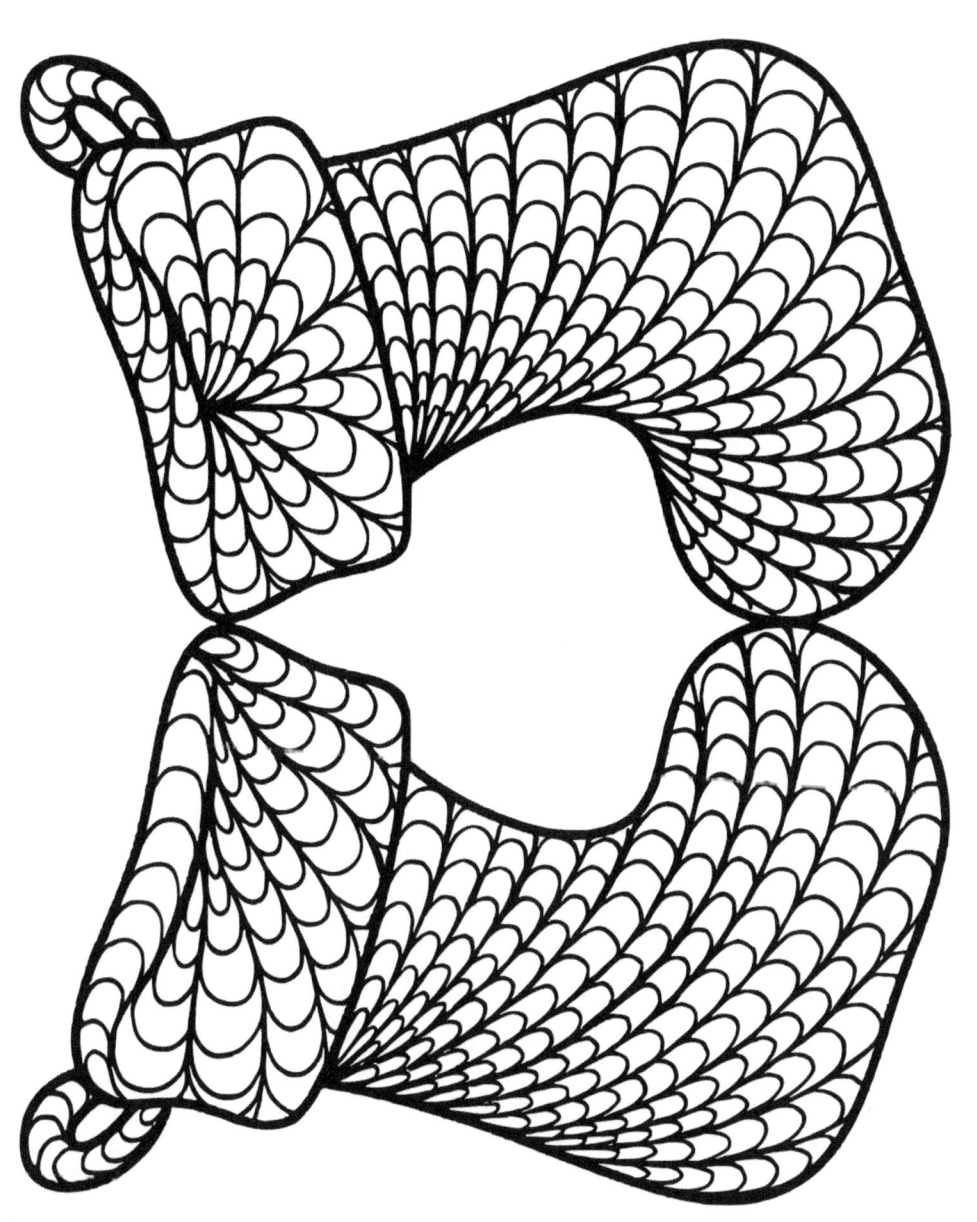

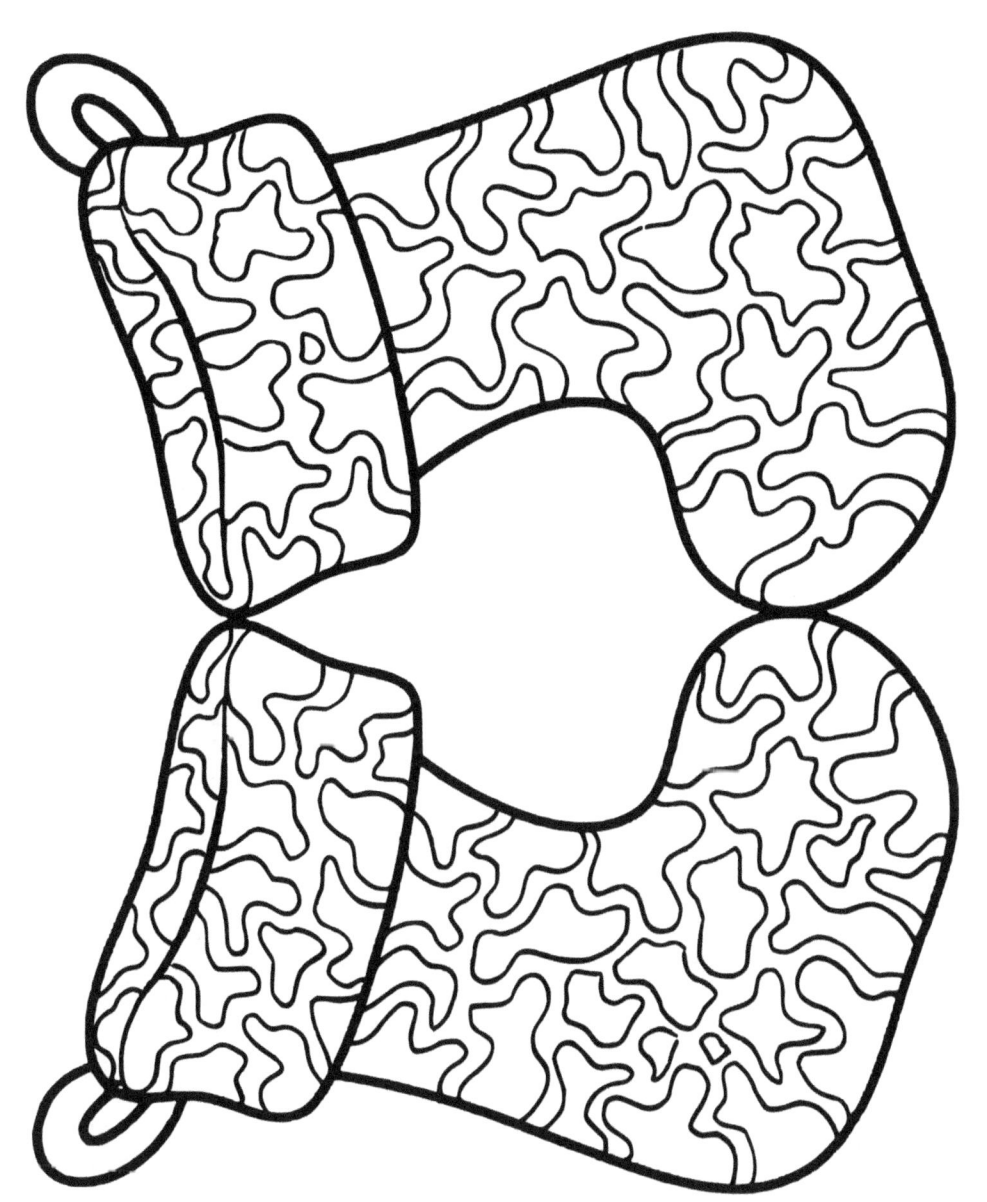

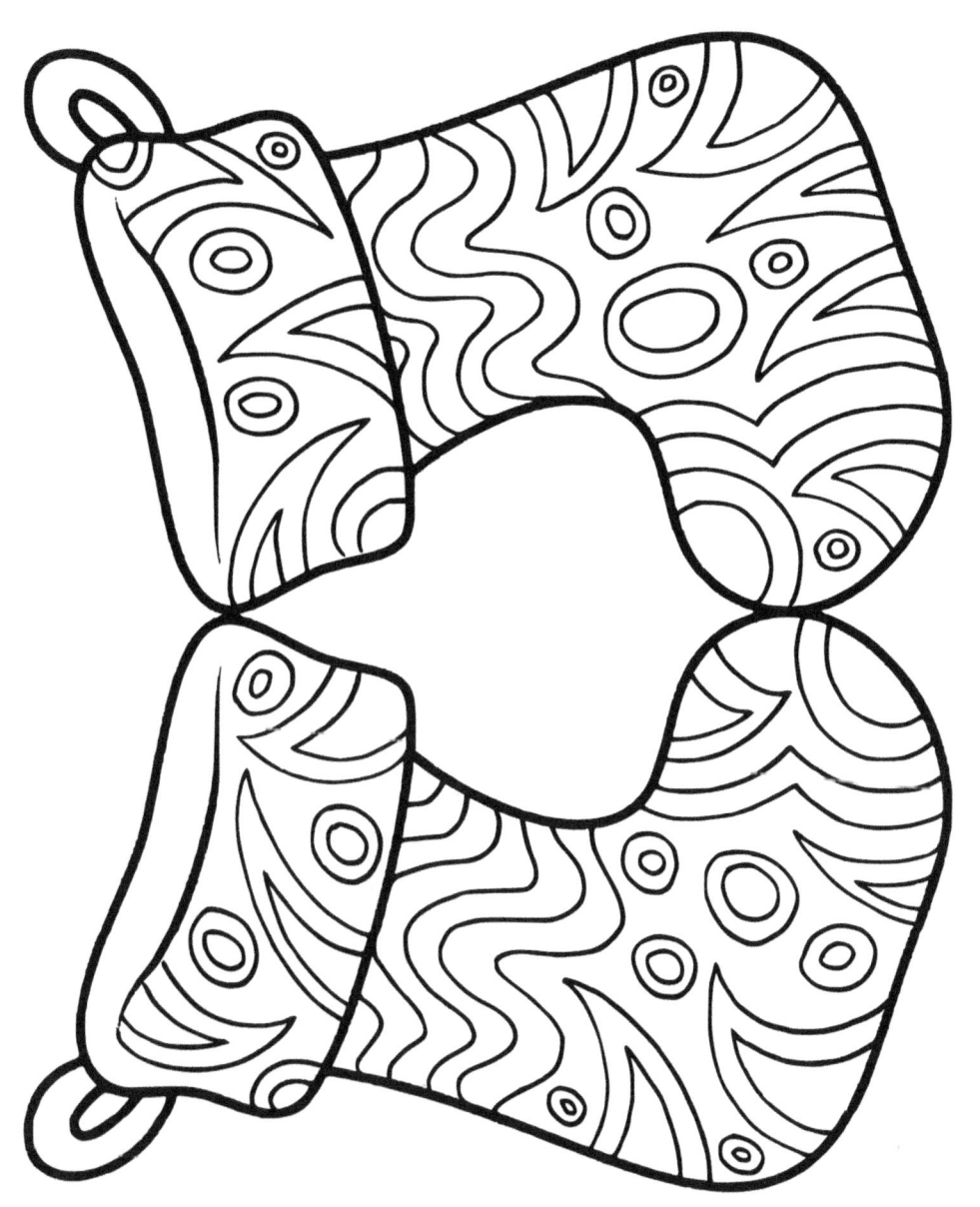

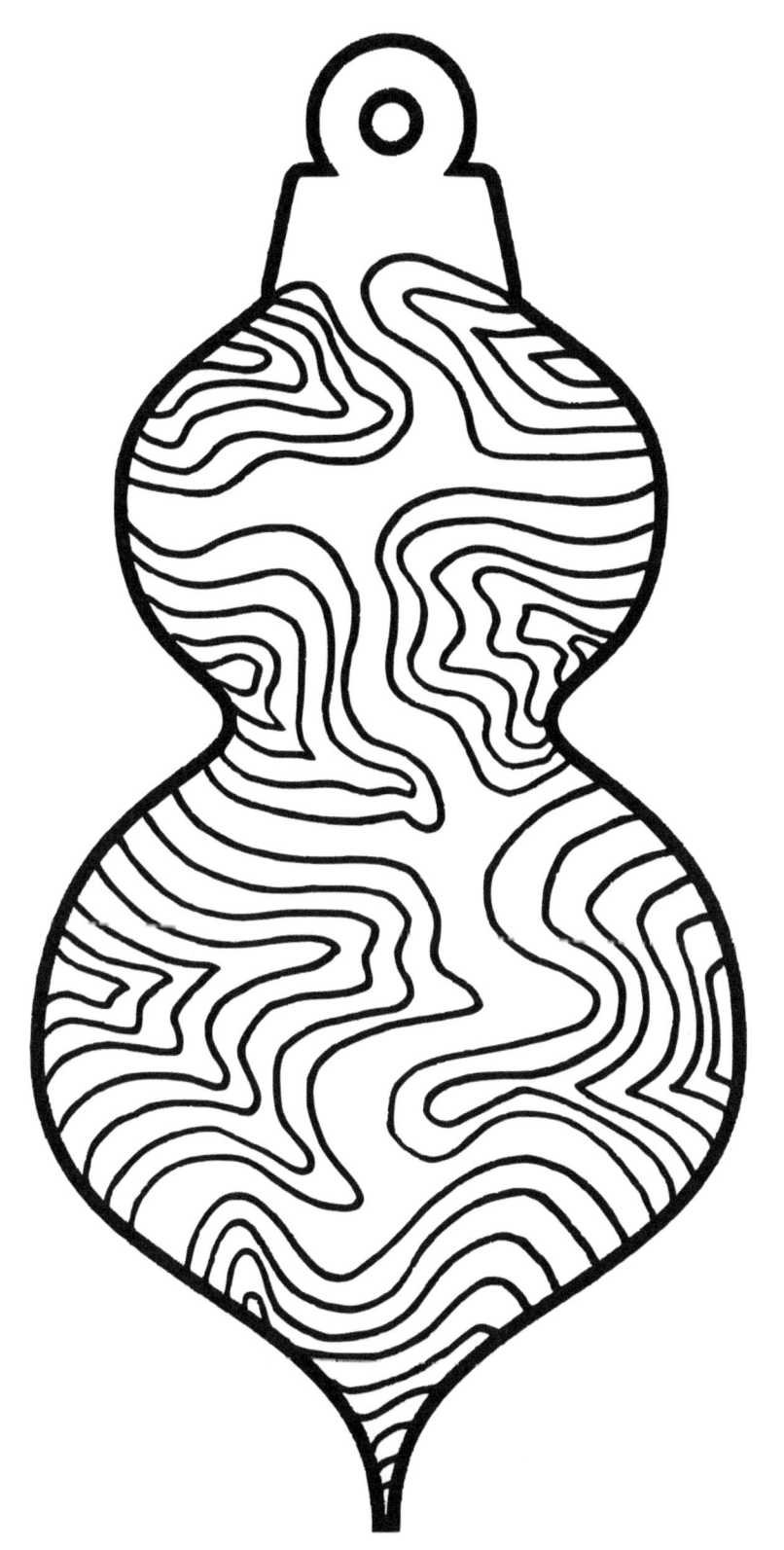

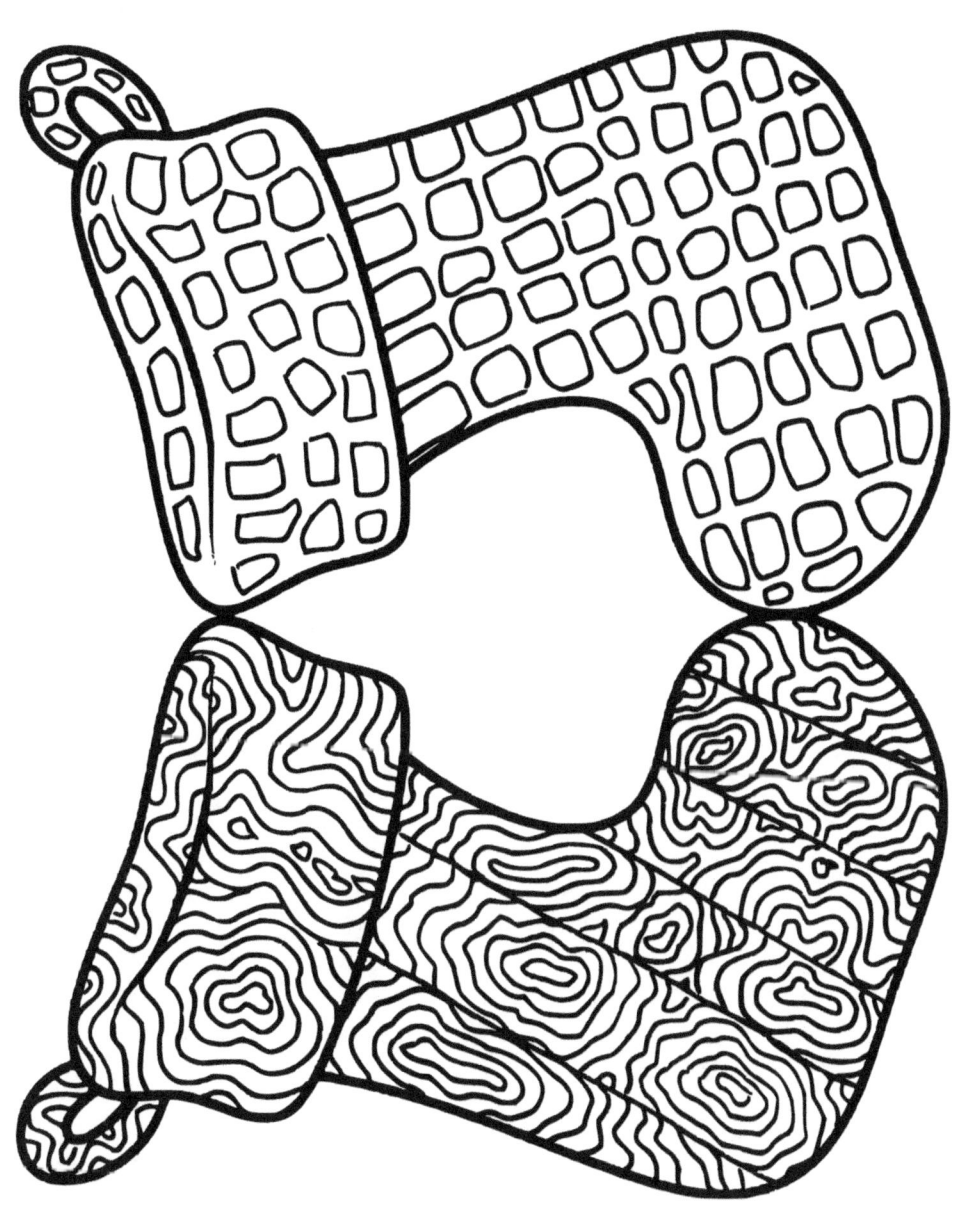

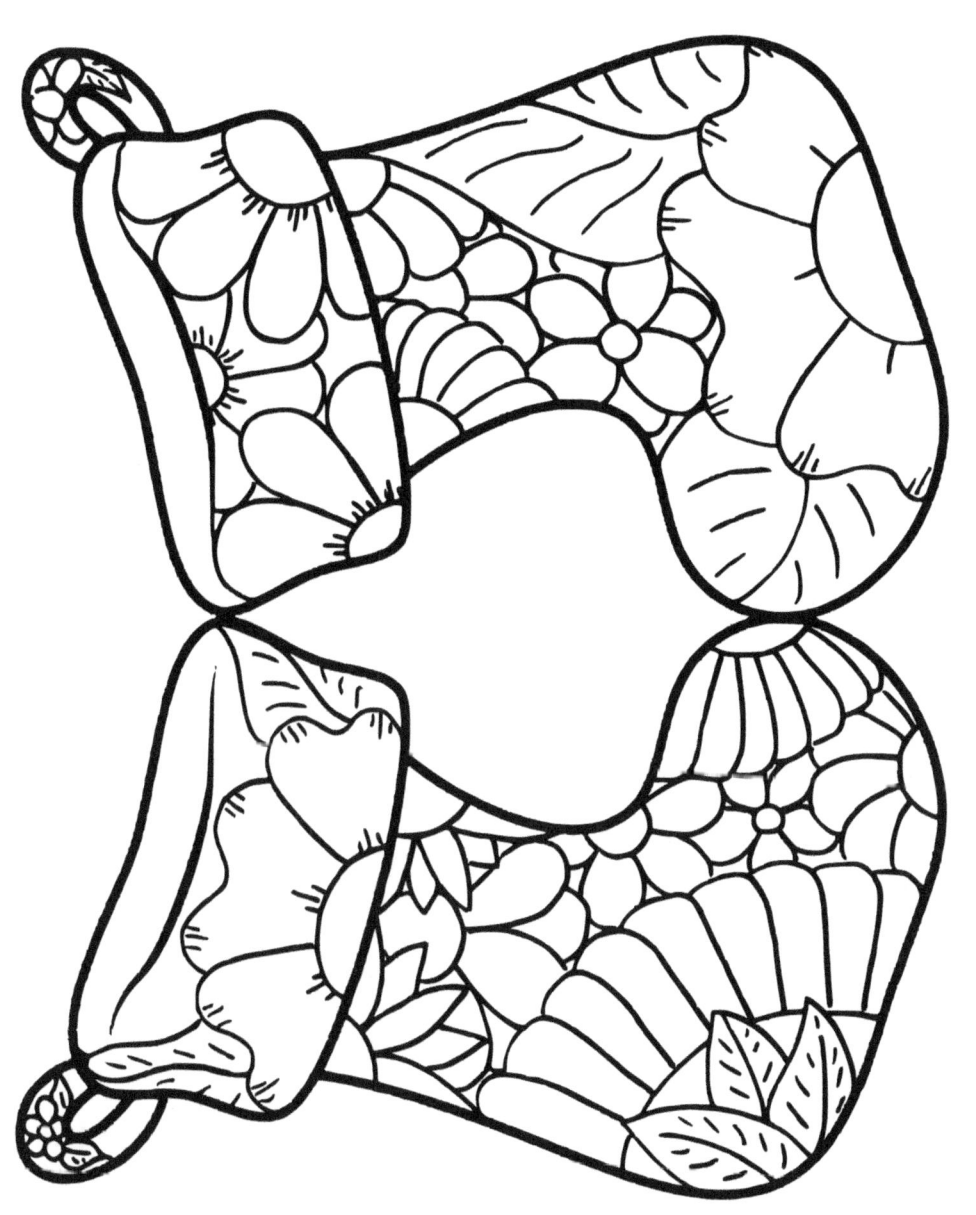

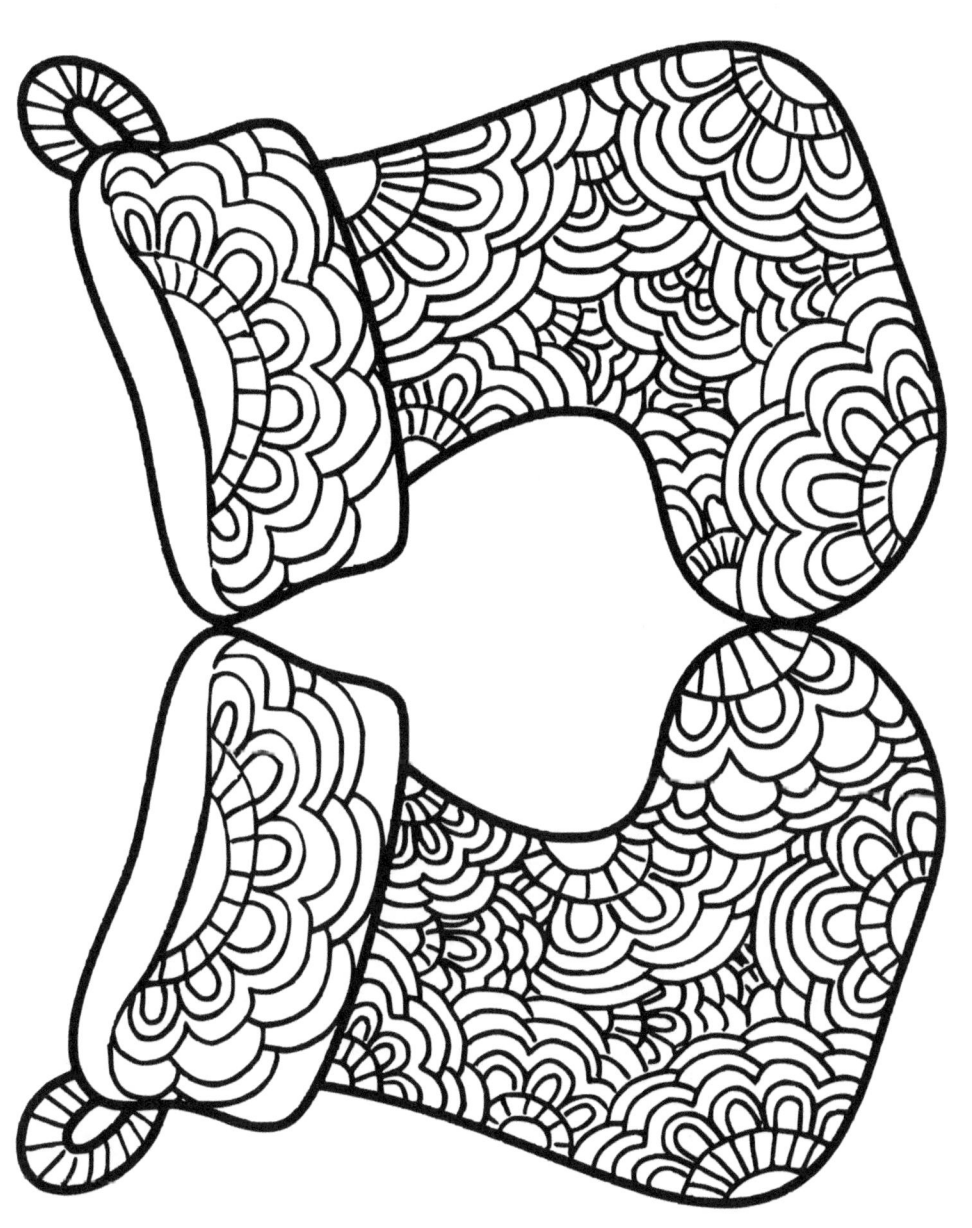

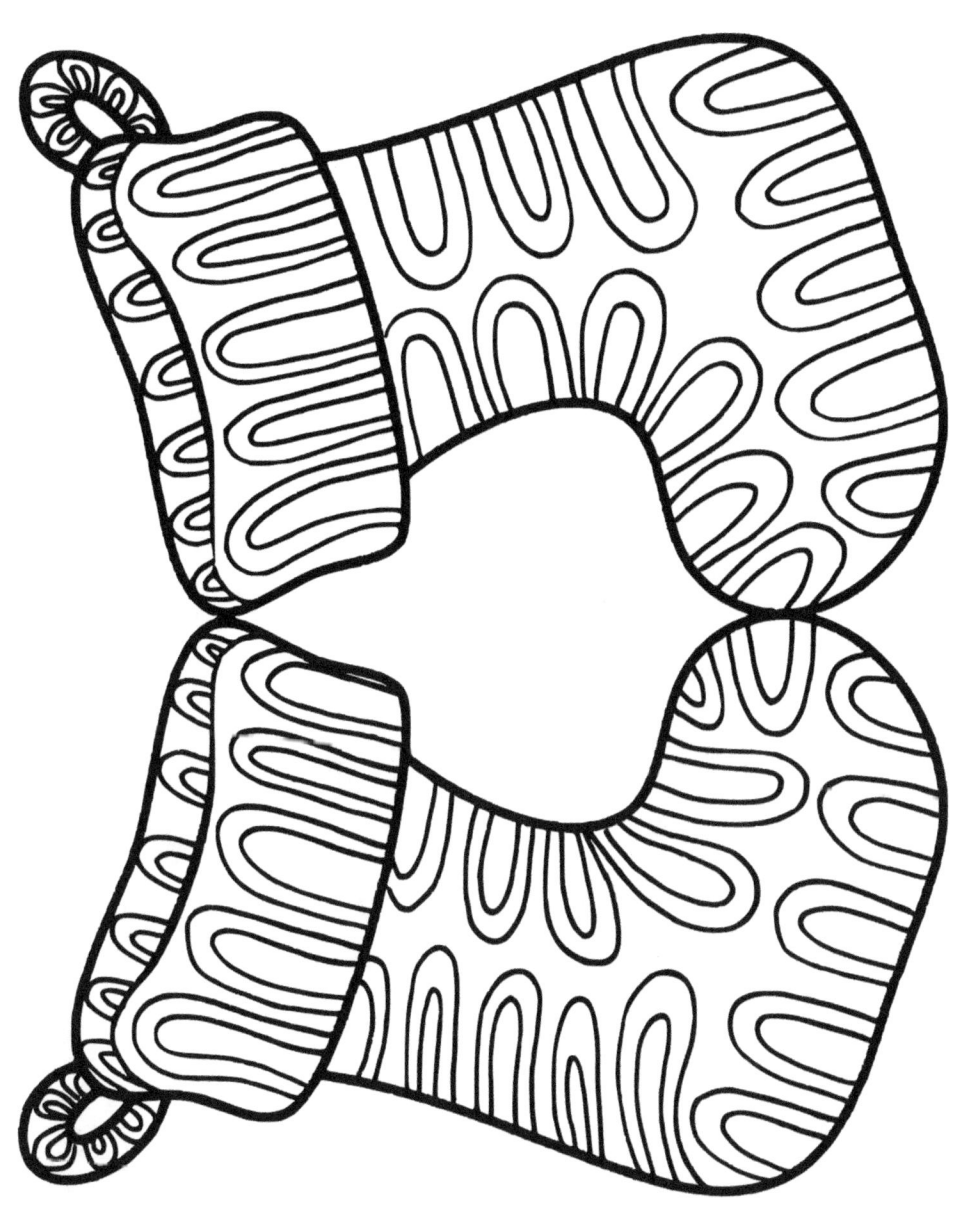

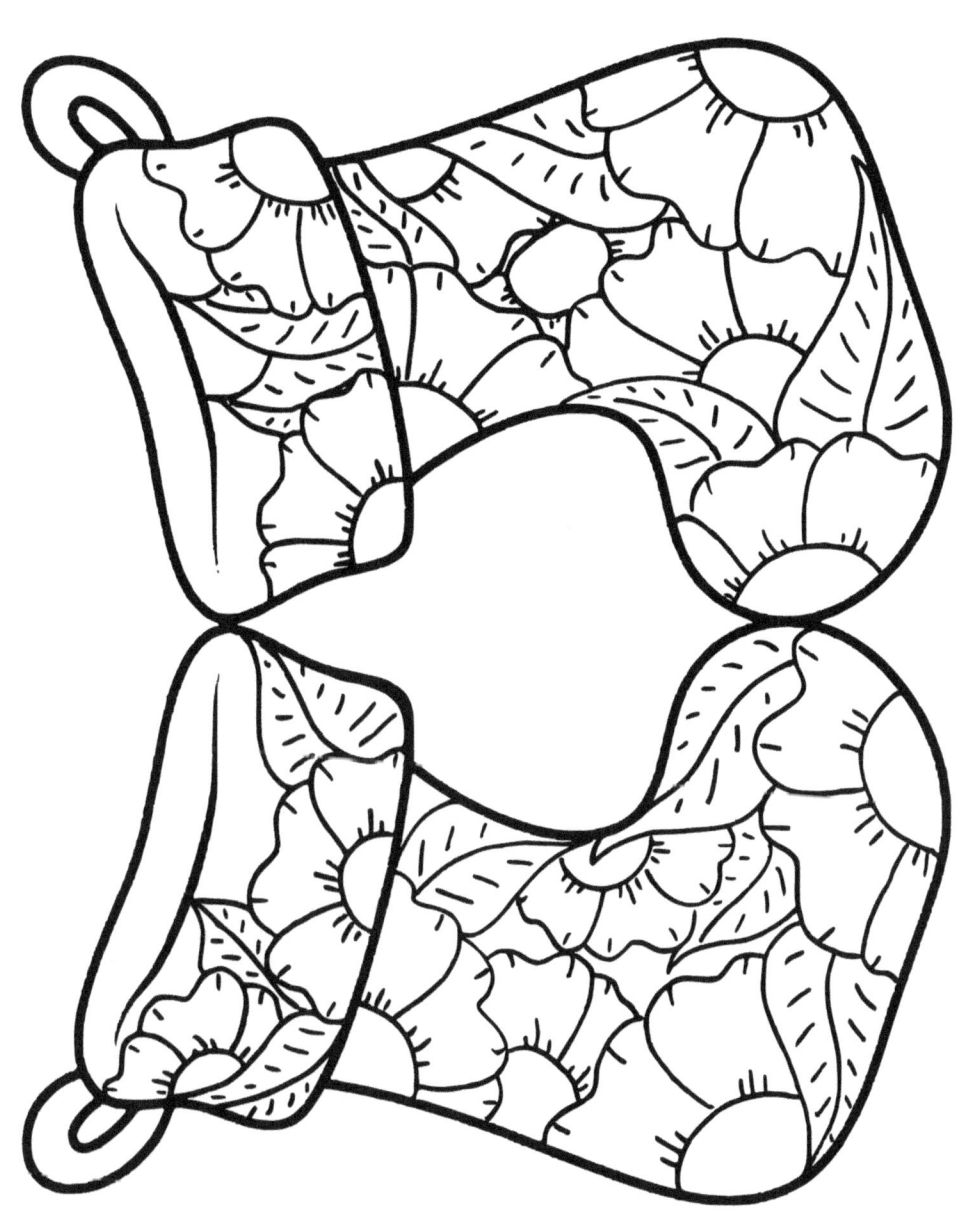

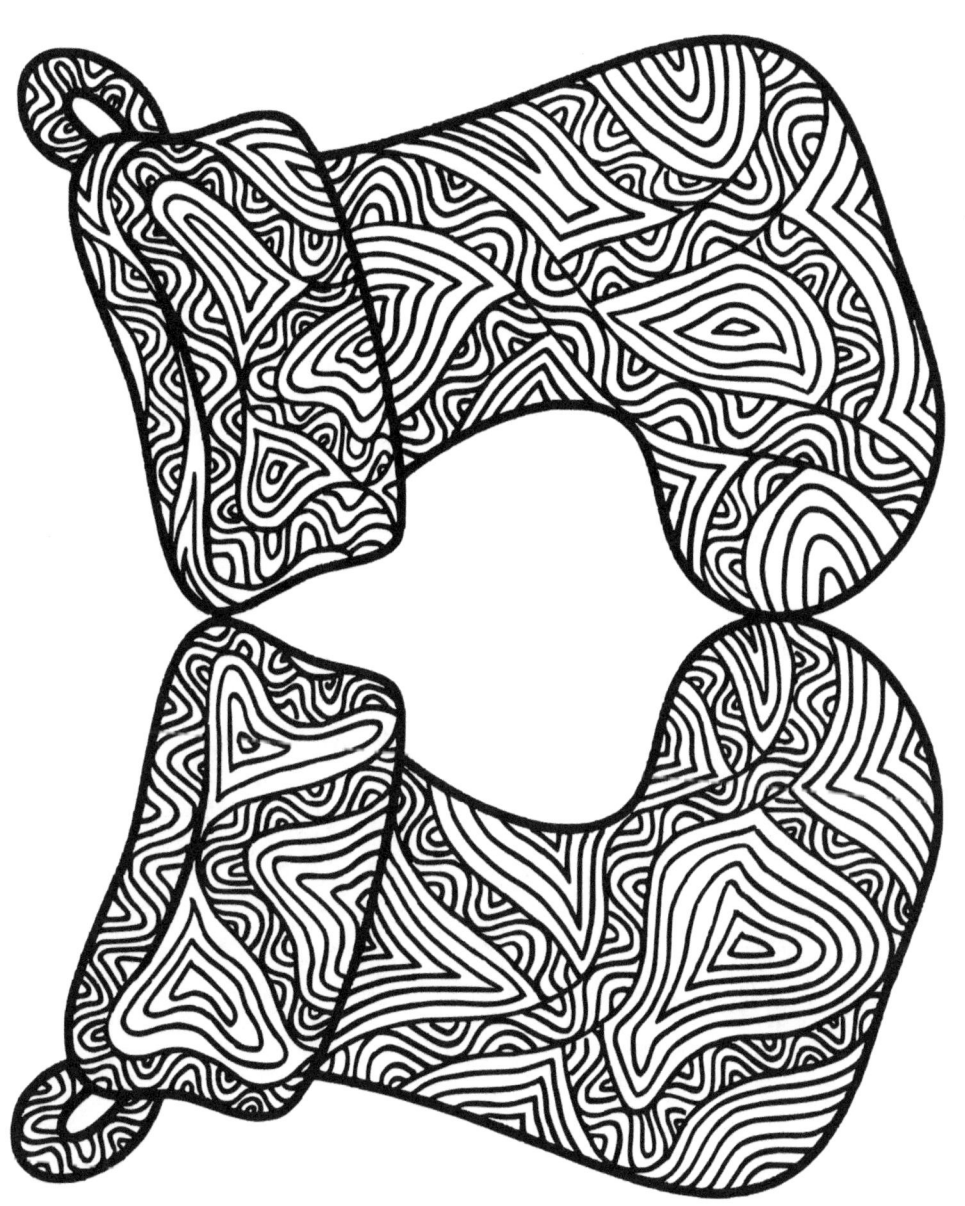

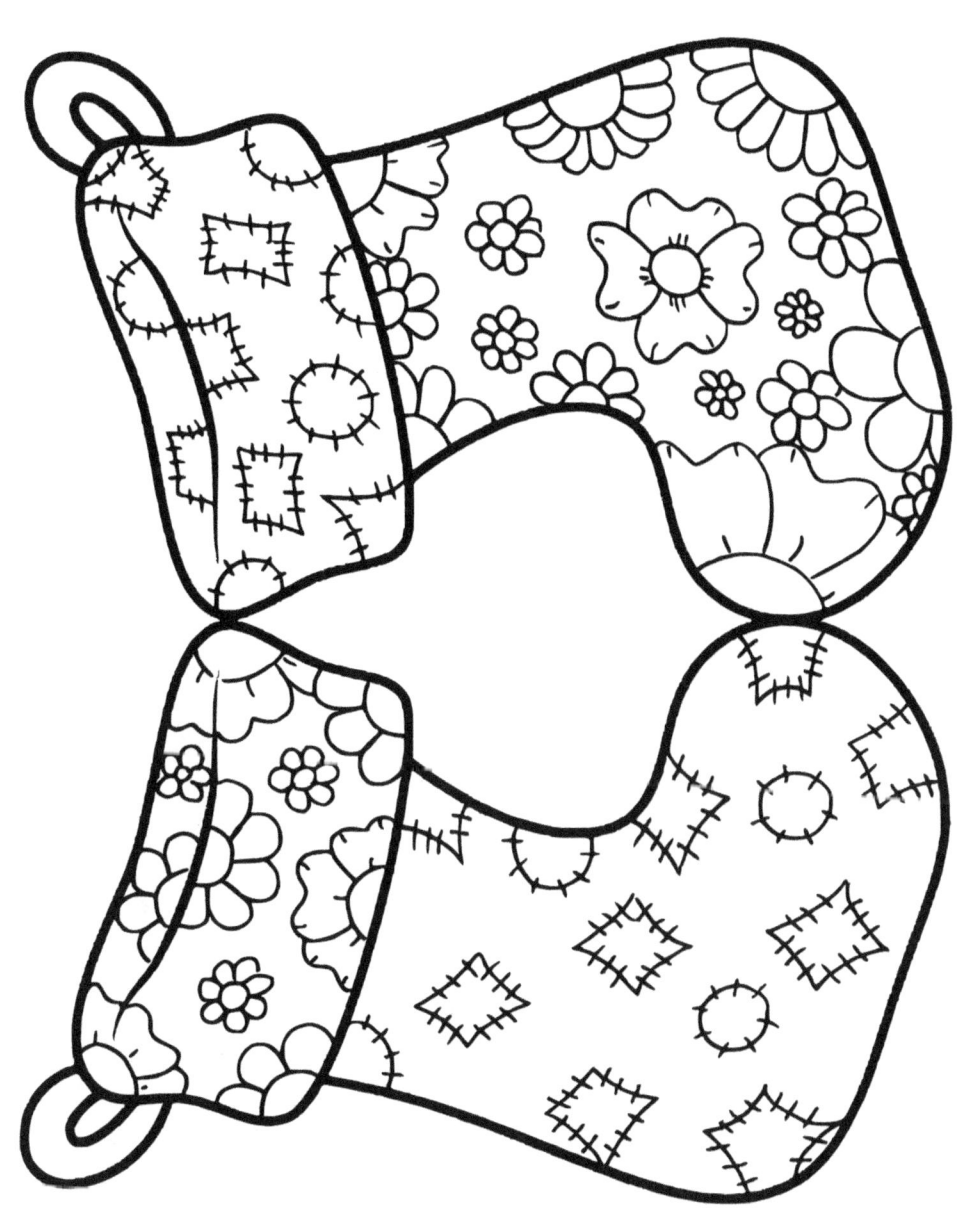

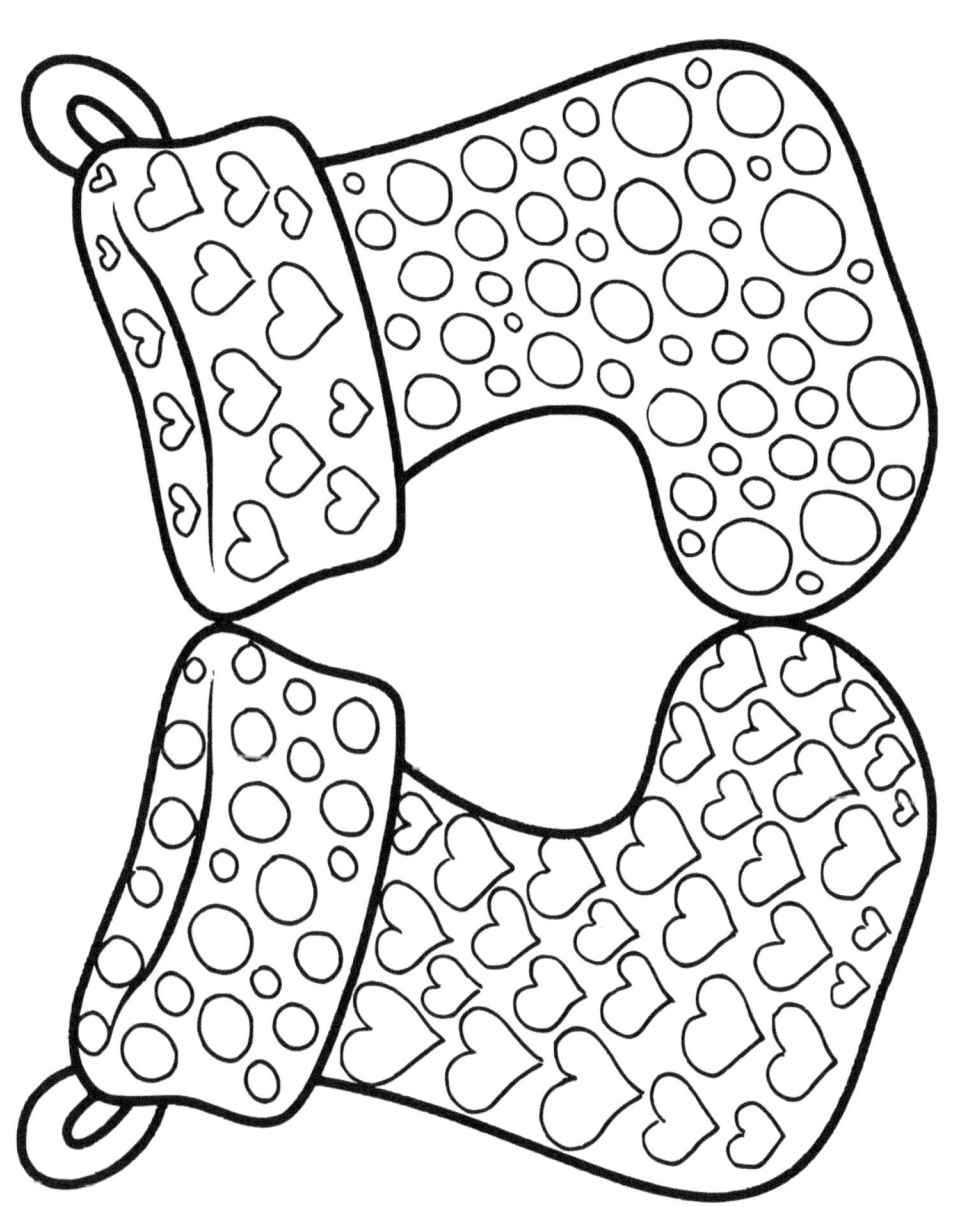

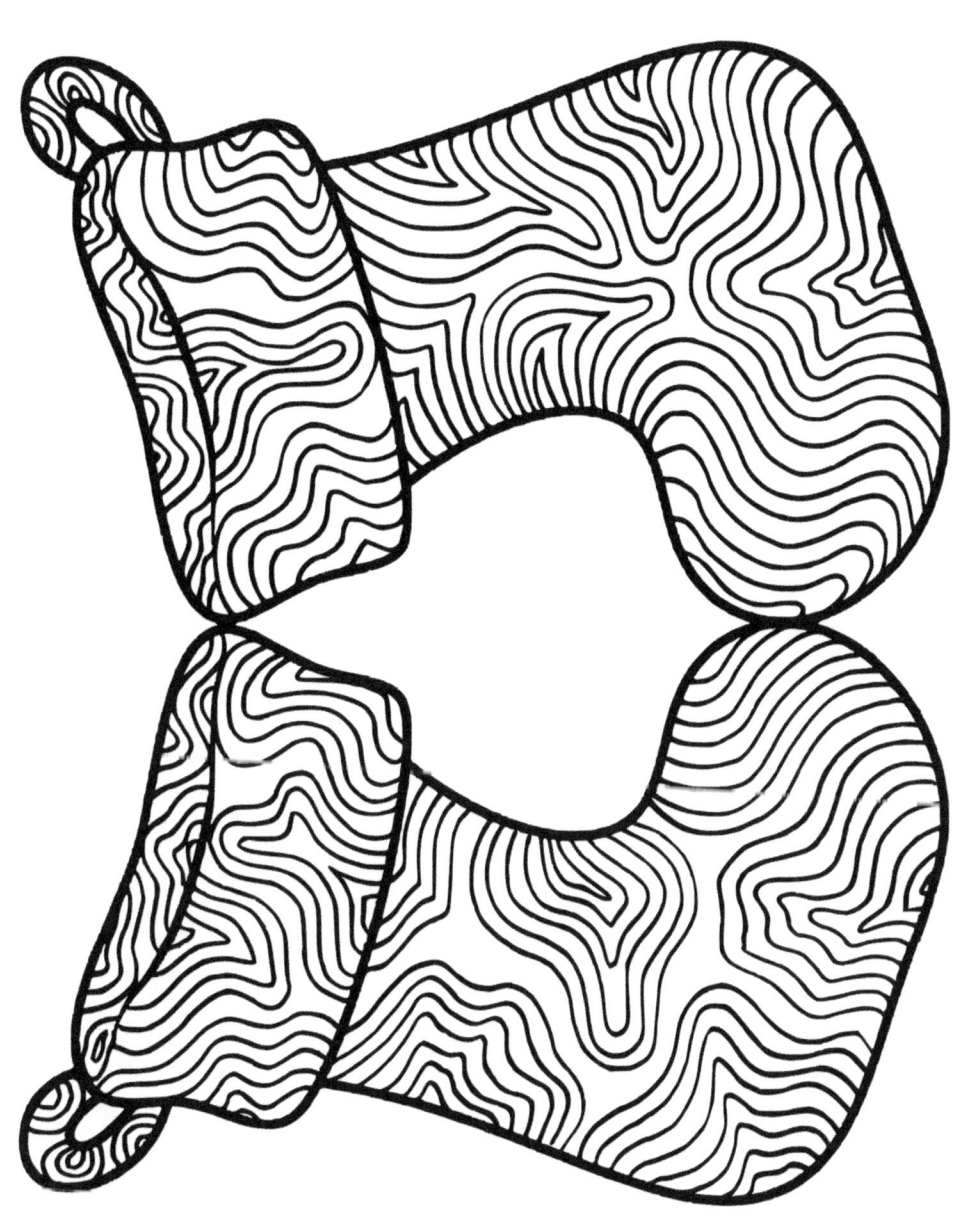

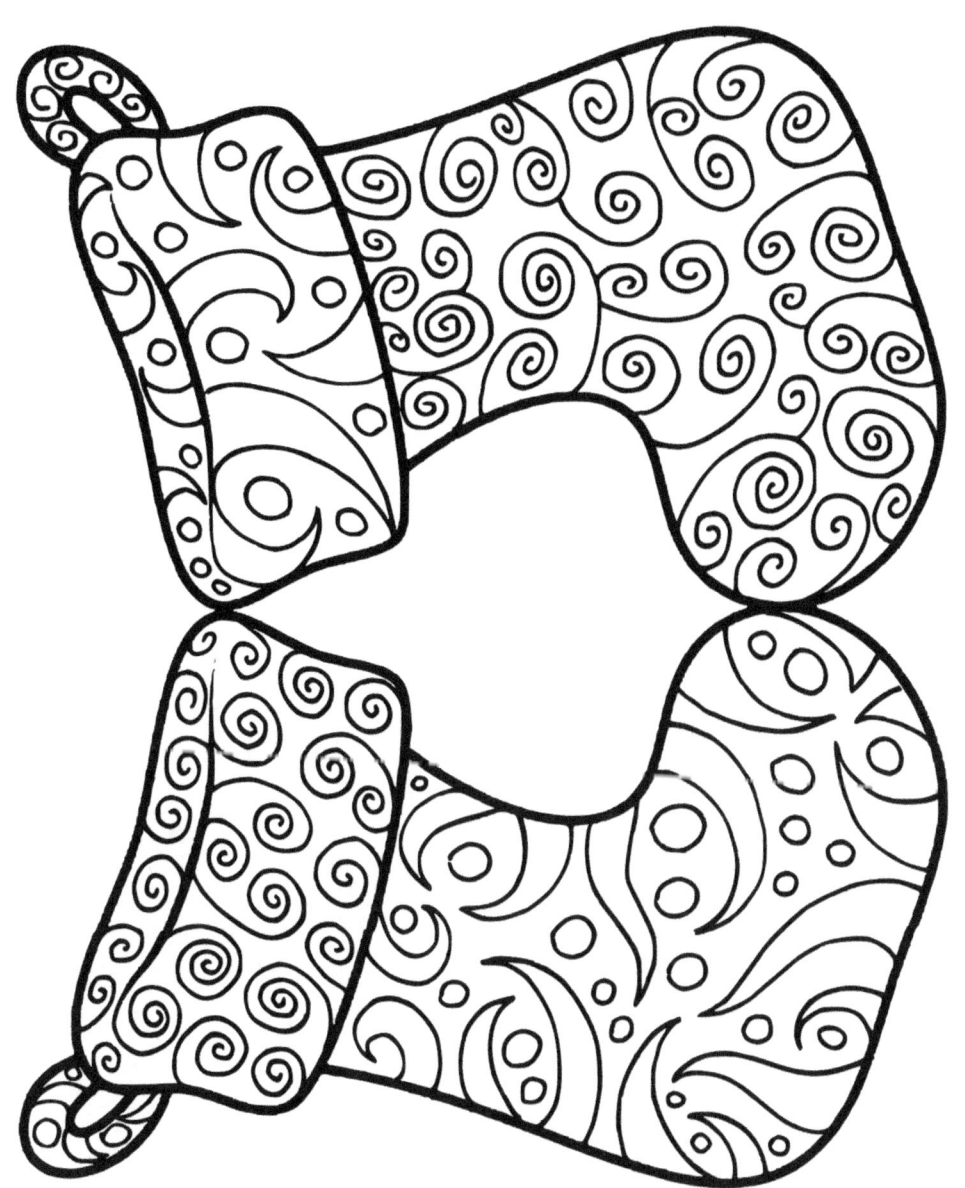

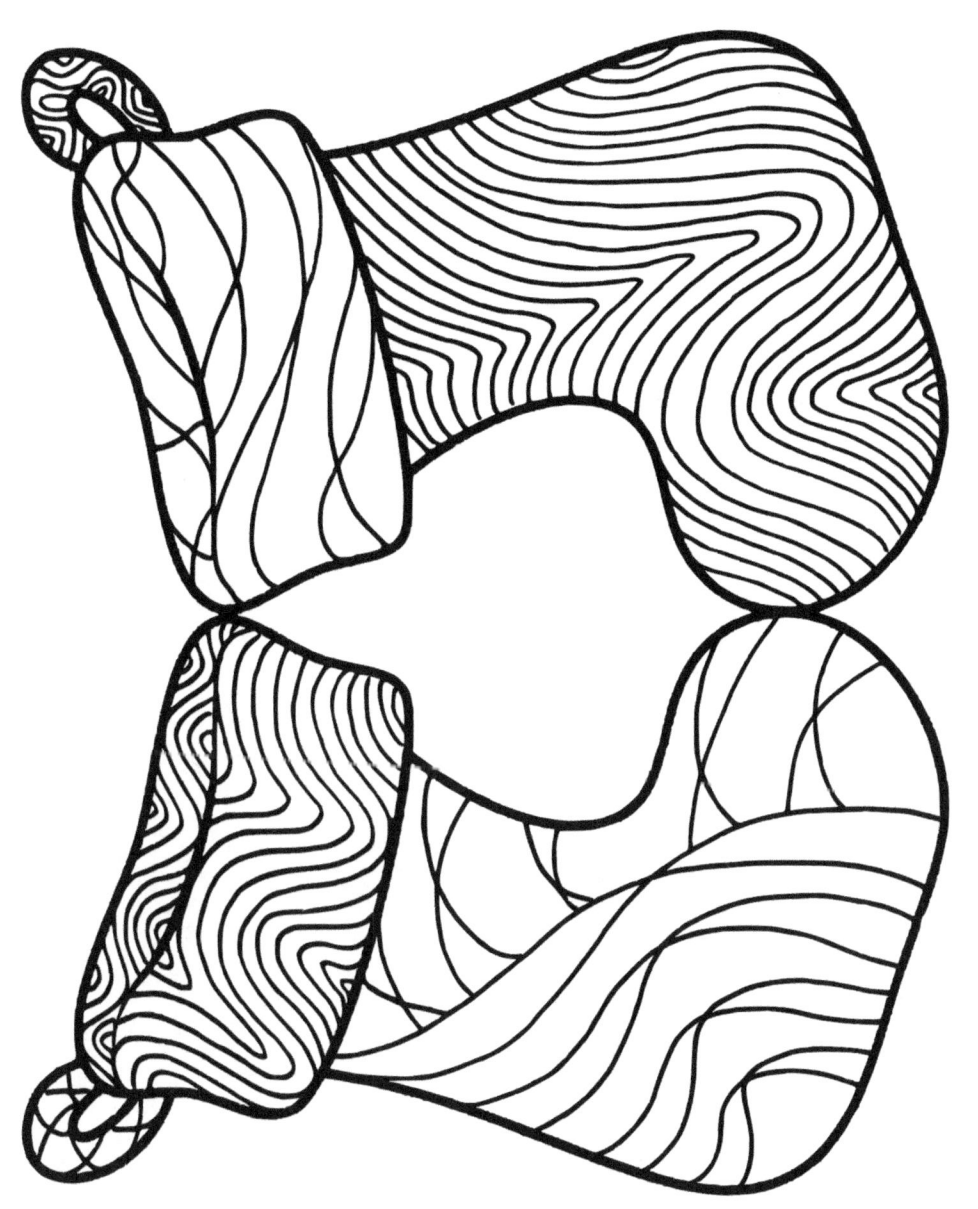

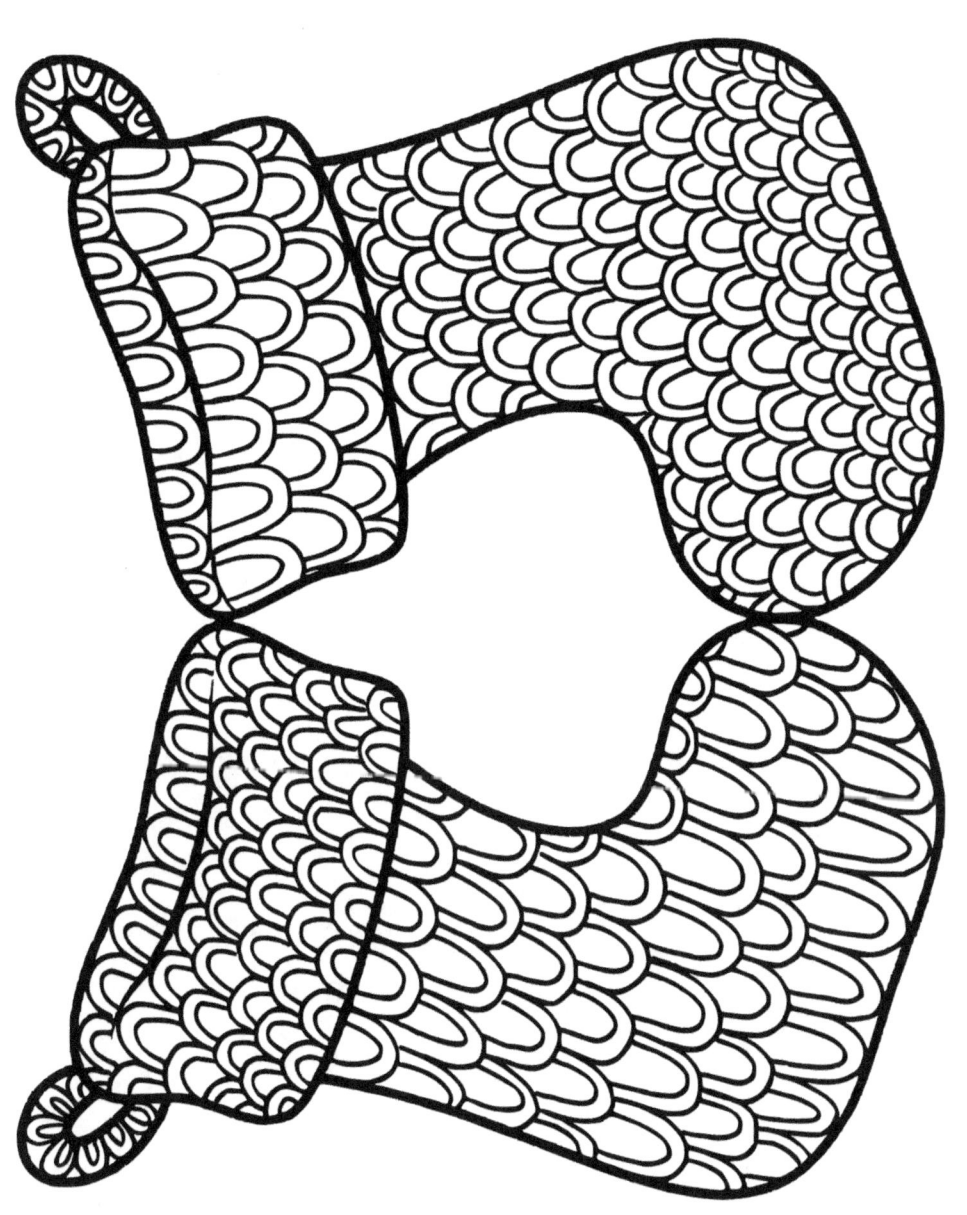

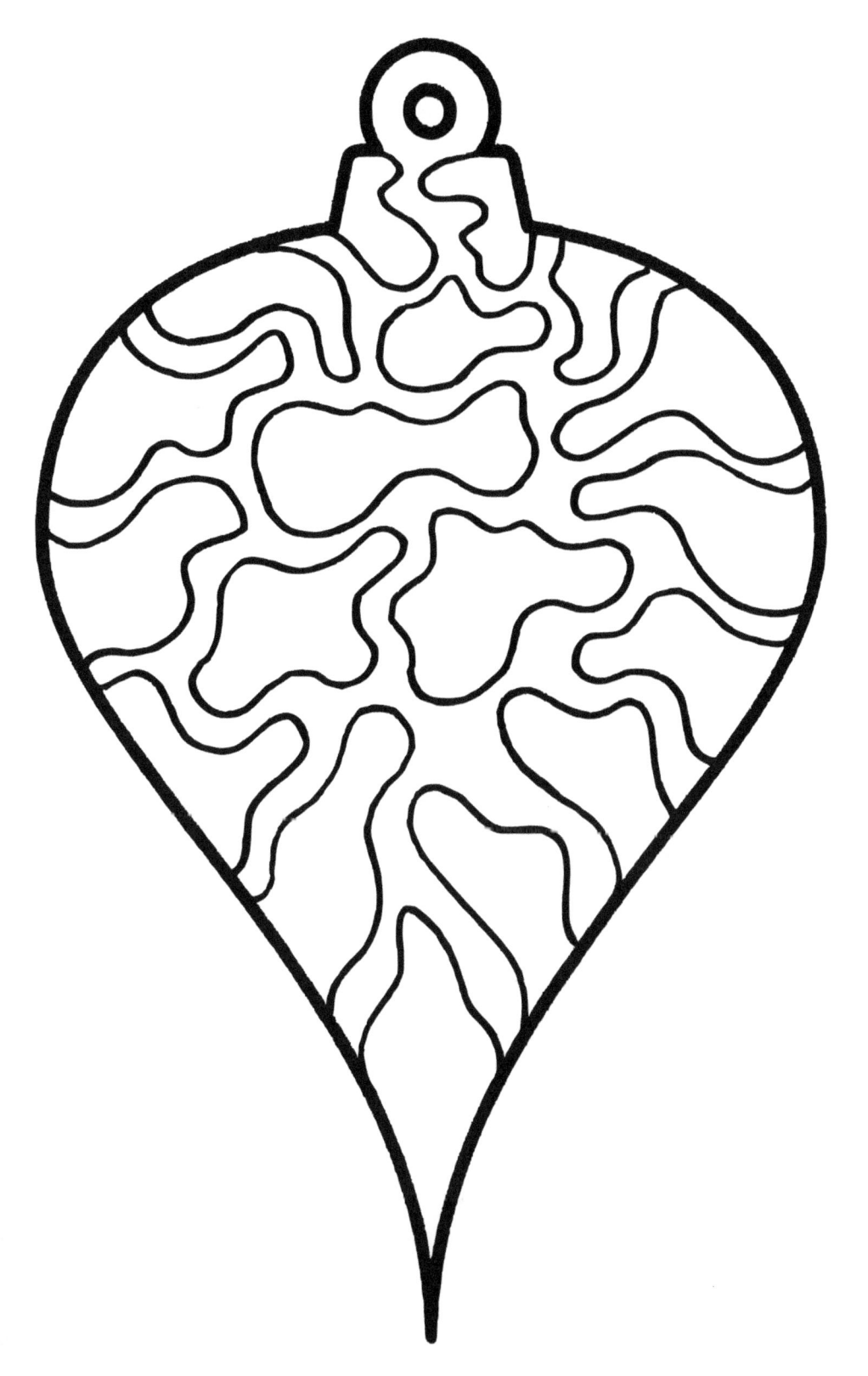

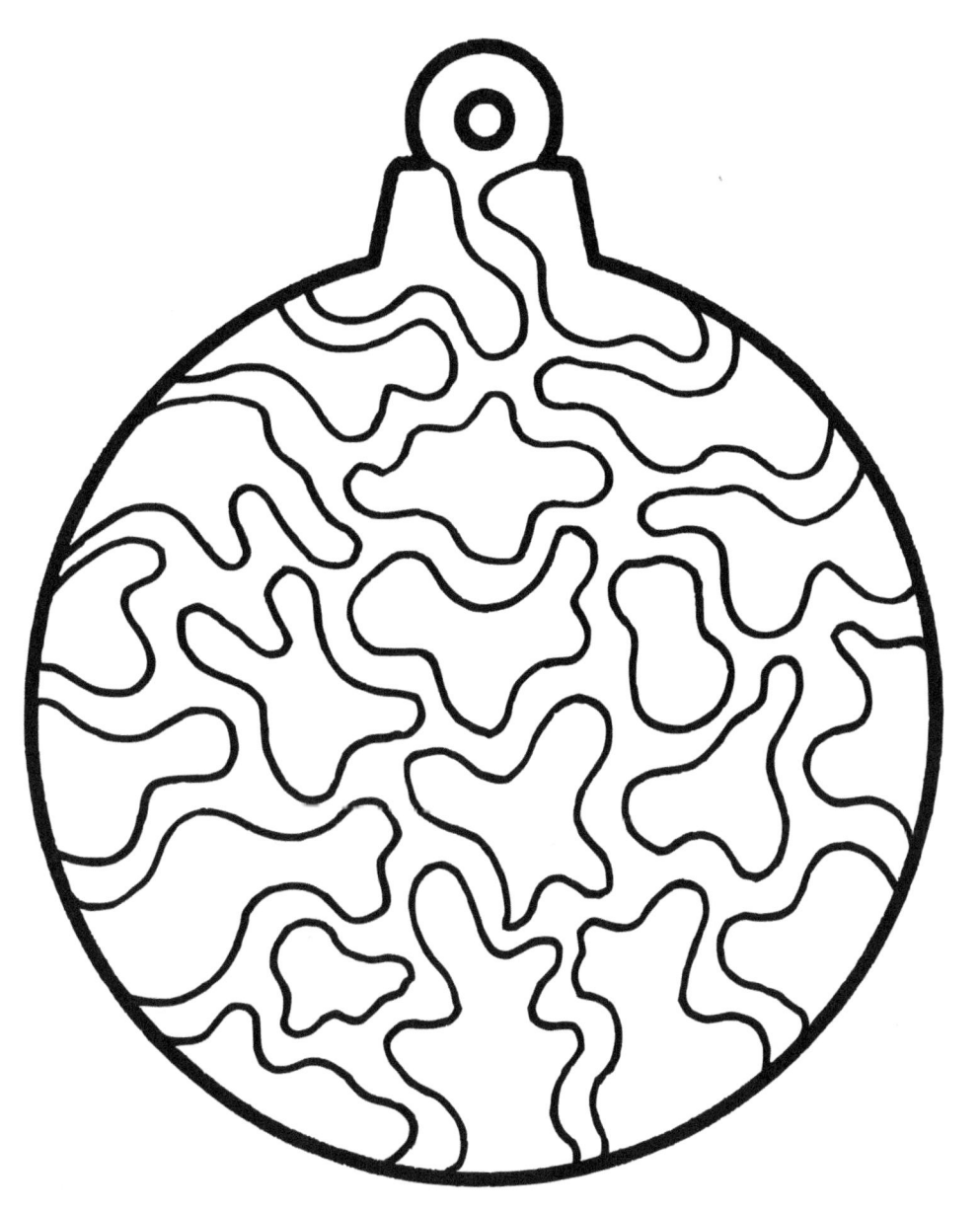

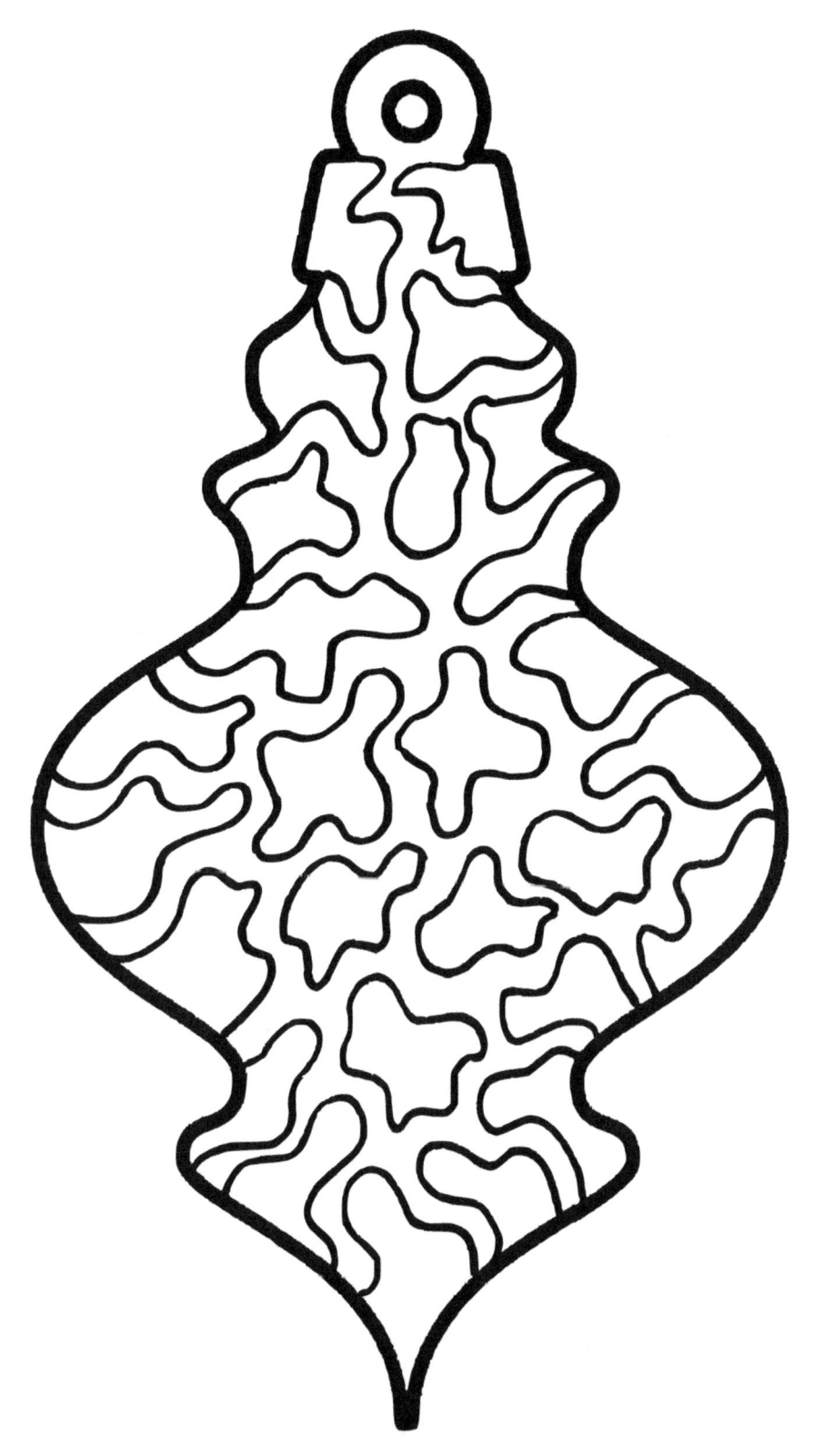

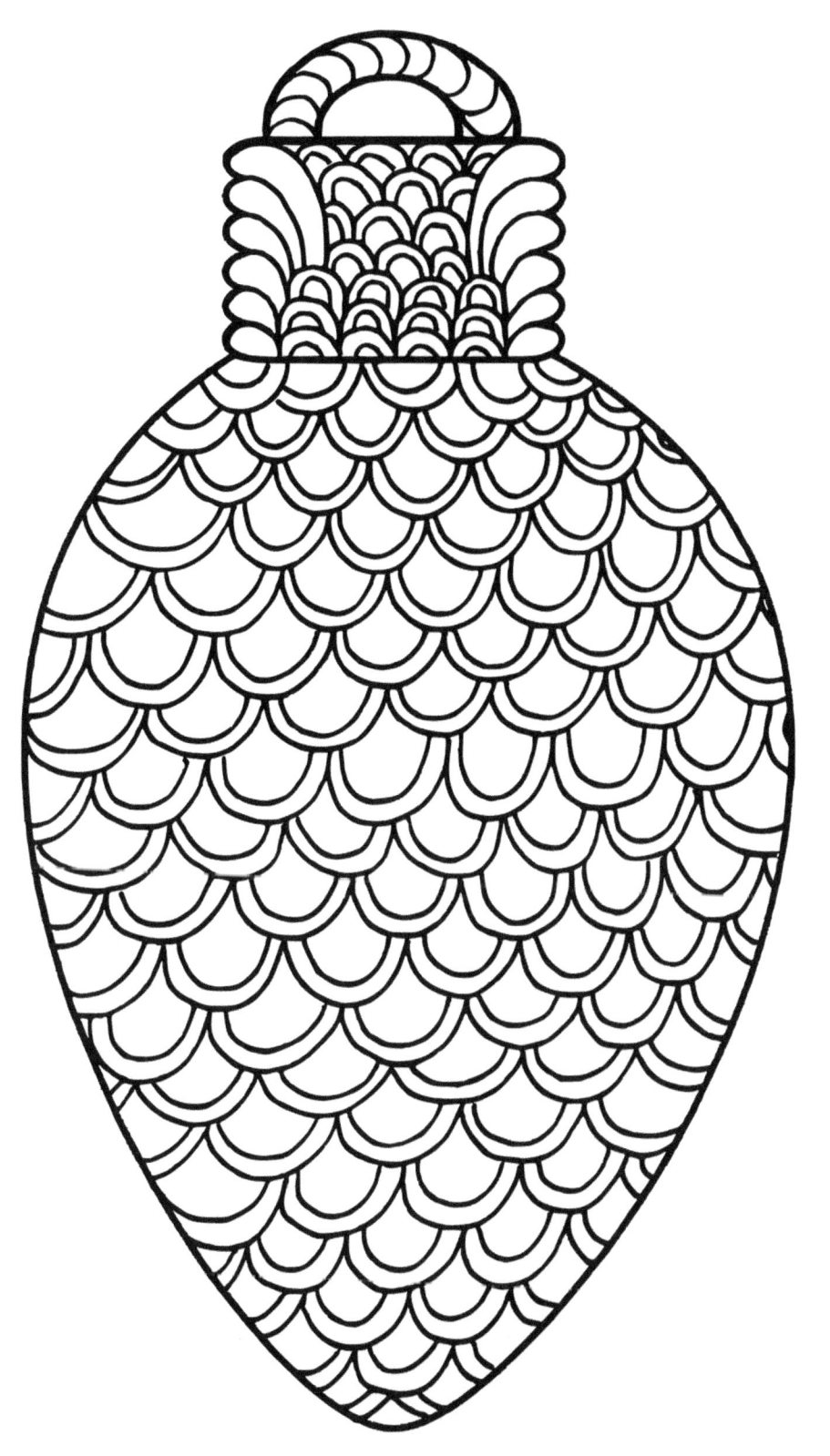

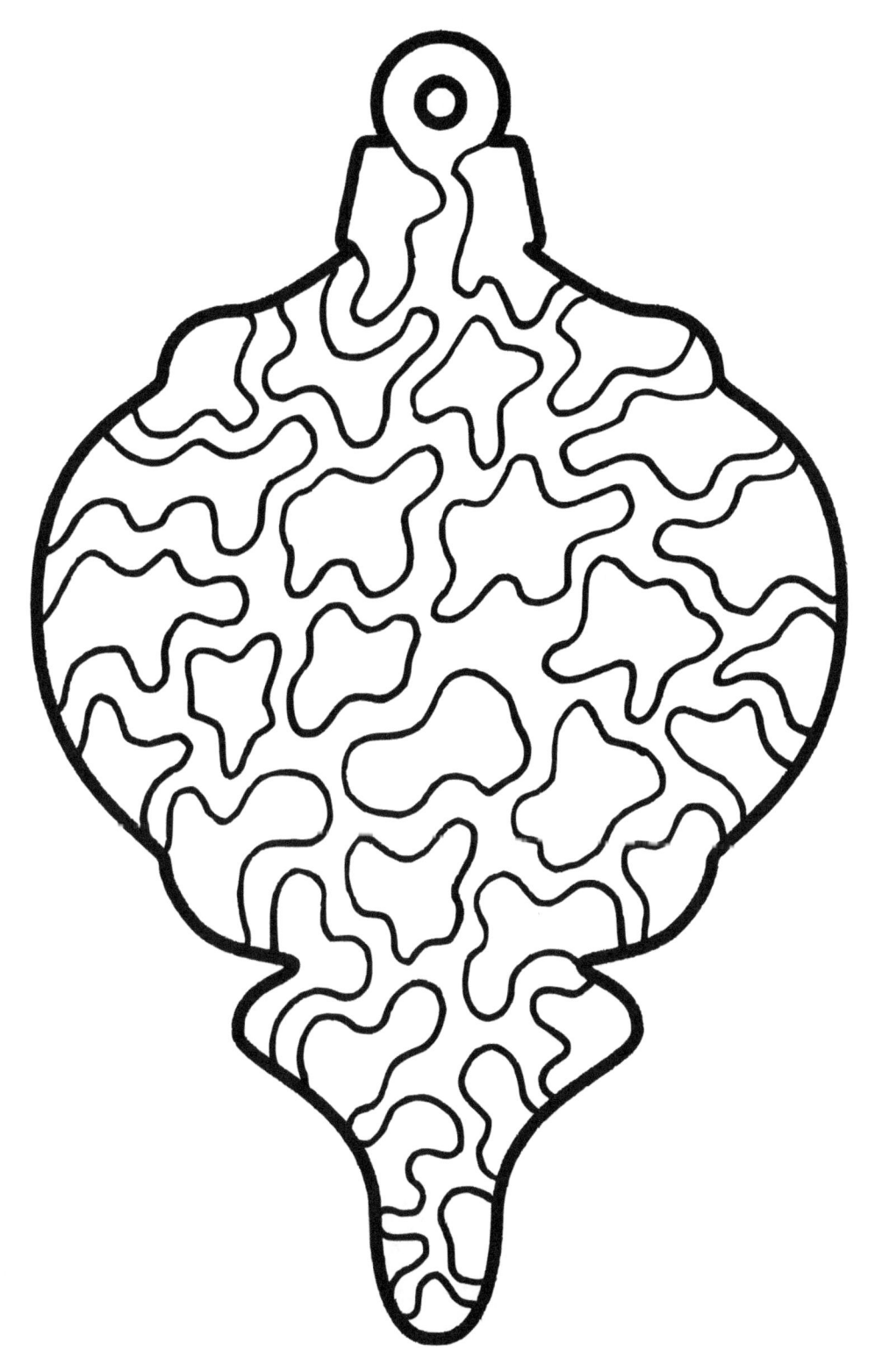

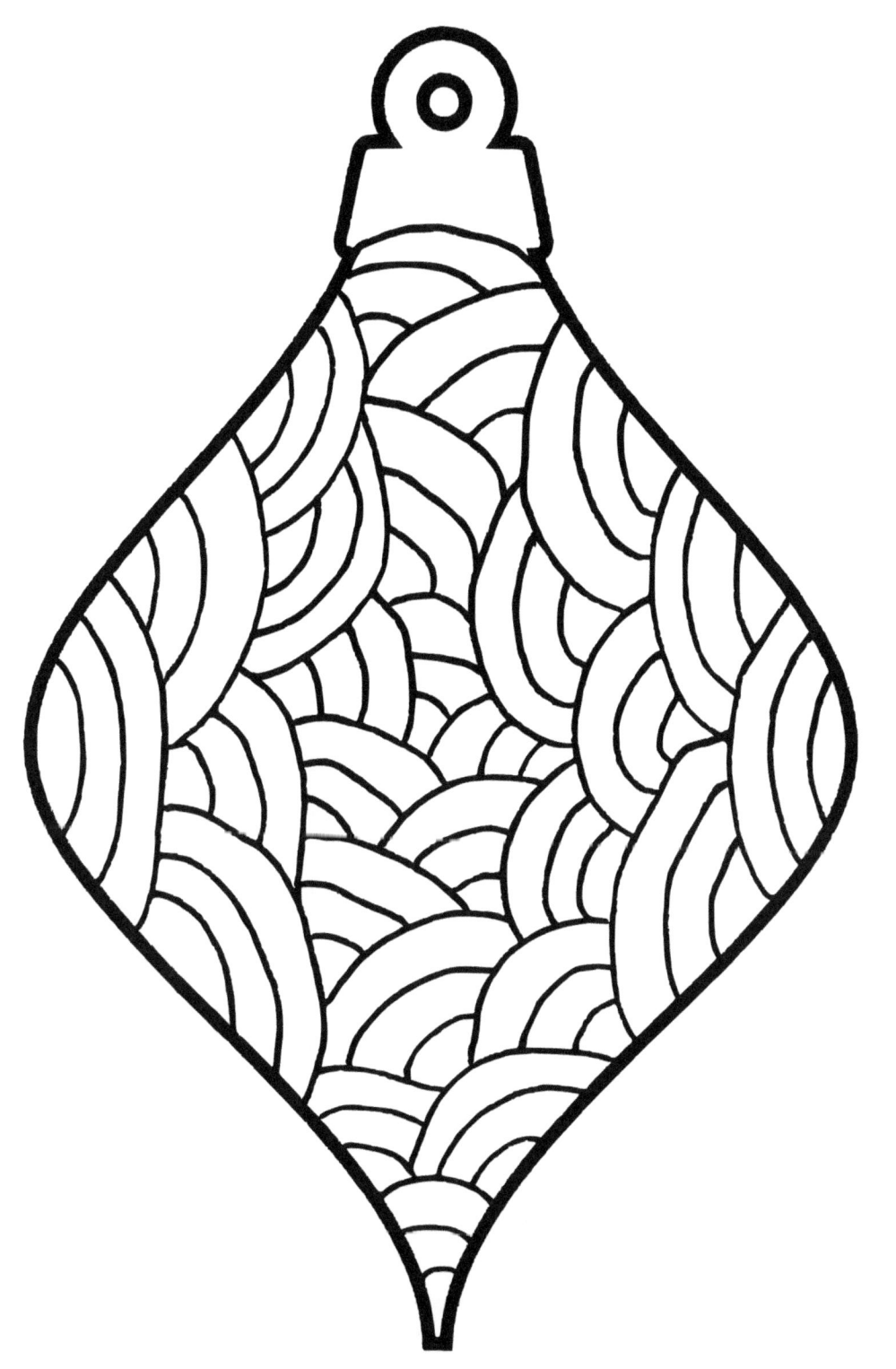

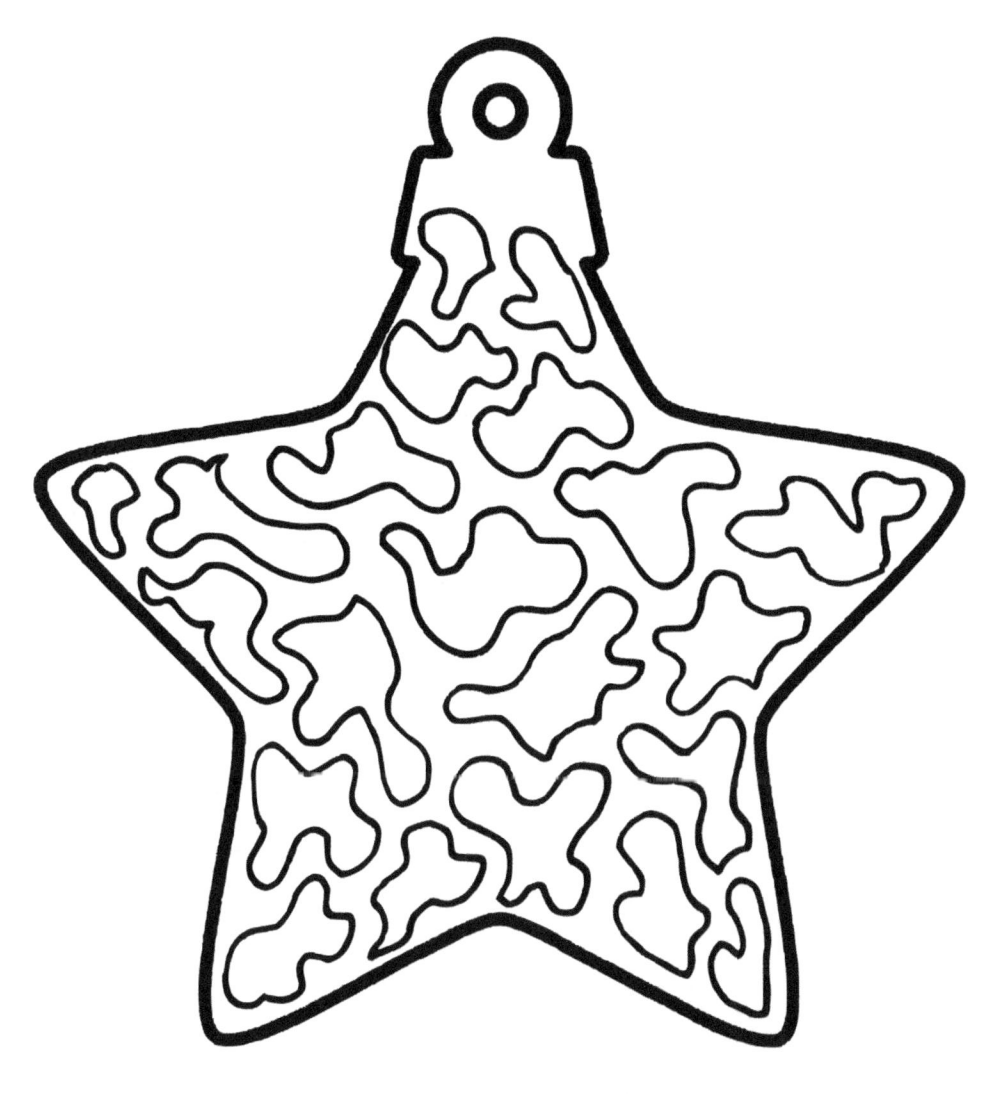

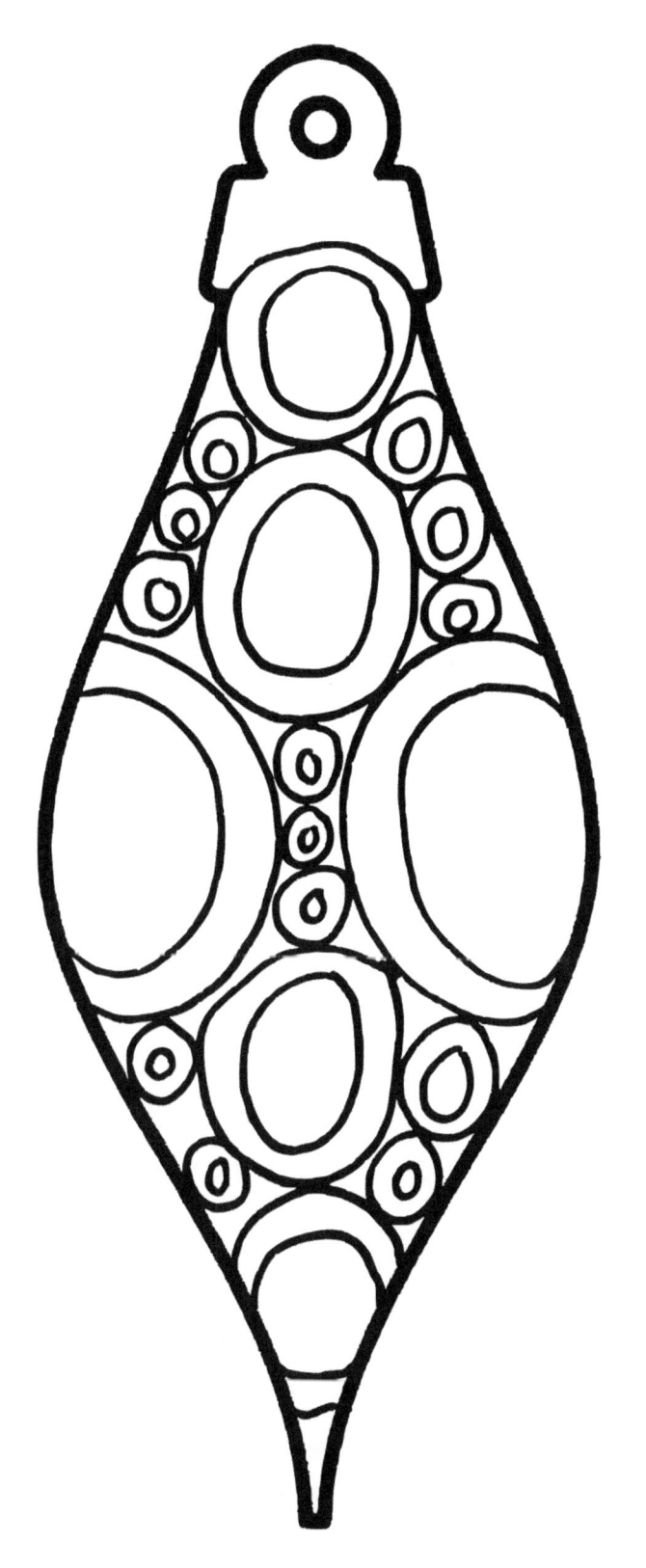

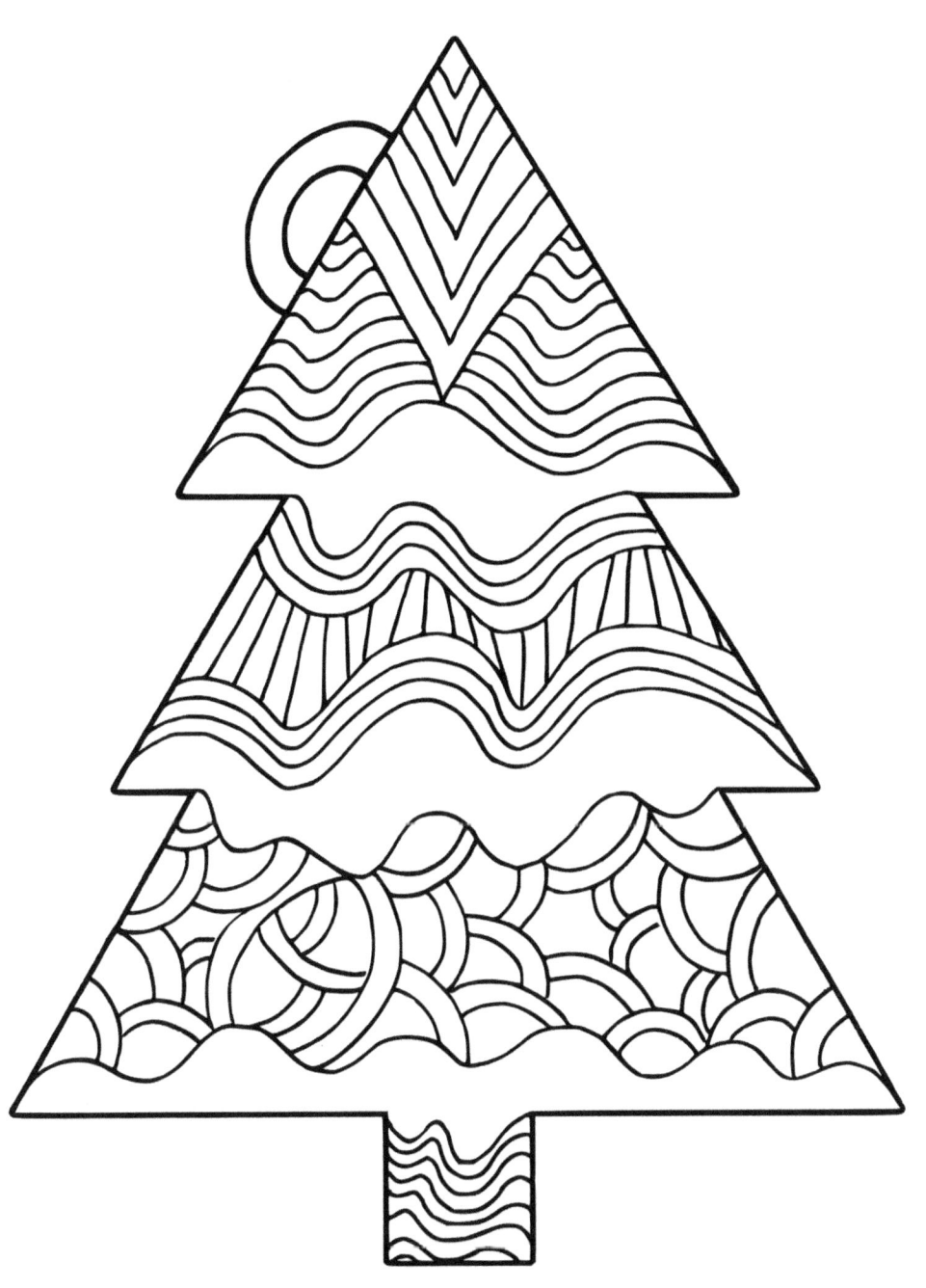

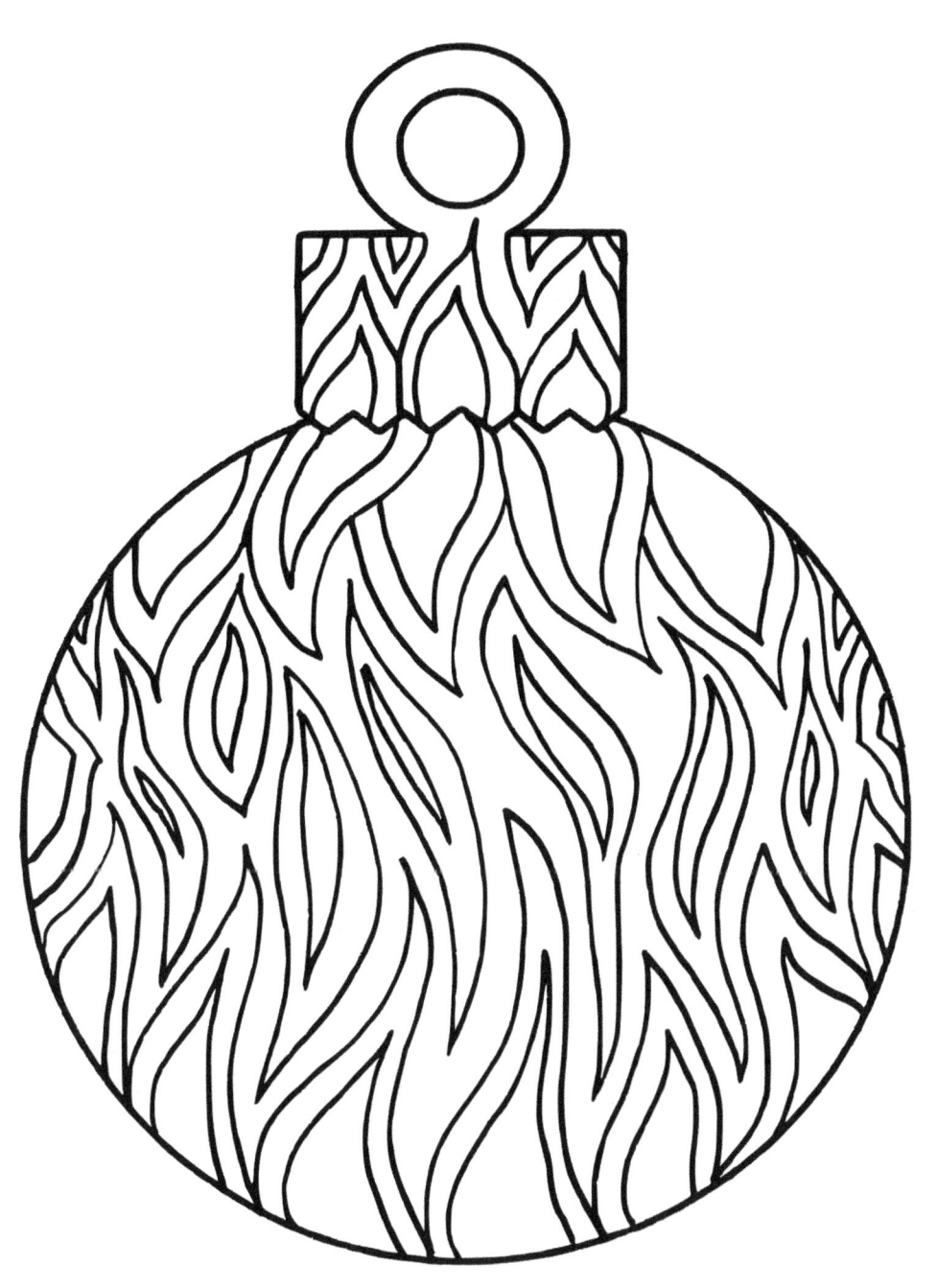

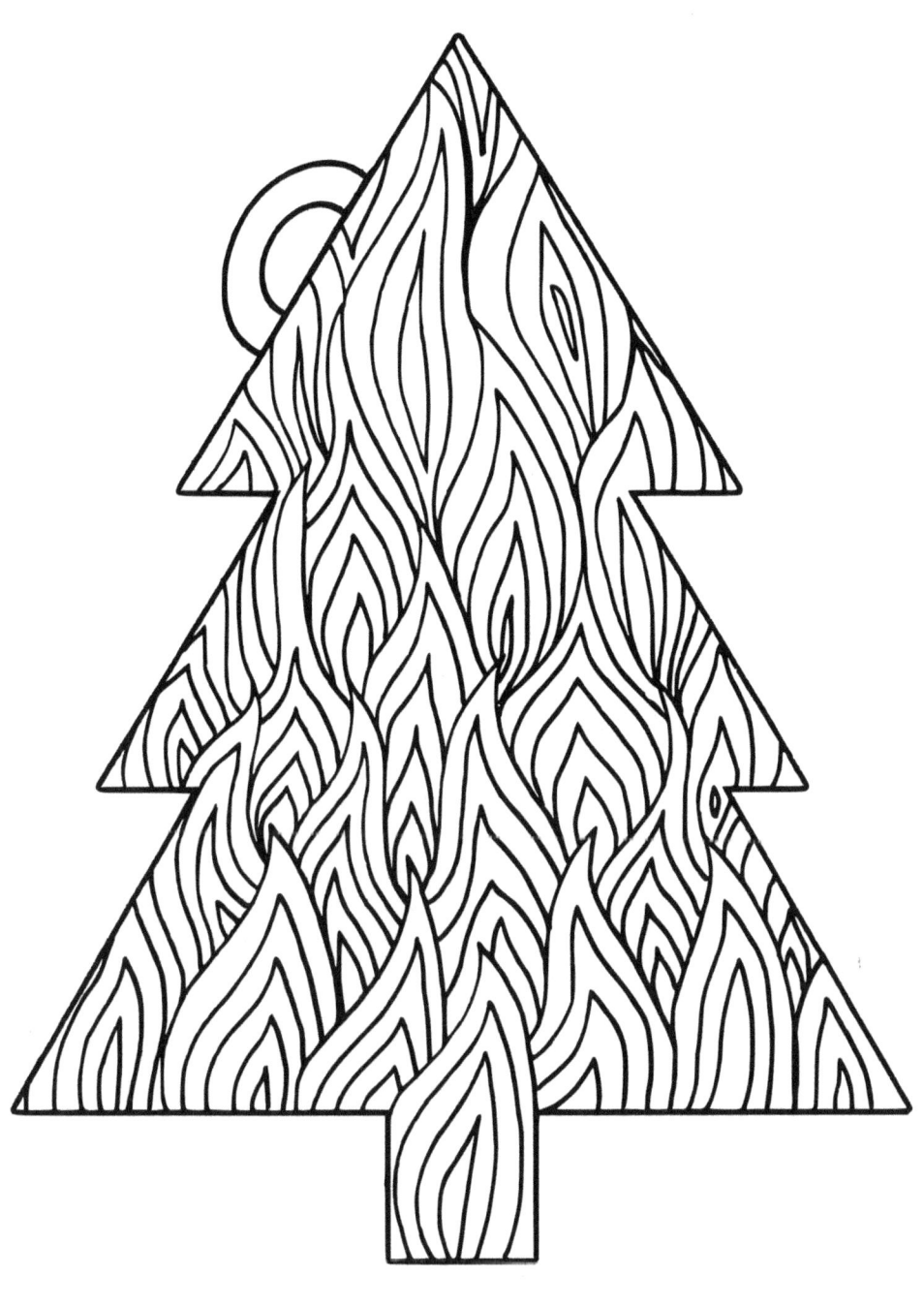

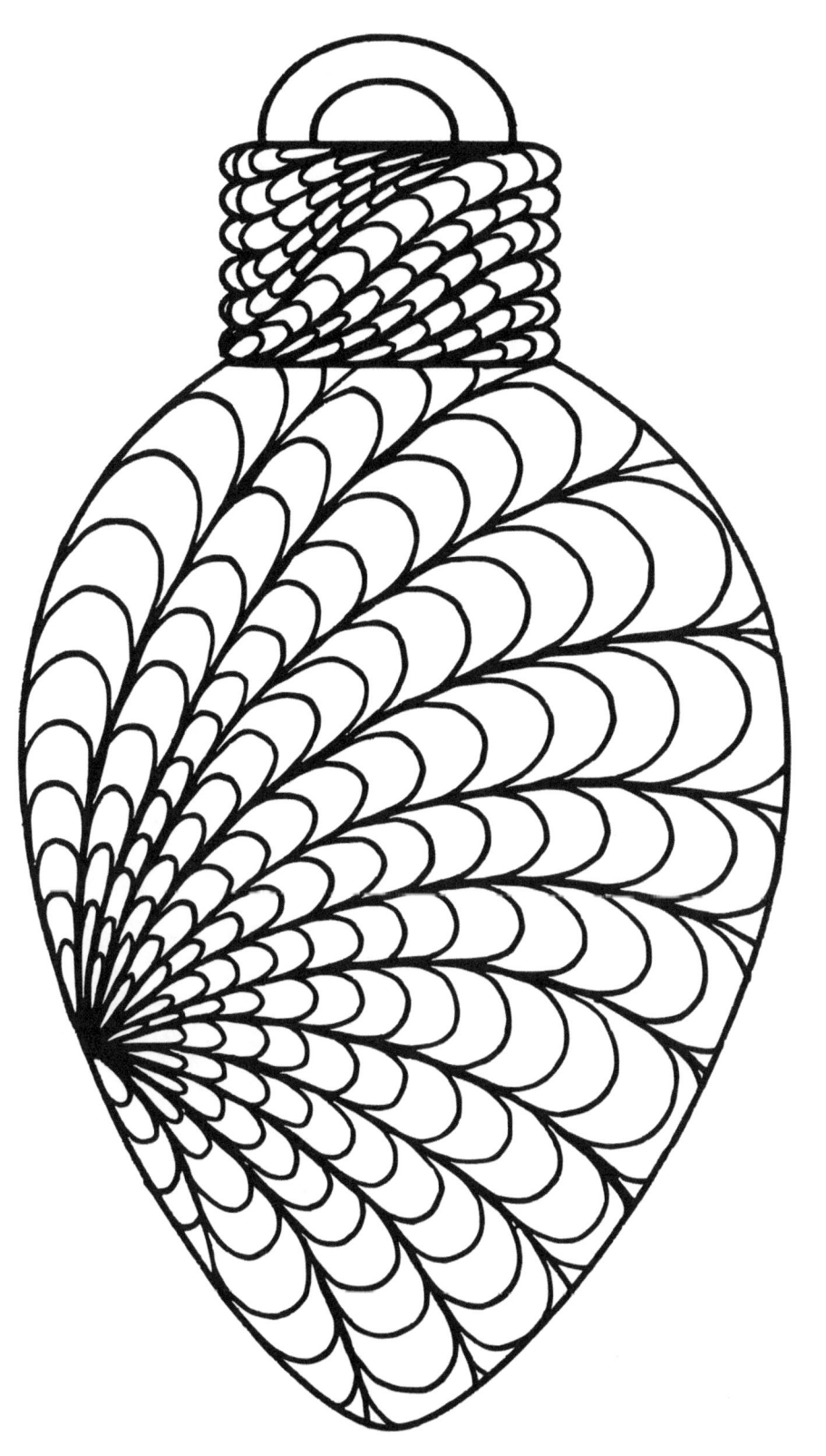

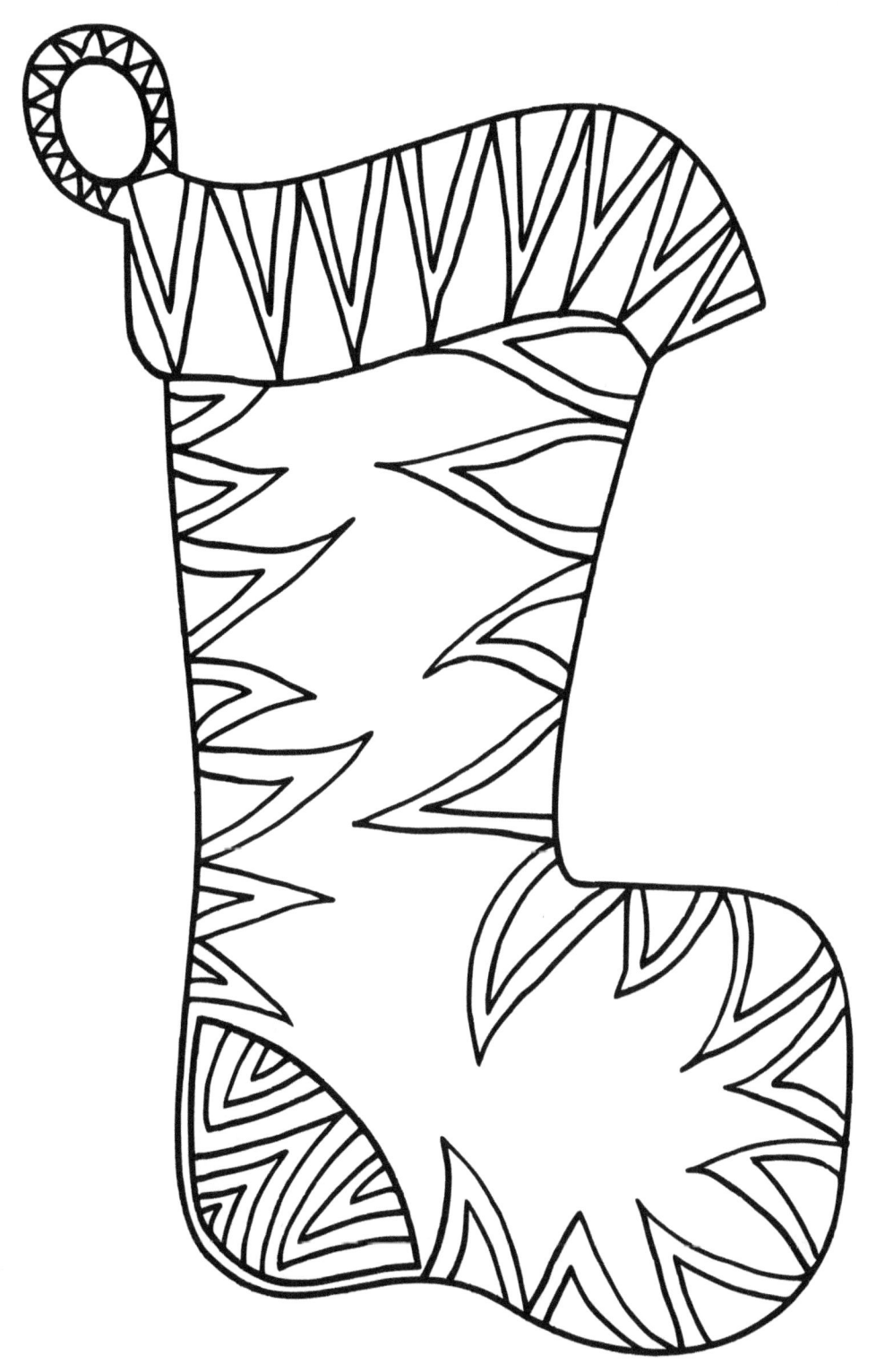

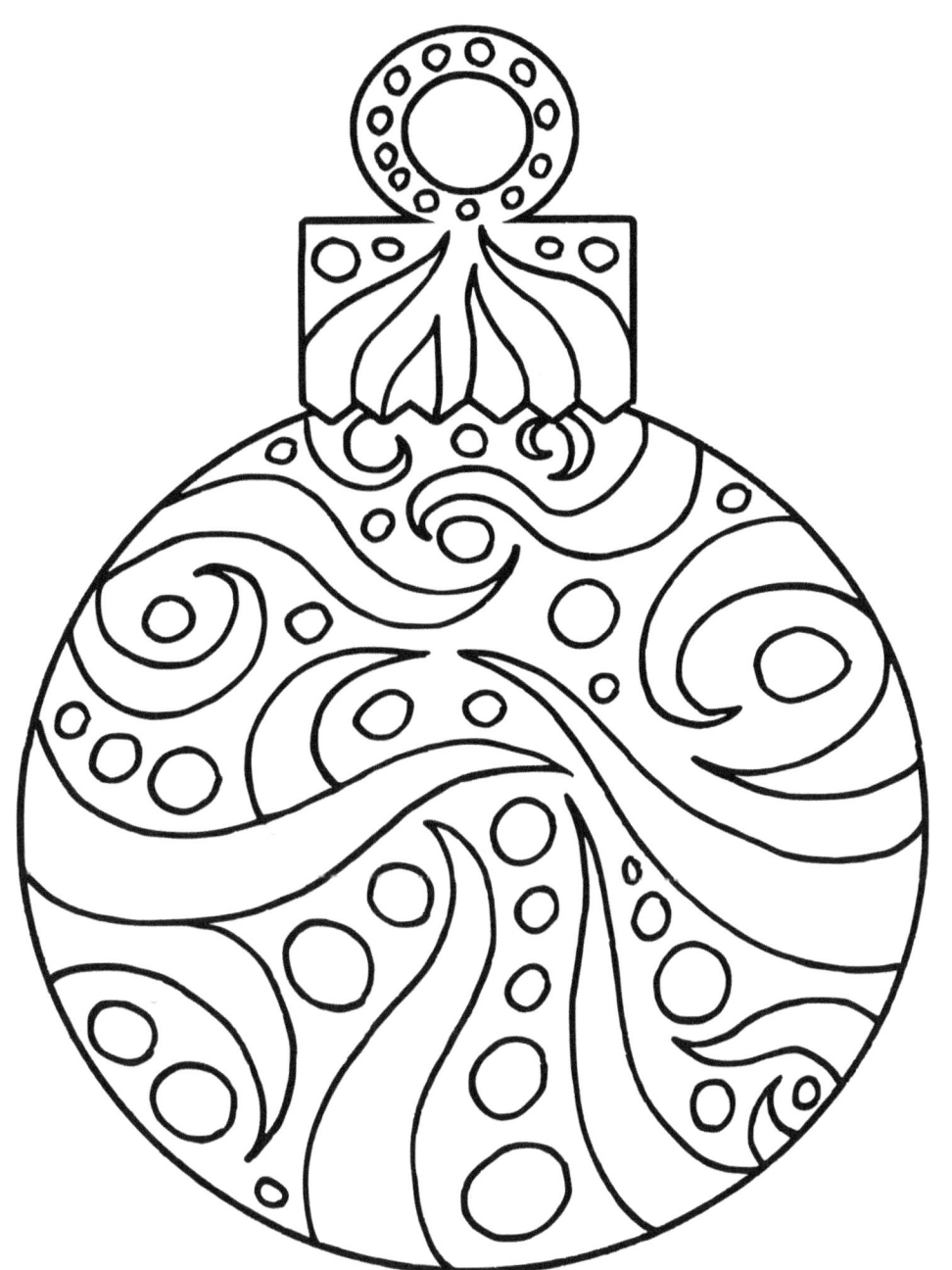

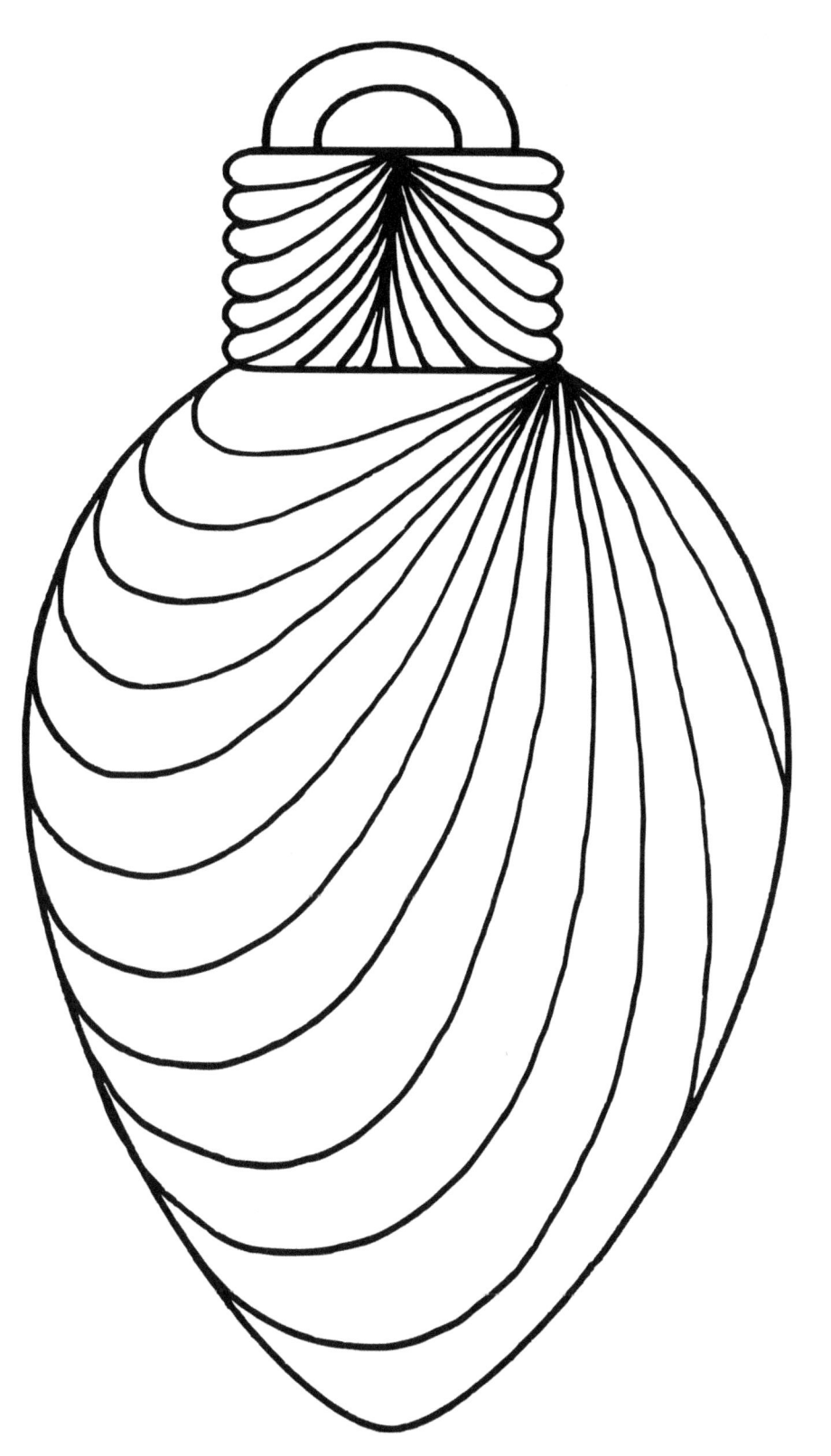

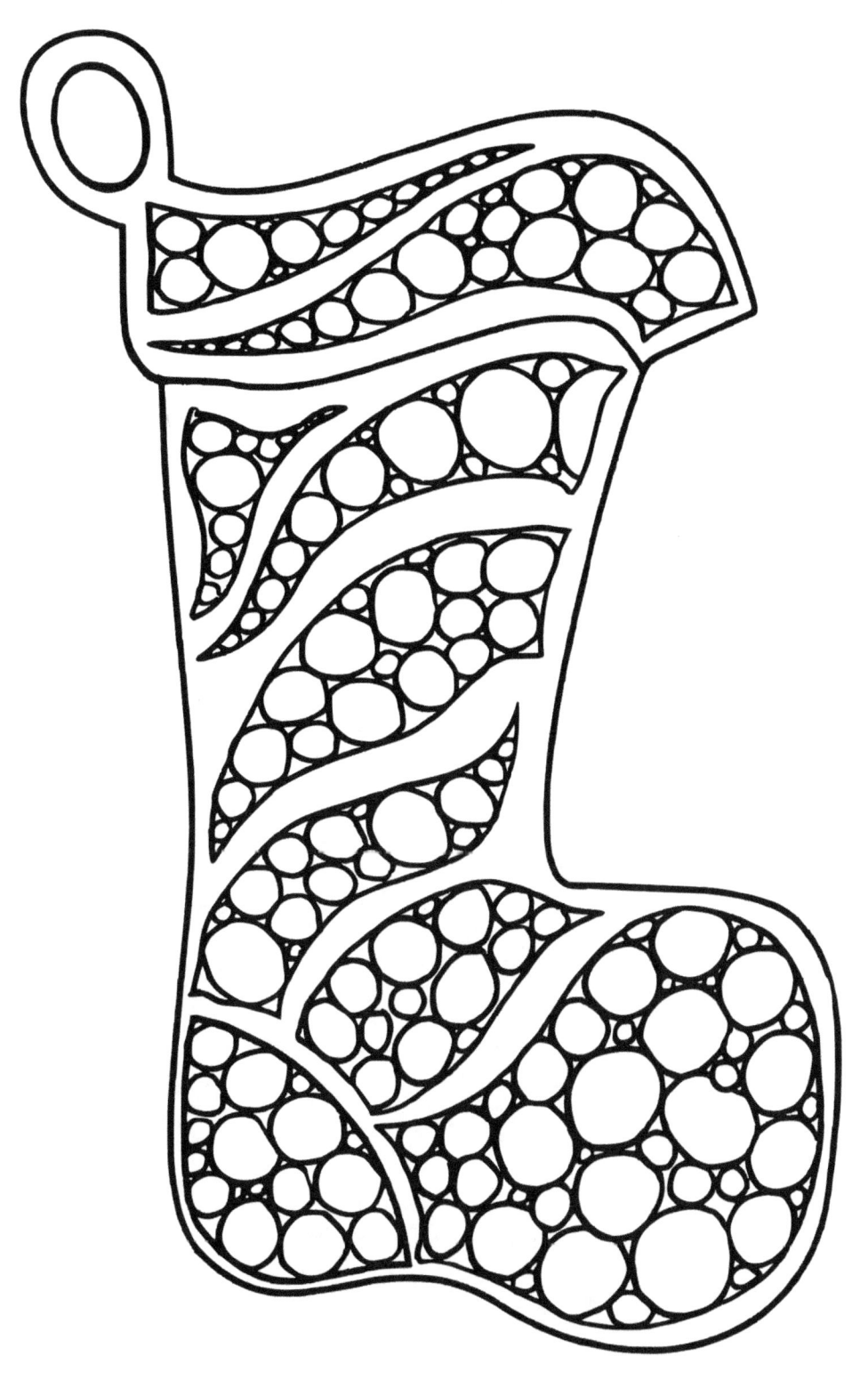

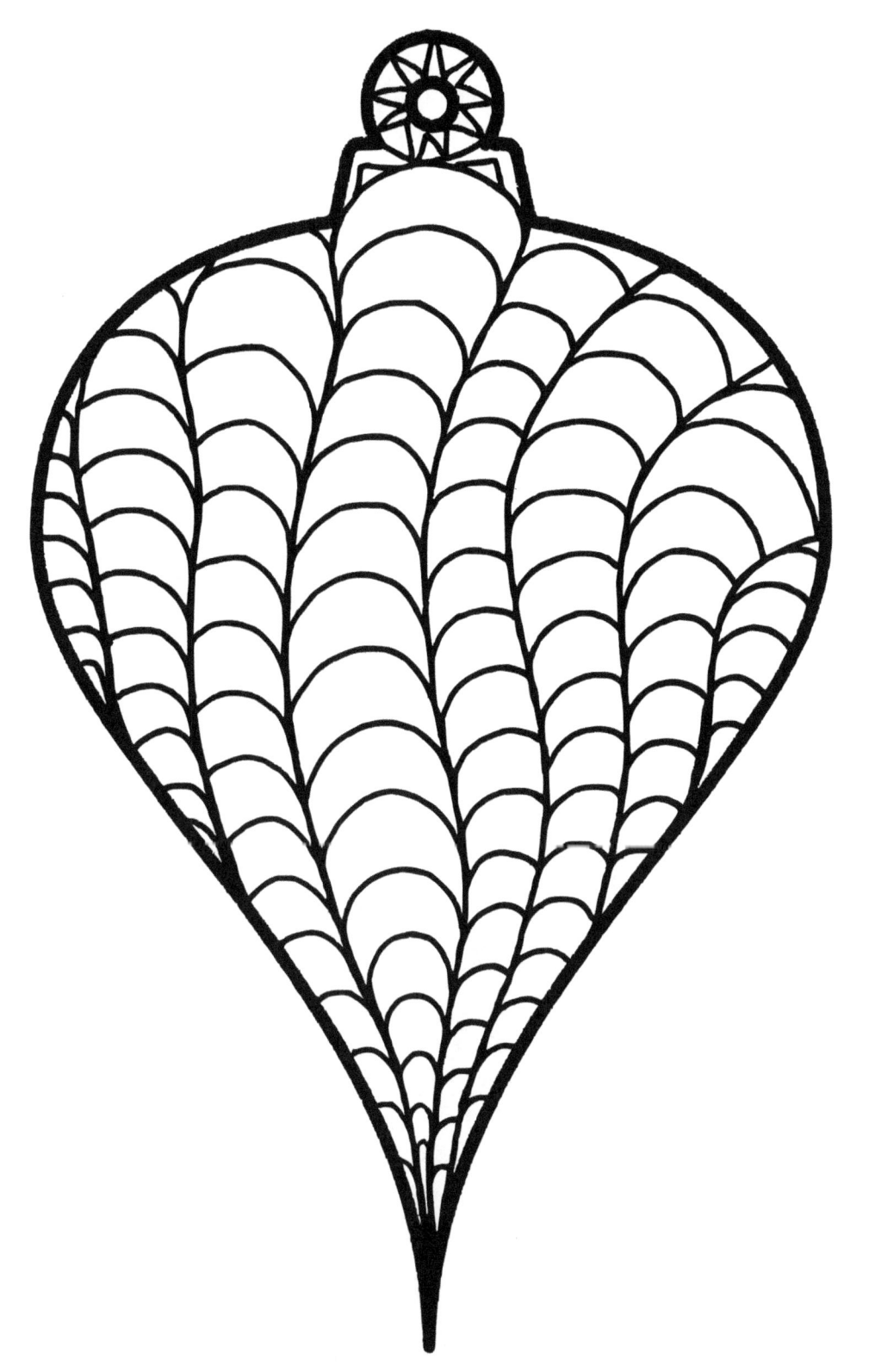

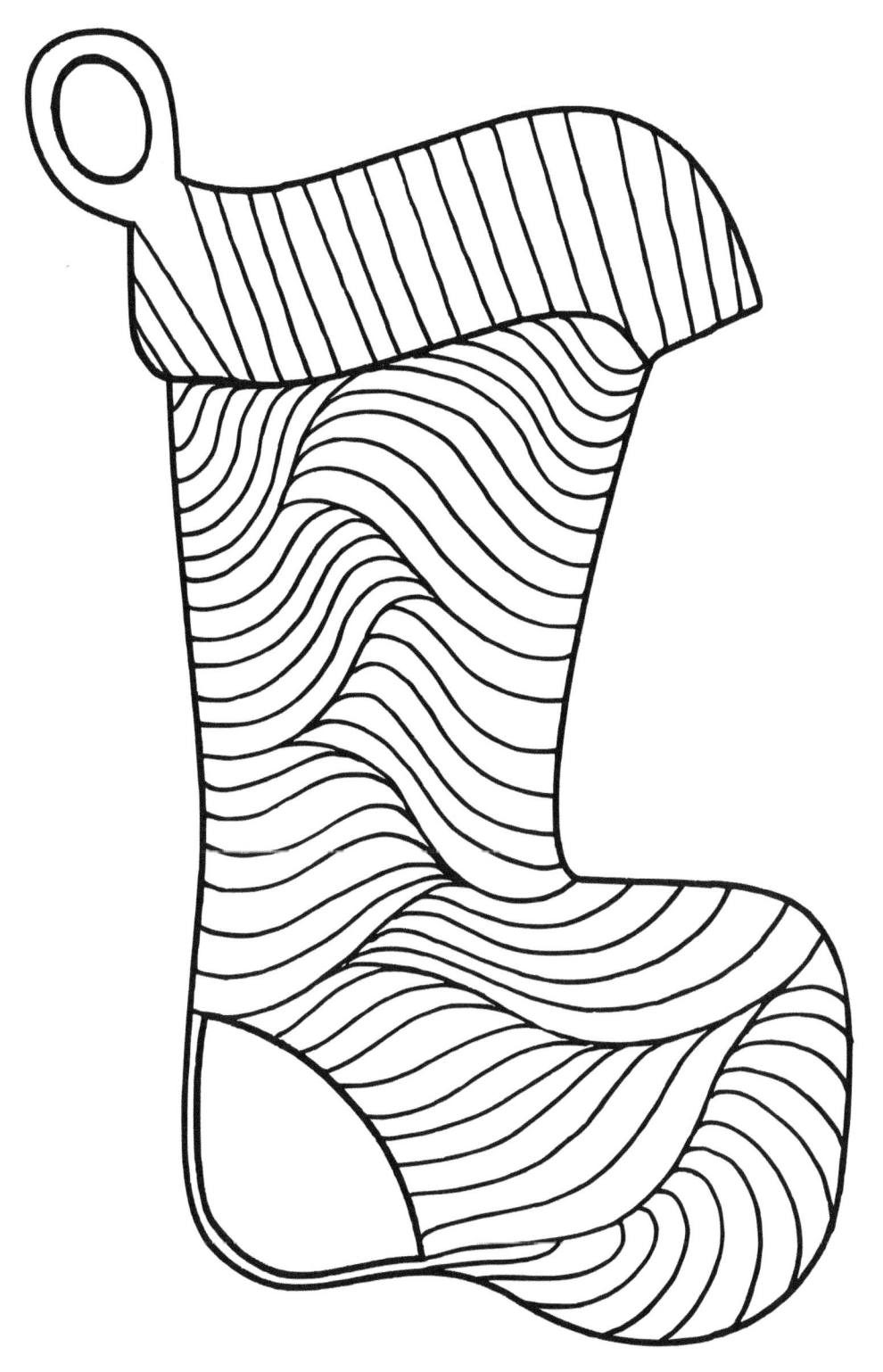

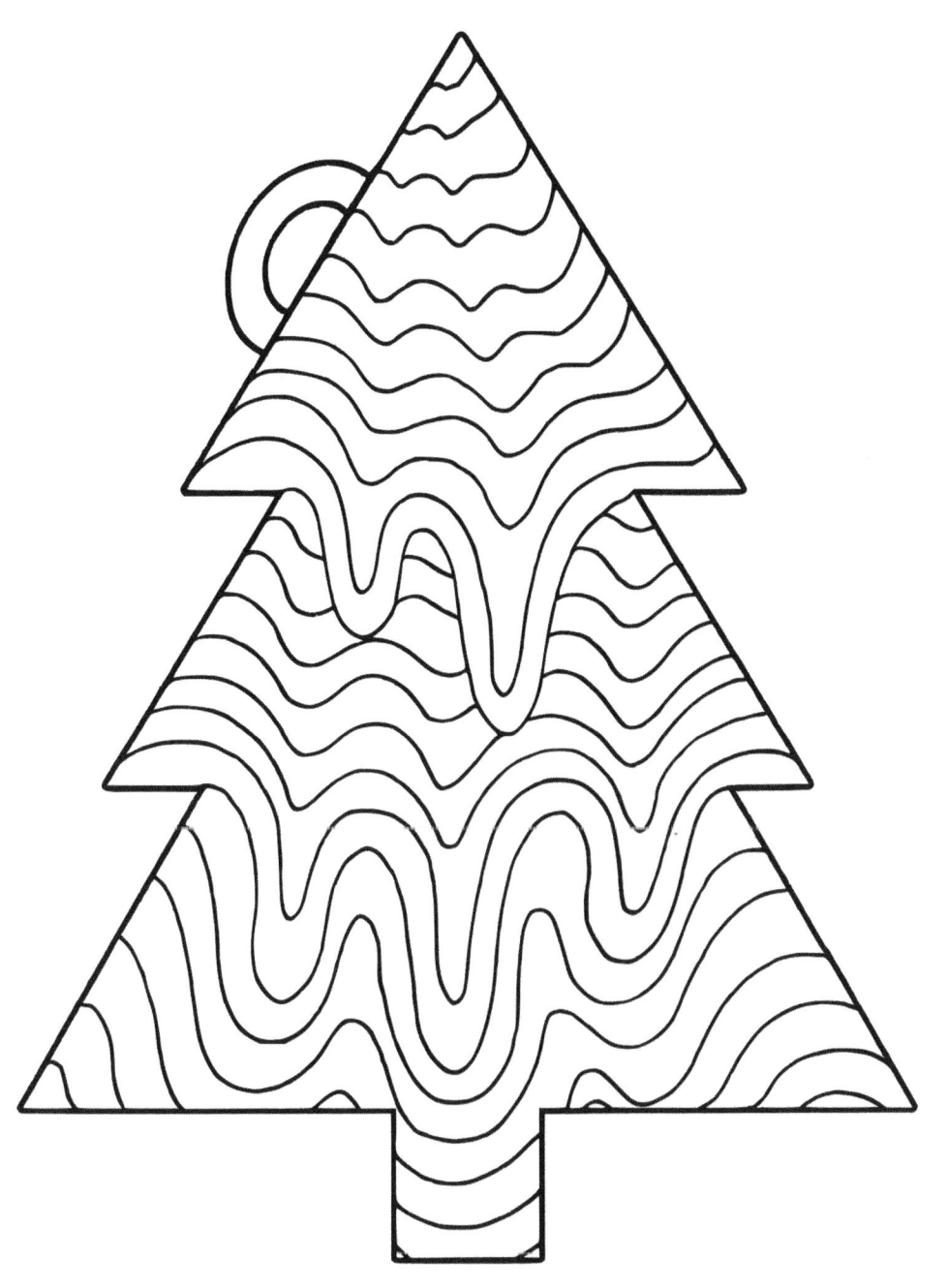

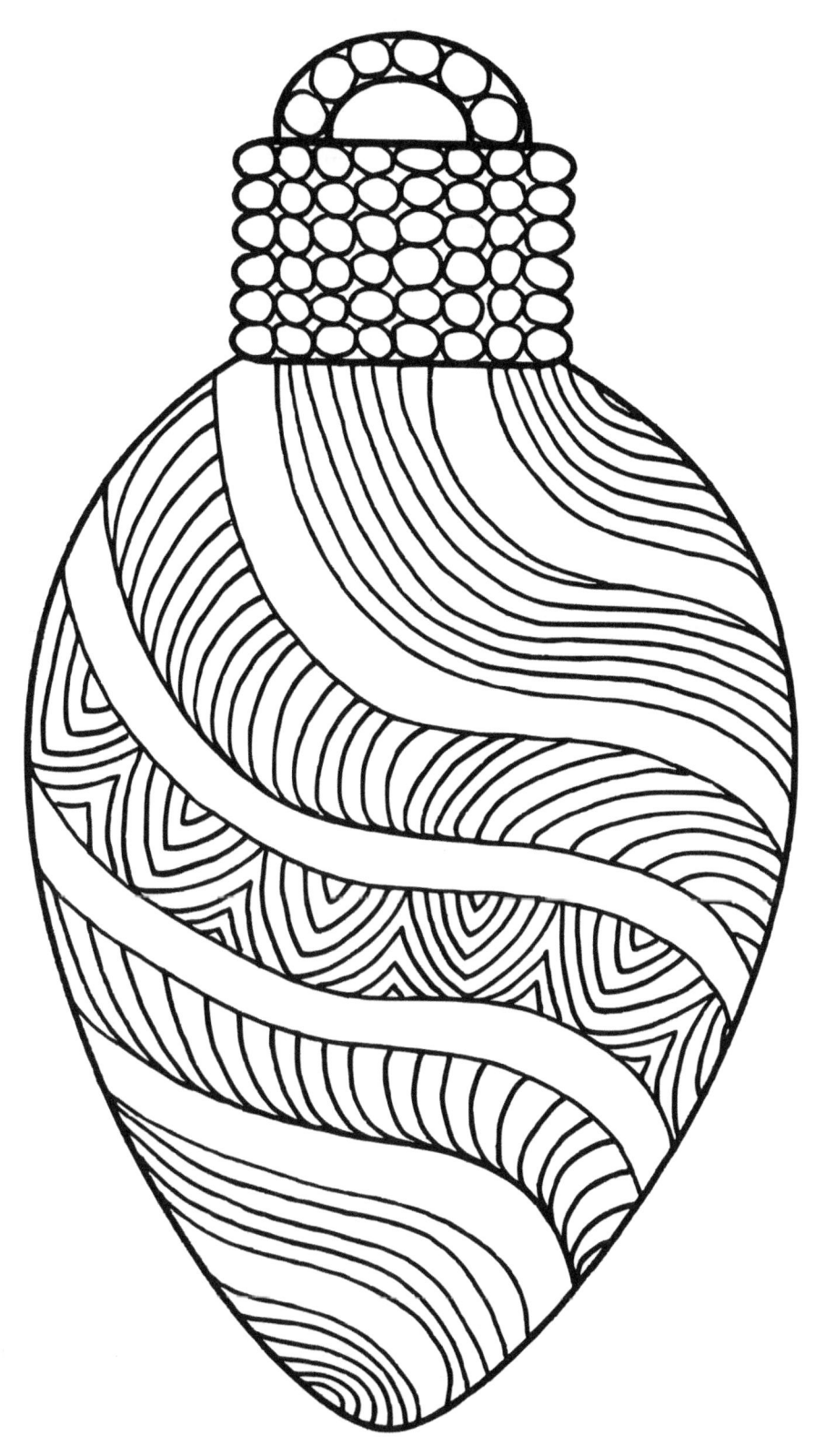

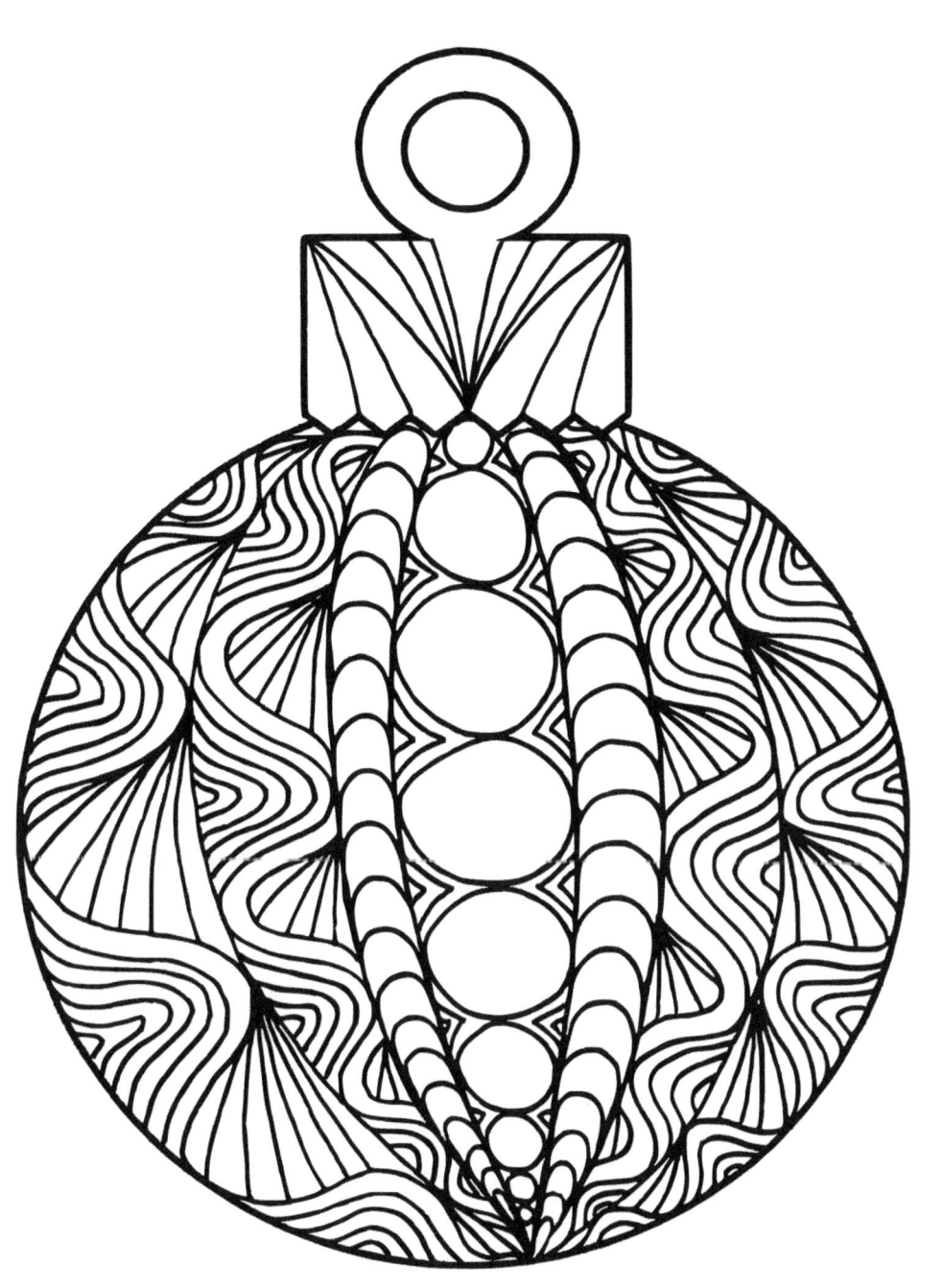

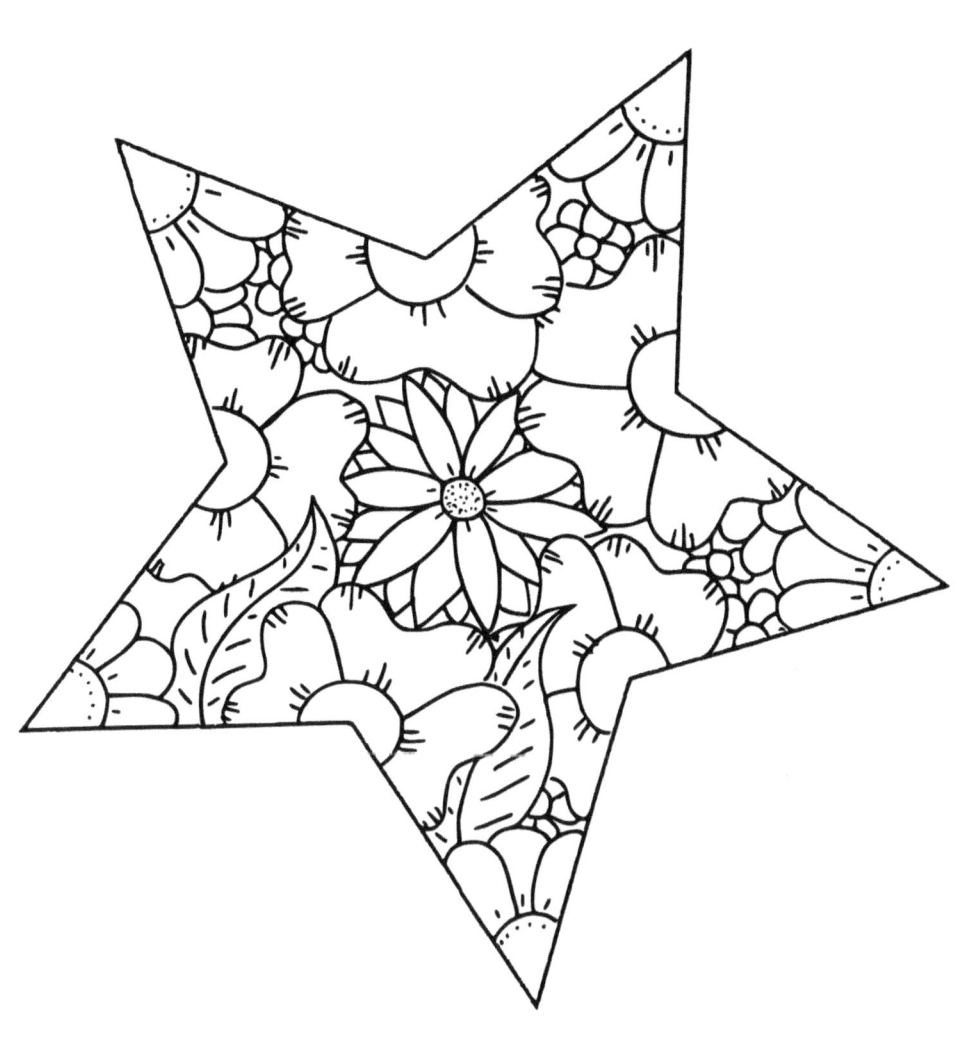

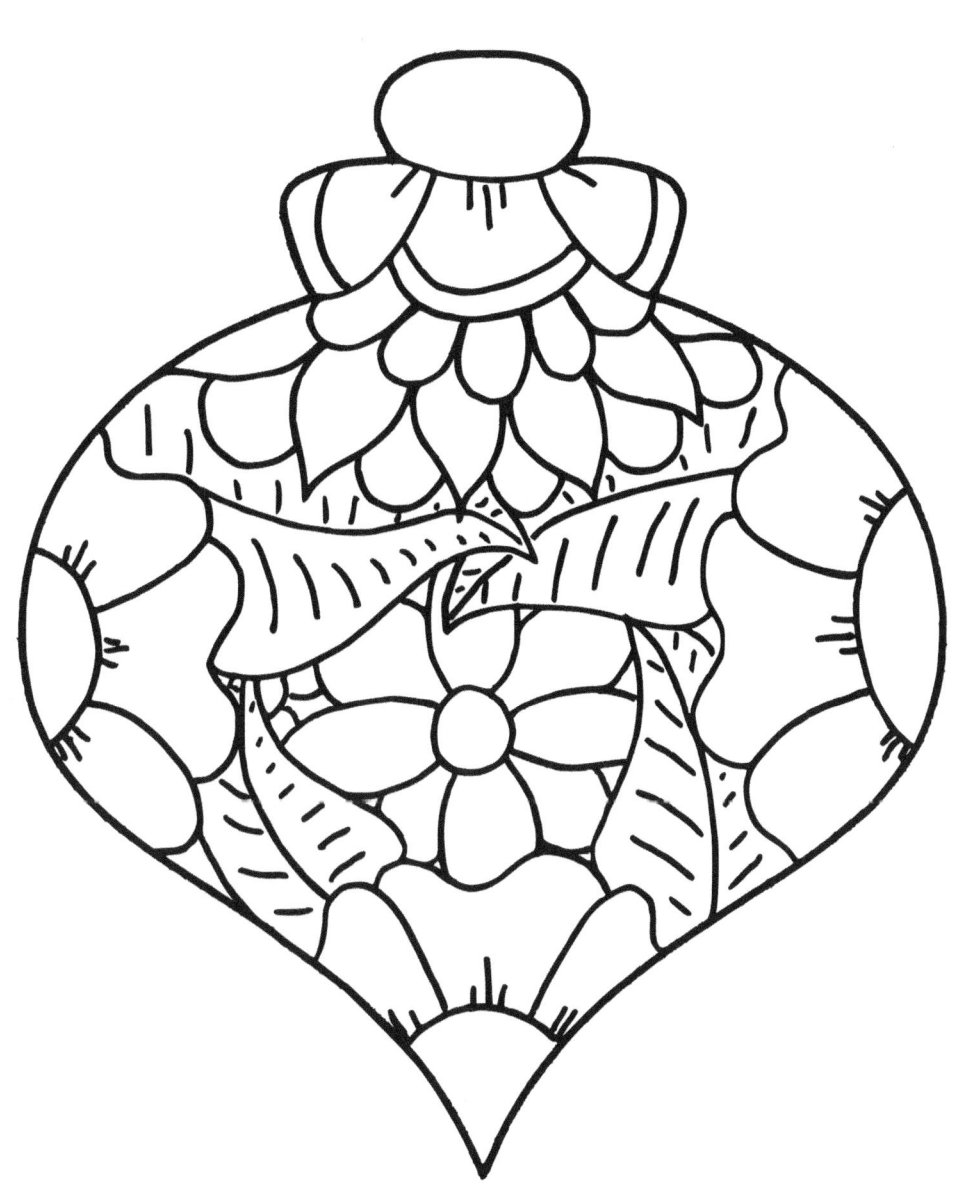

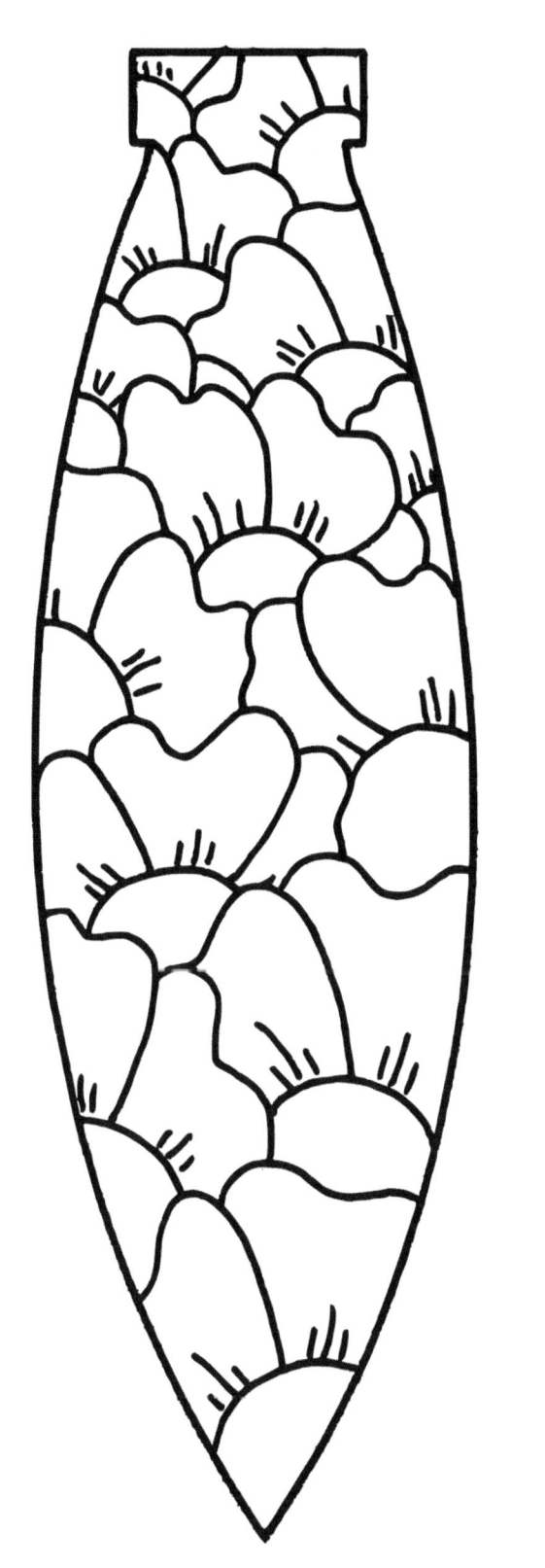

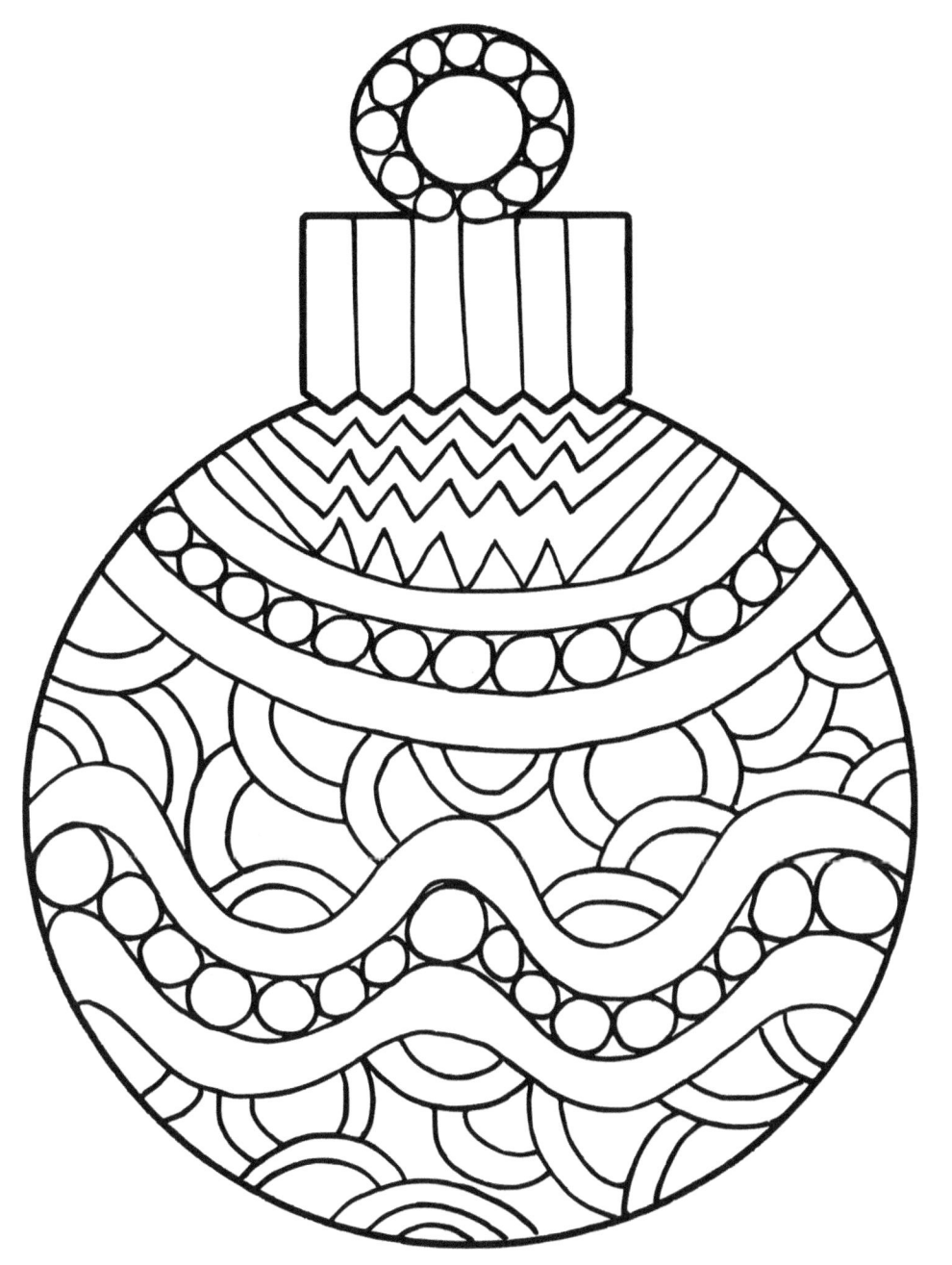

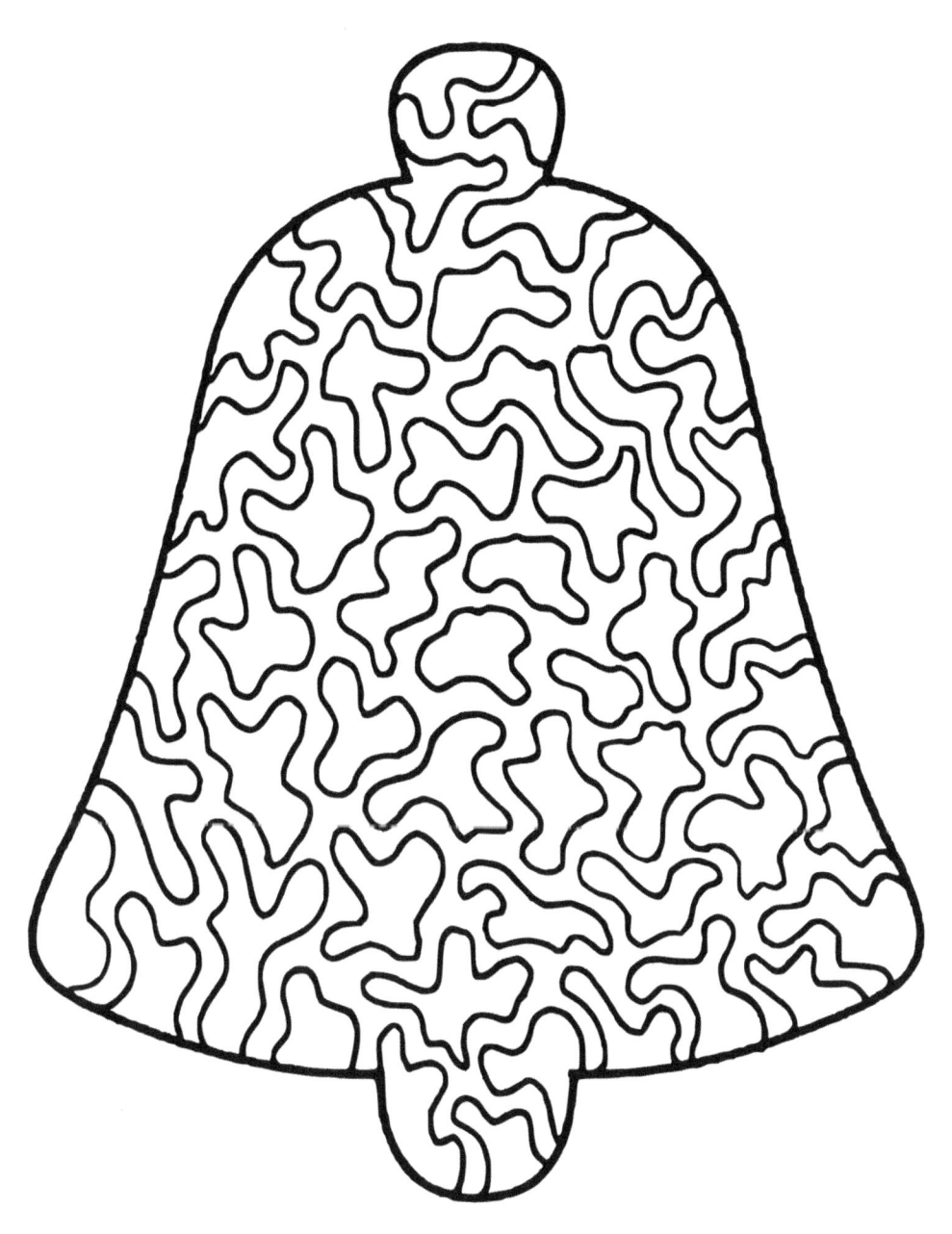

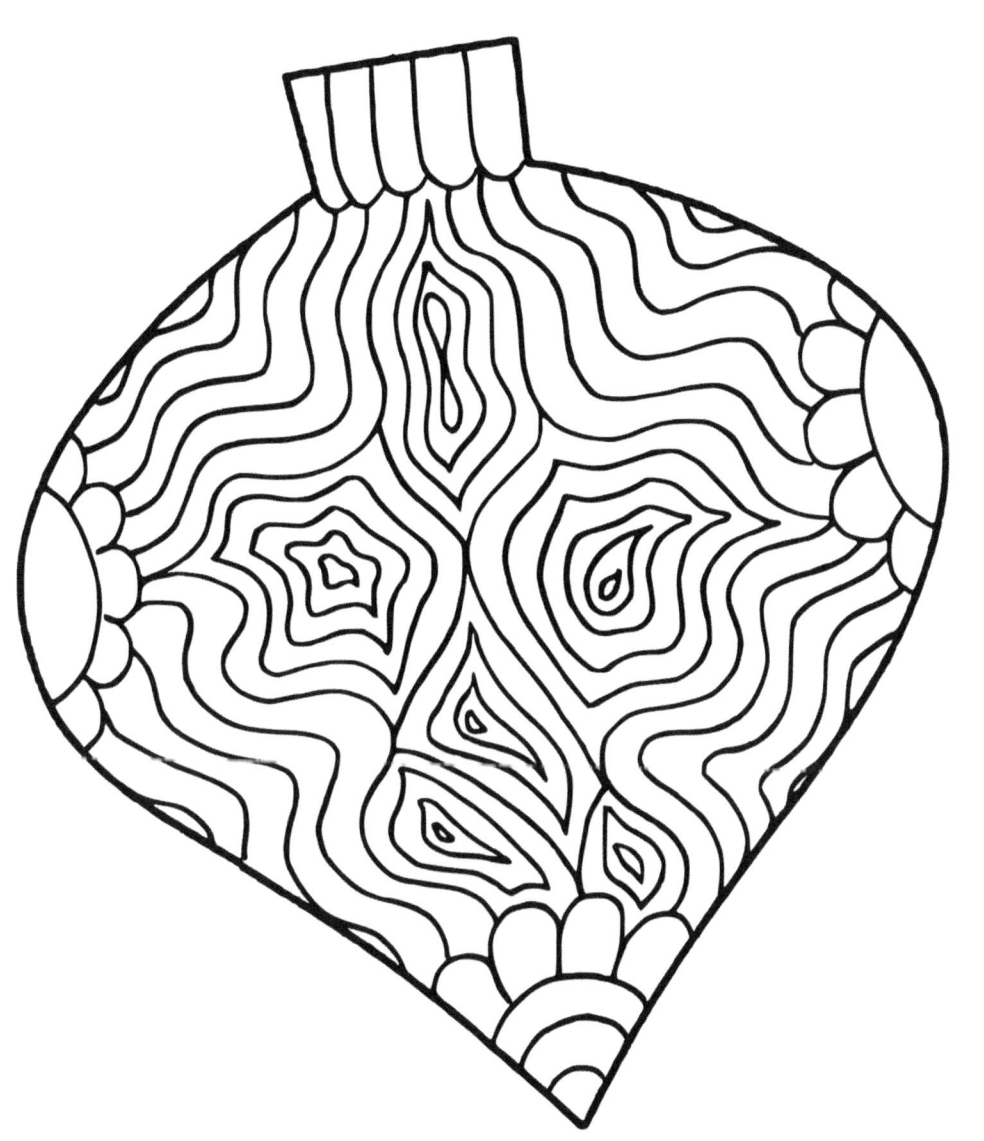

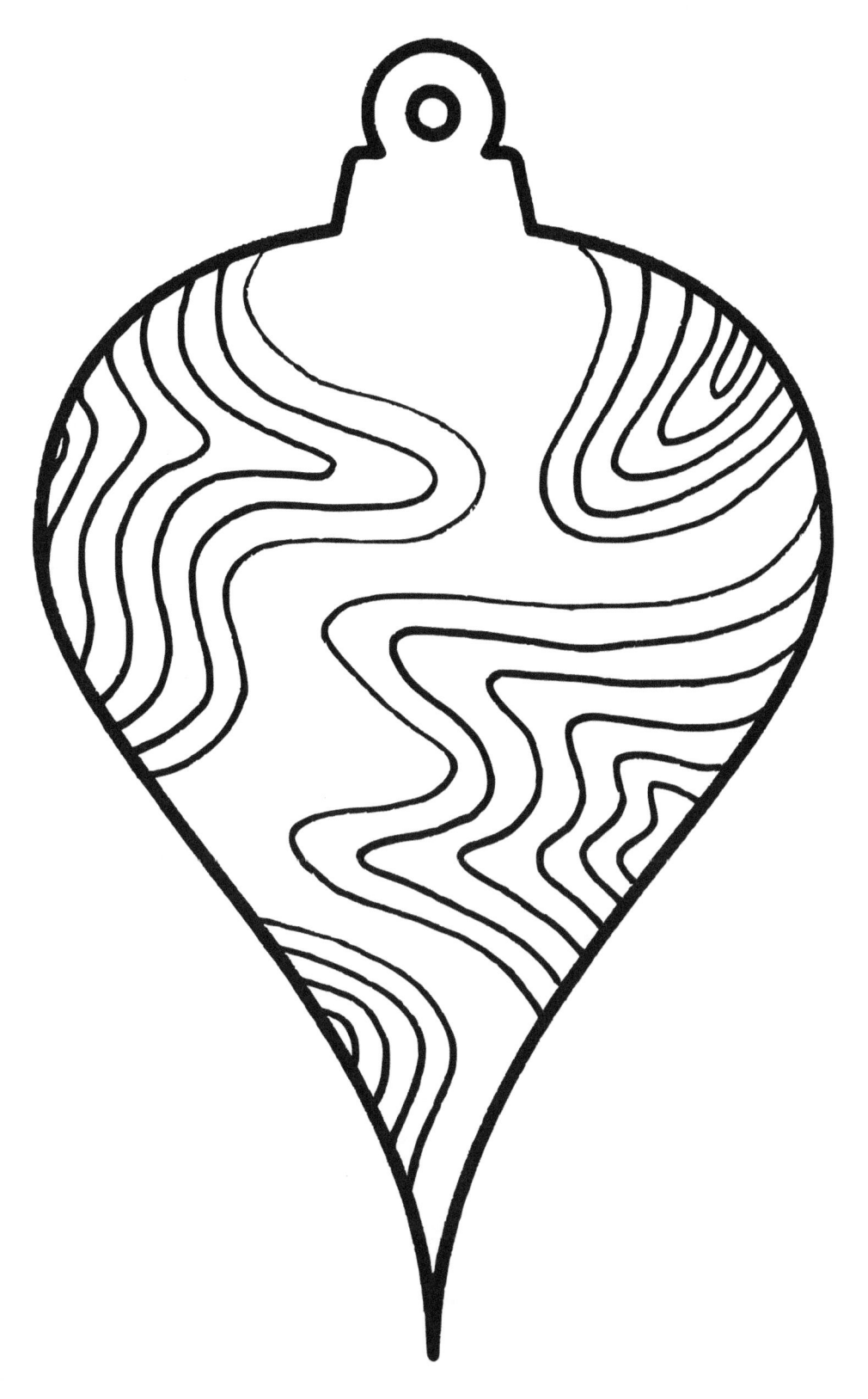

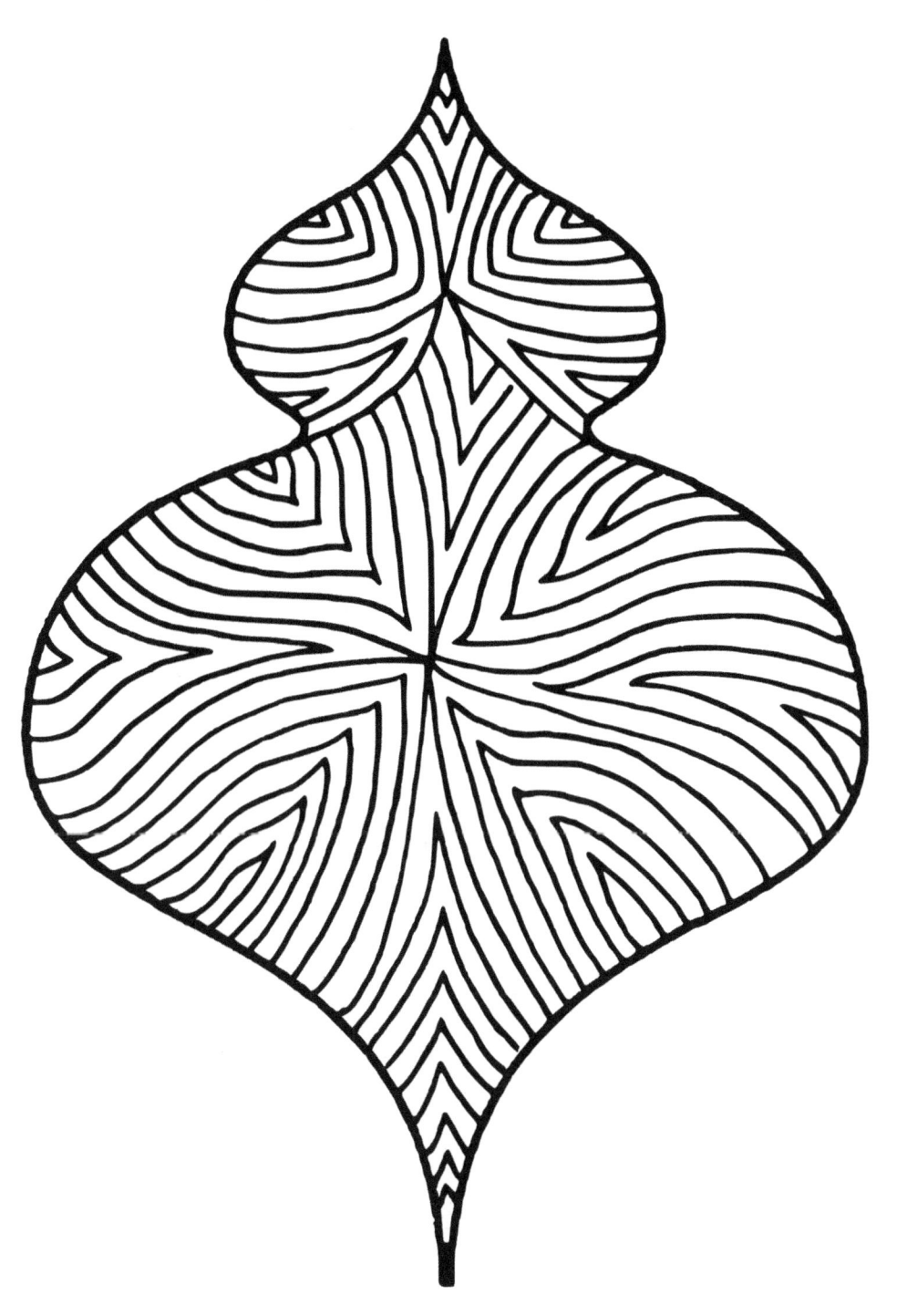

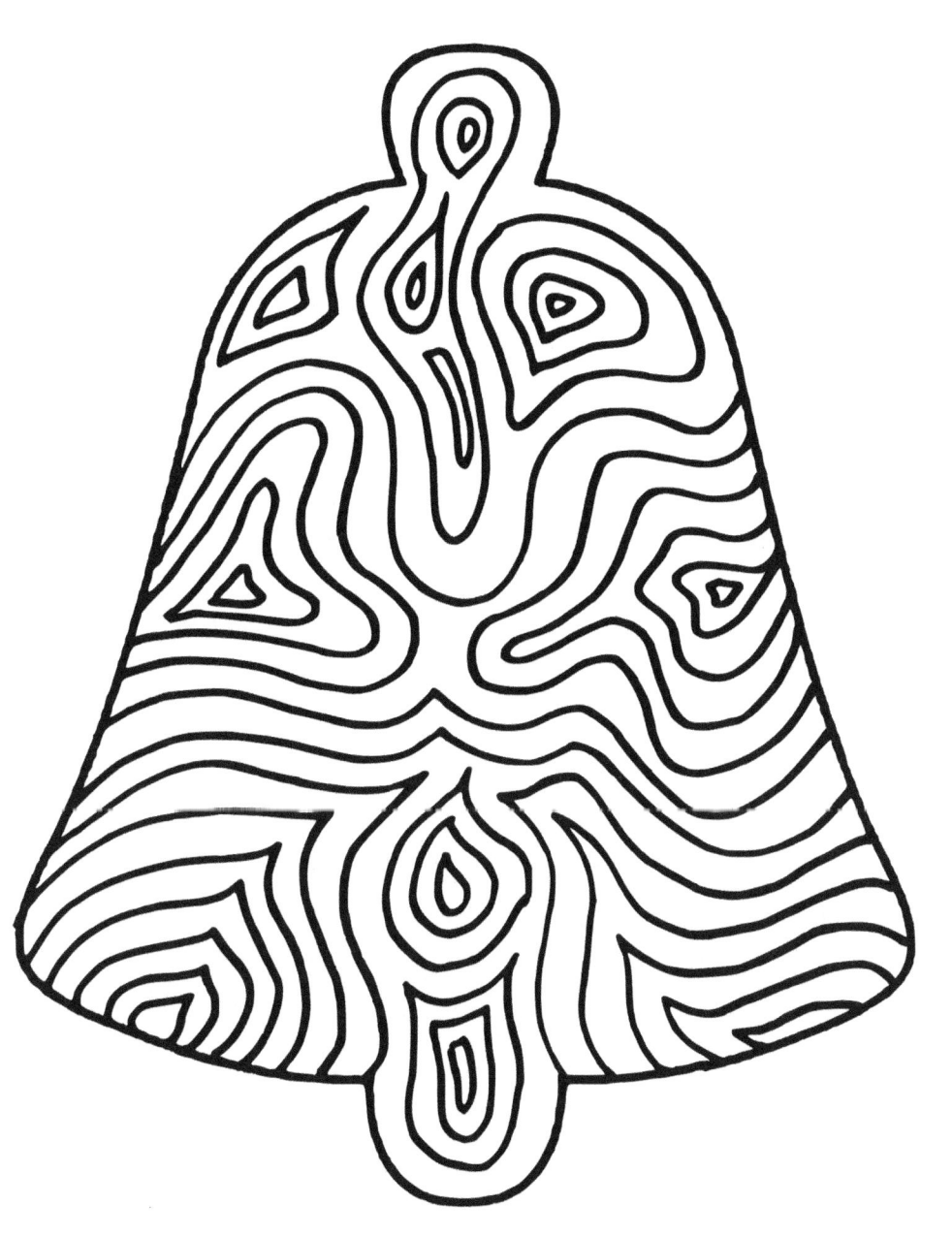

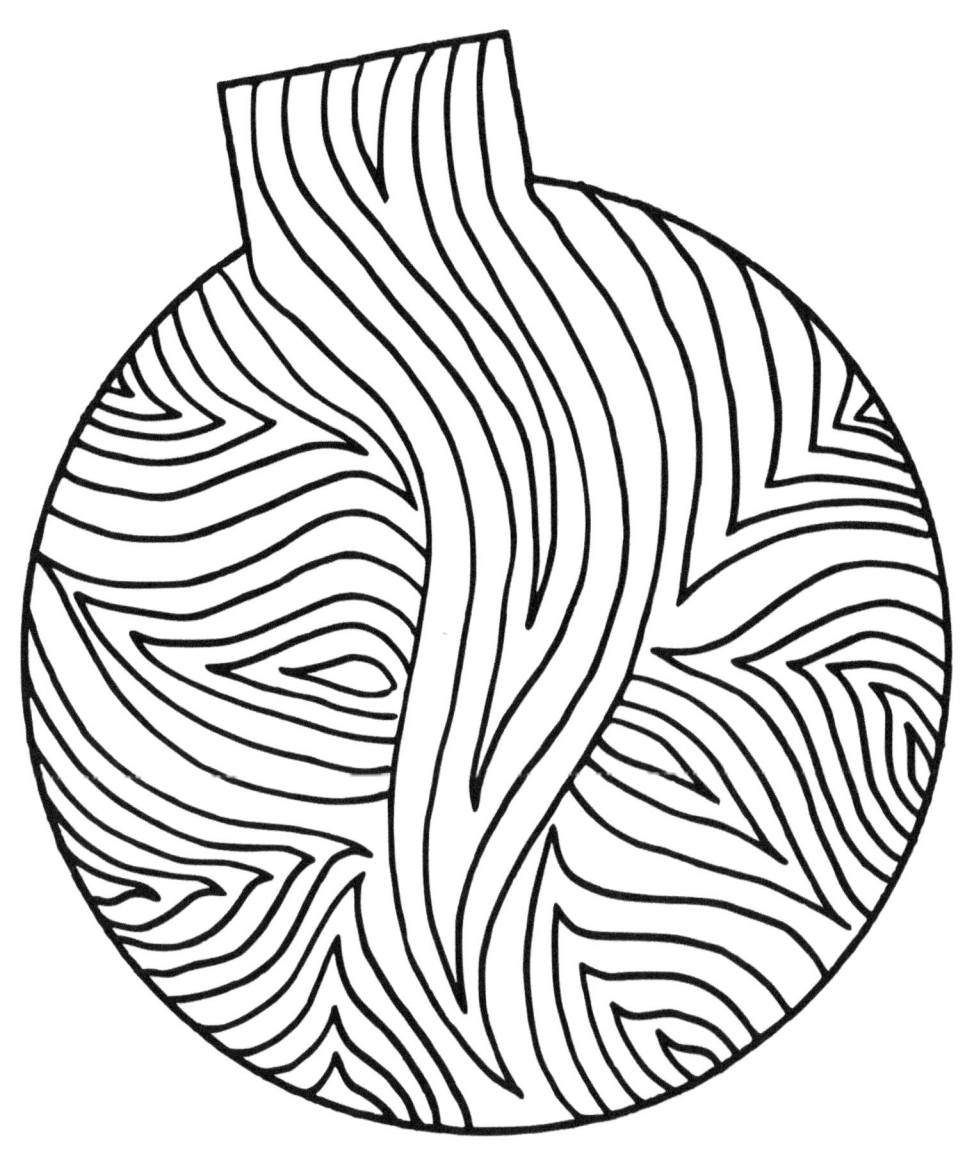

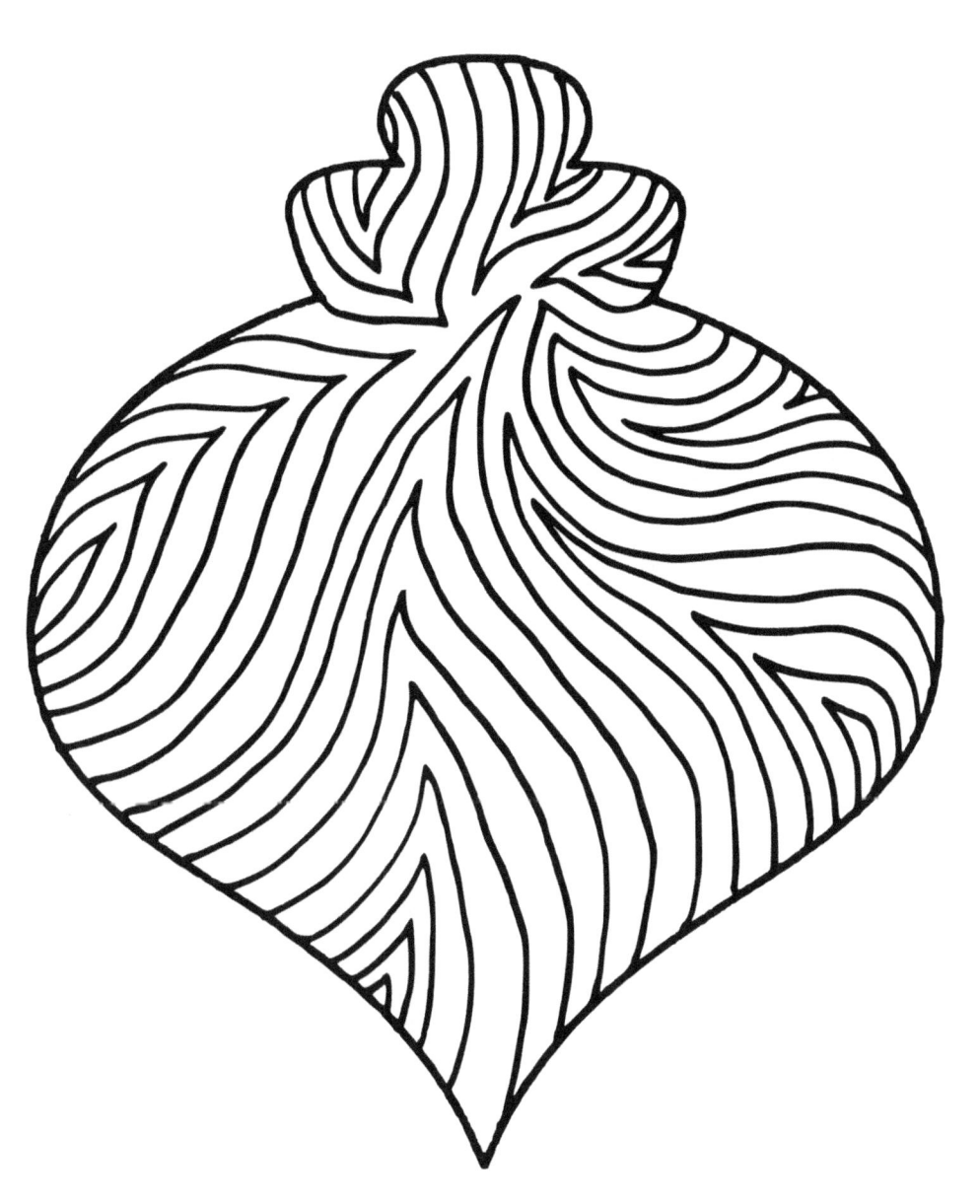

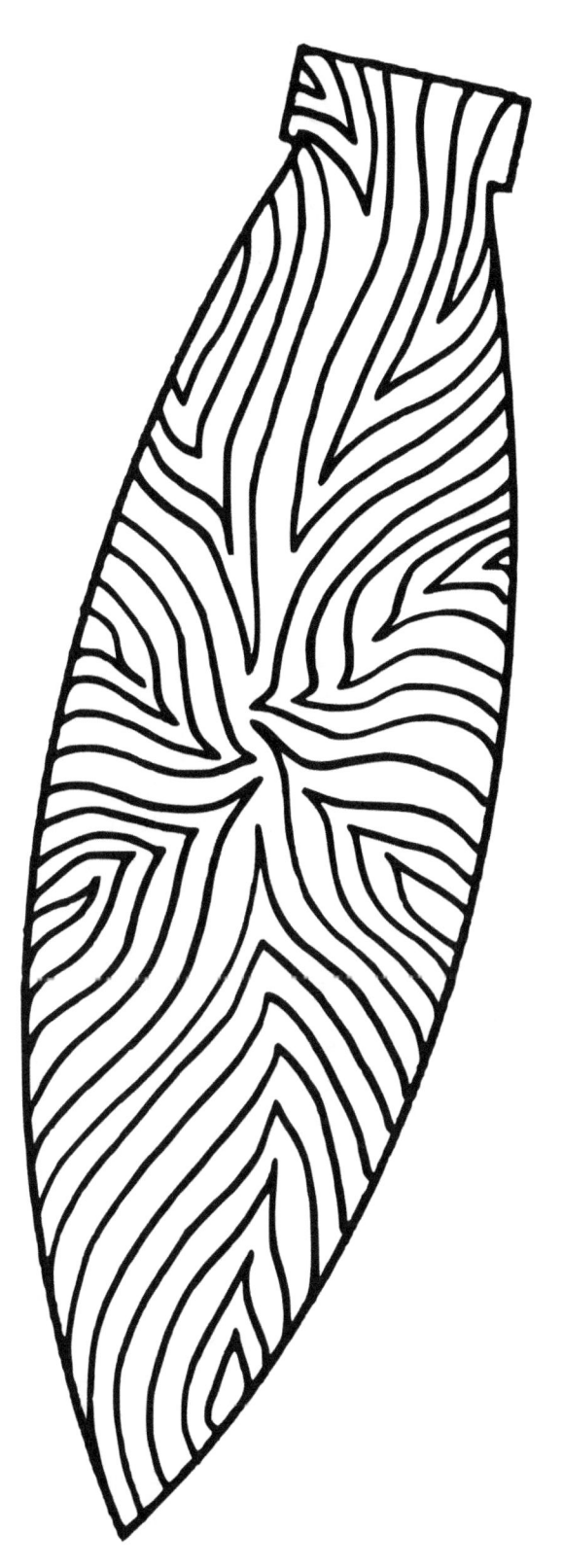

25 Designs from Johanna Ans

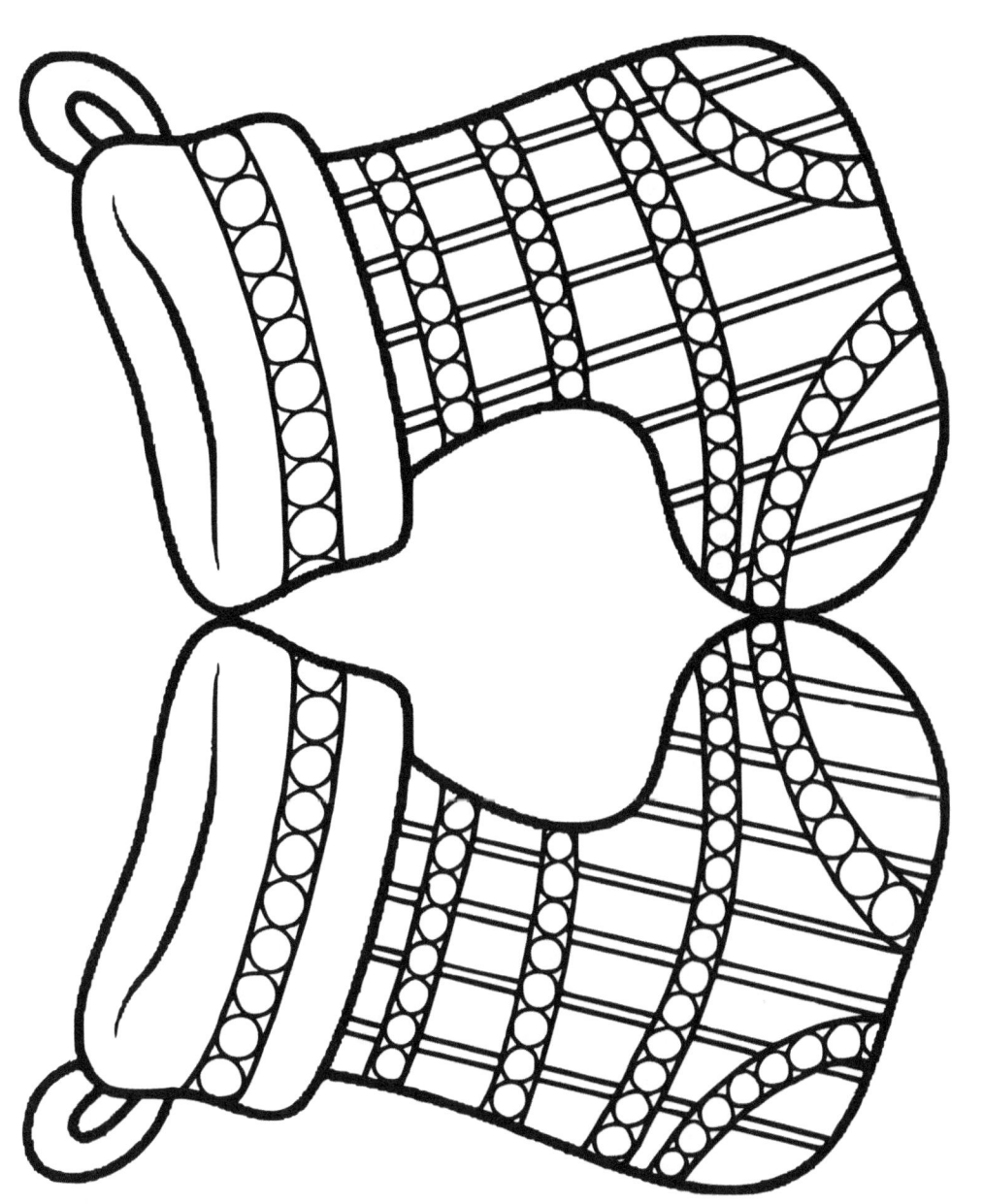

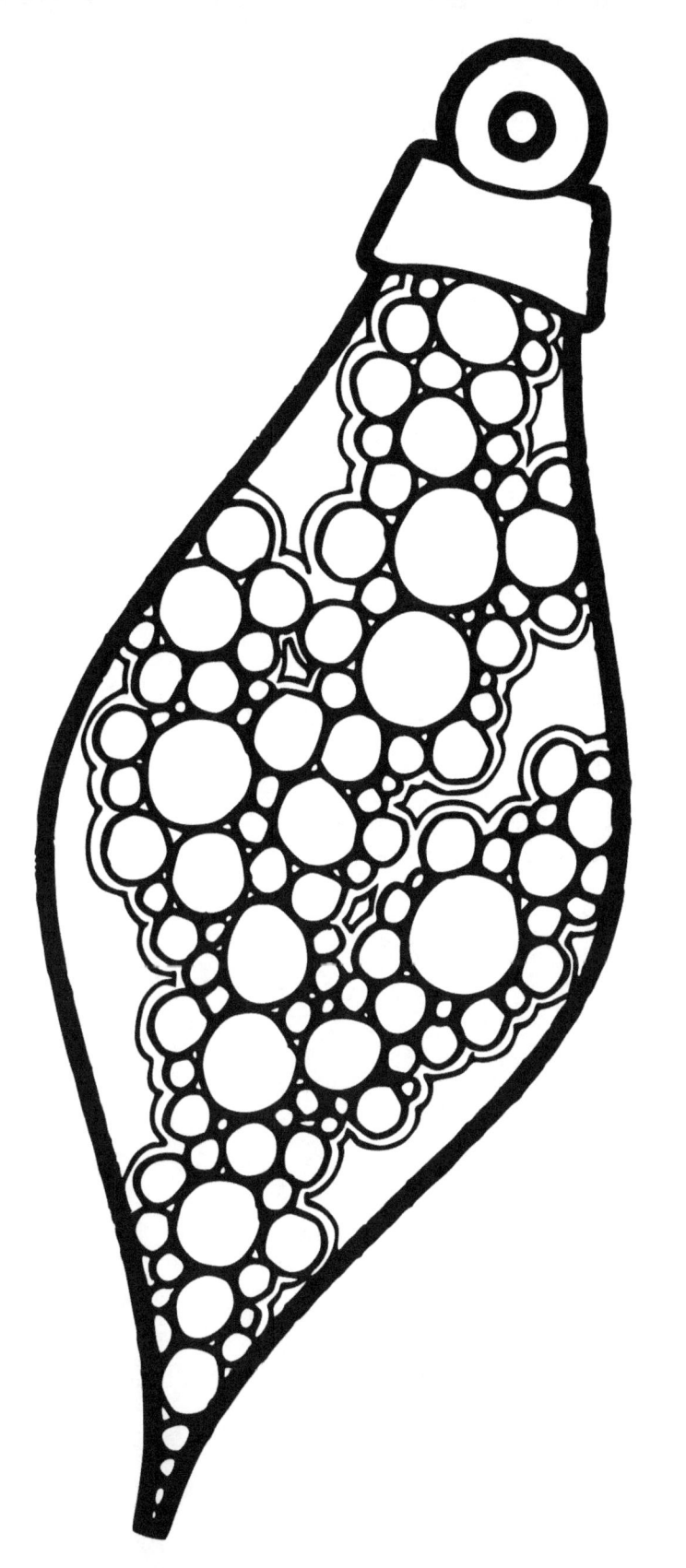

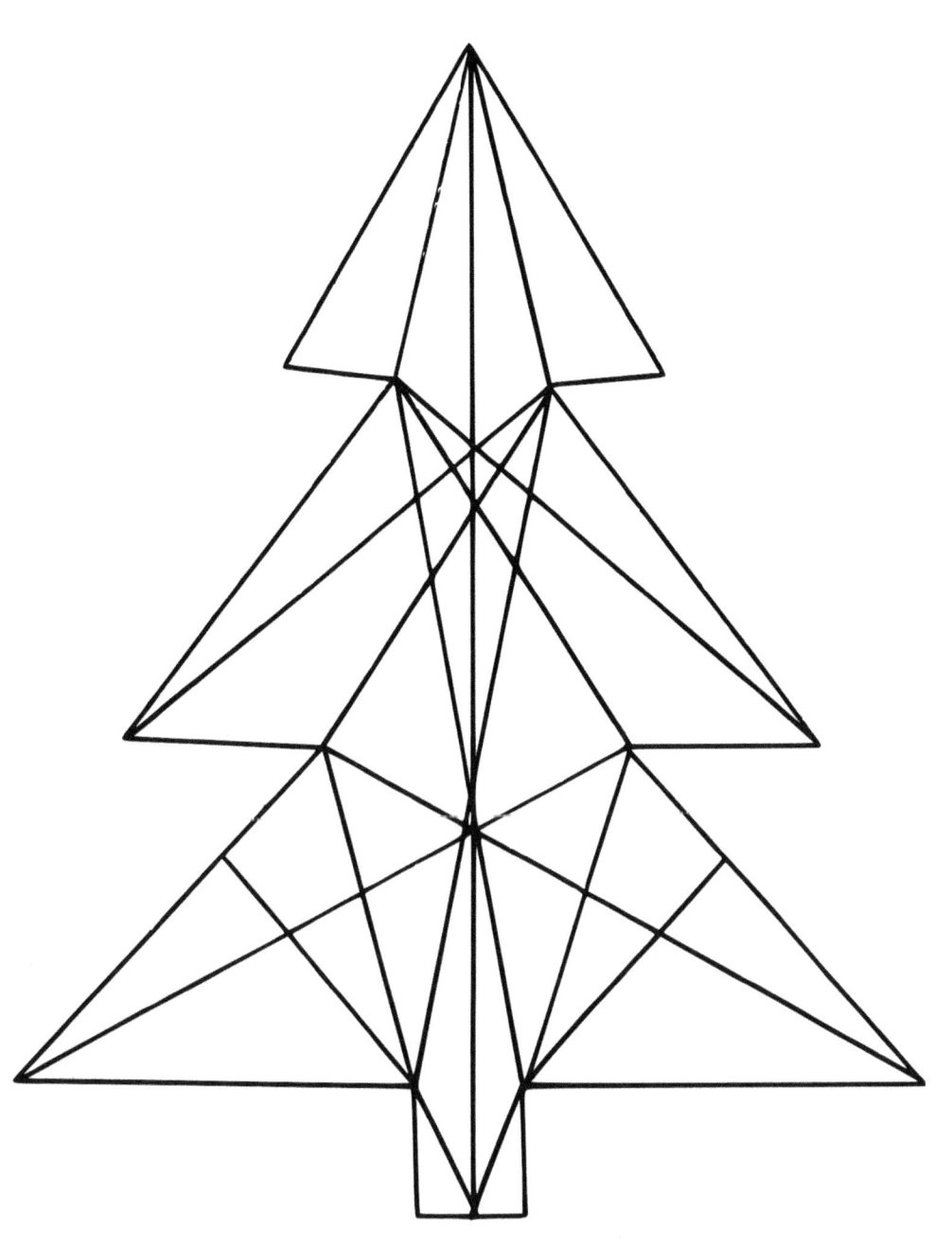

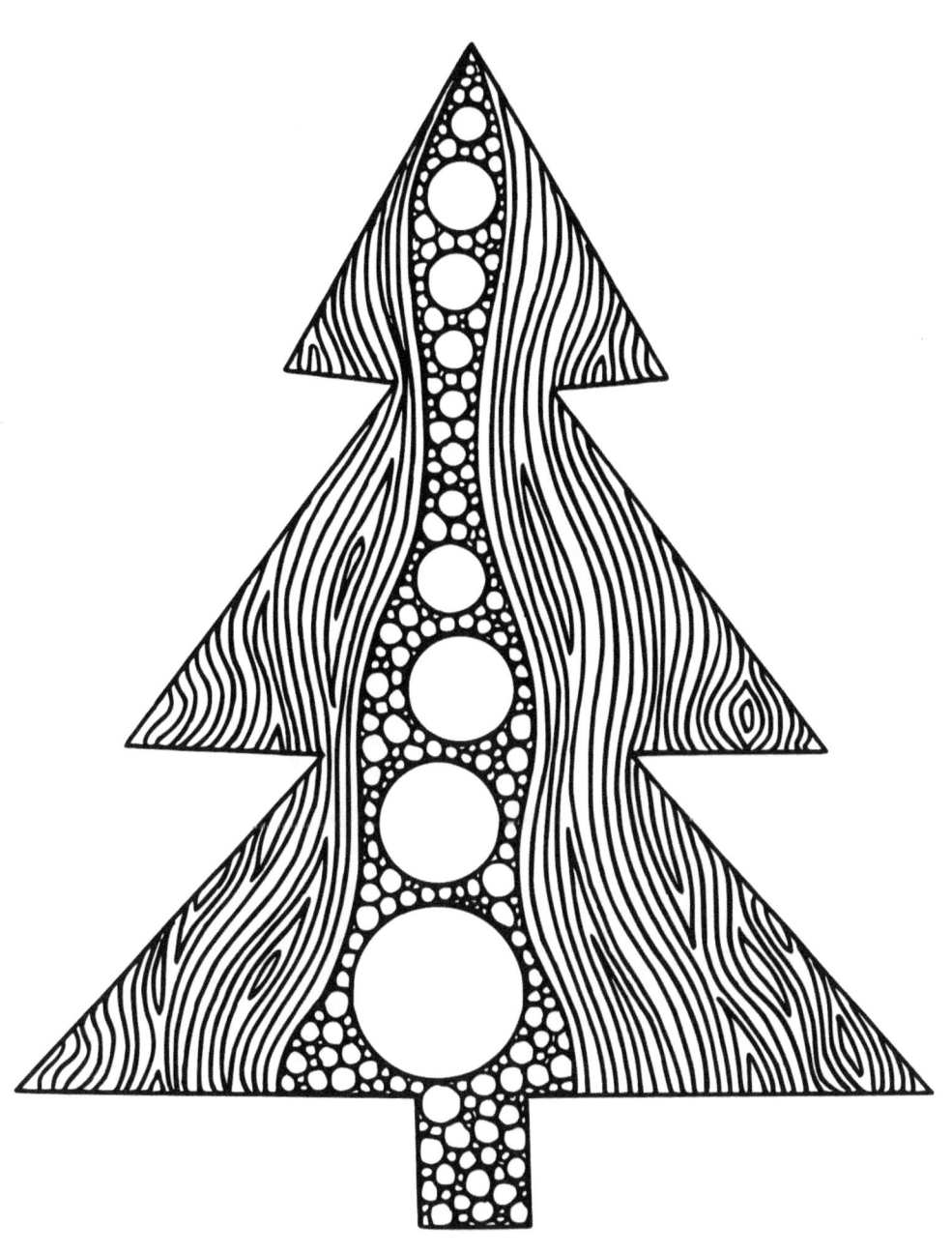

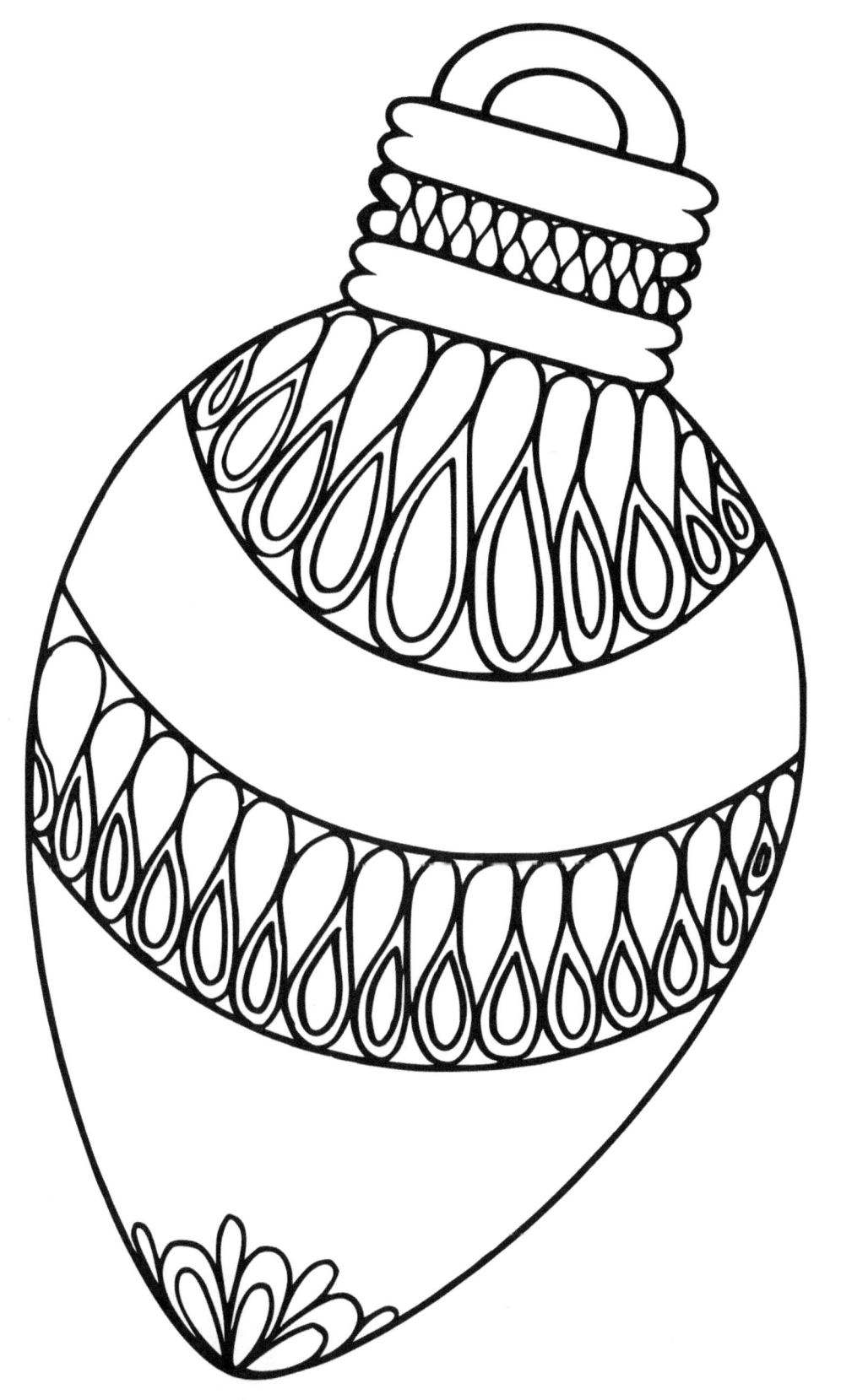

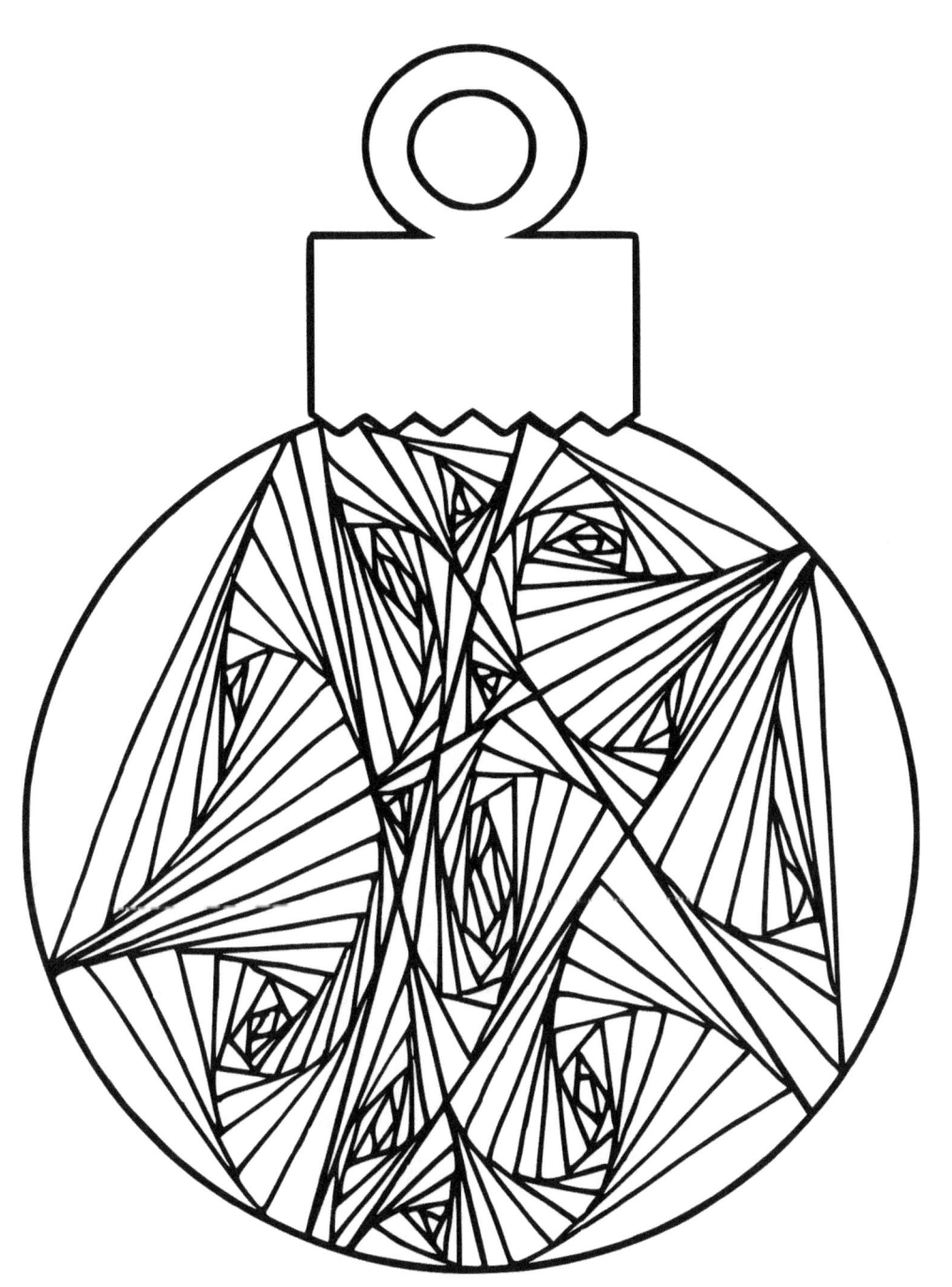

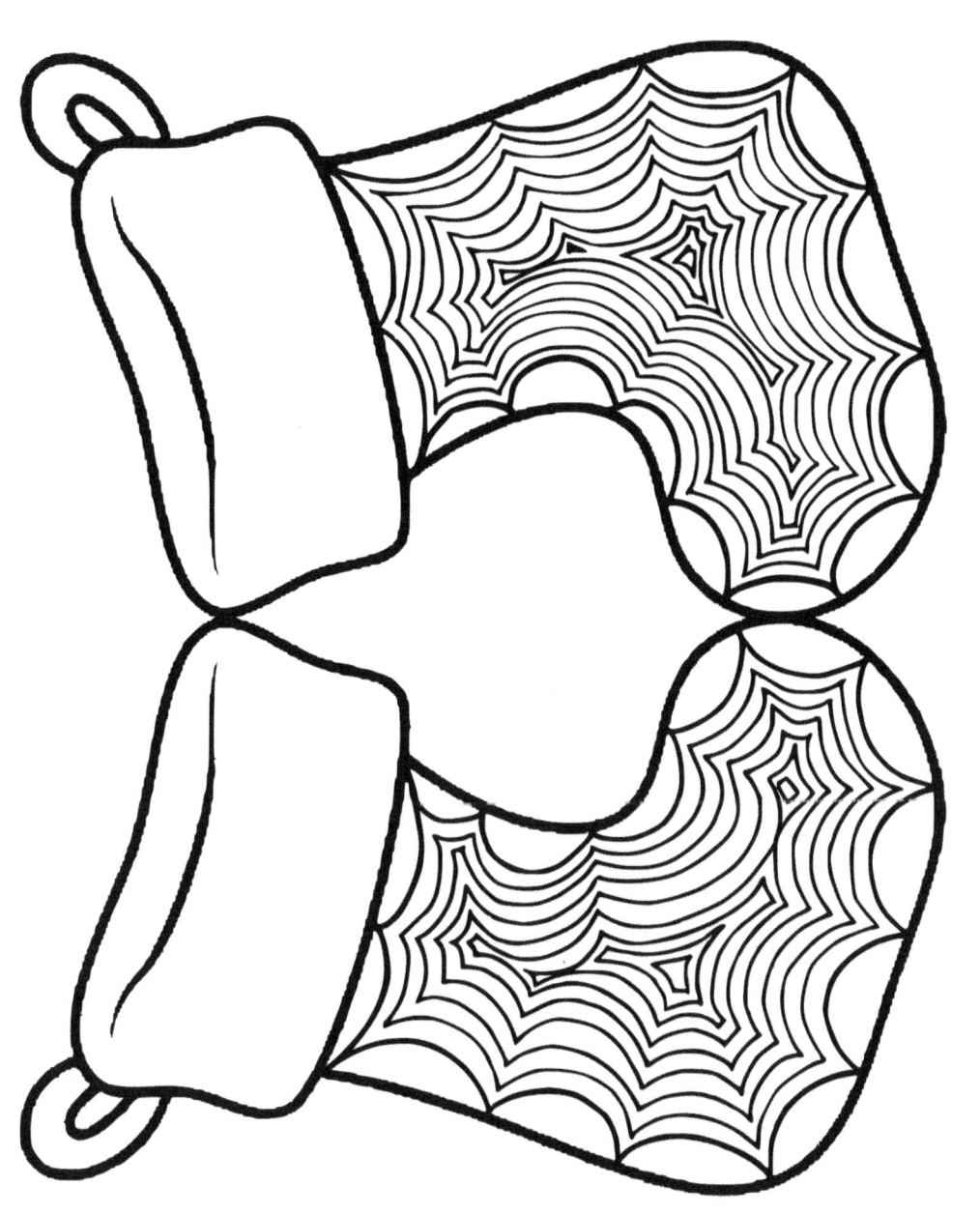

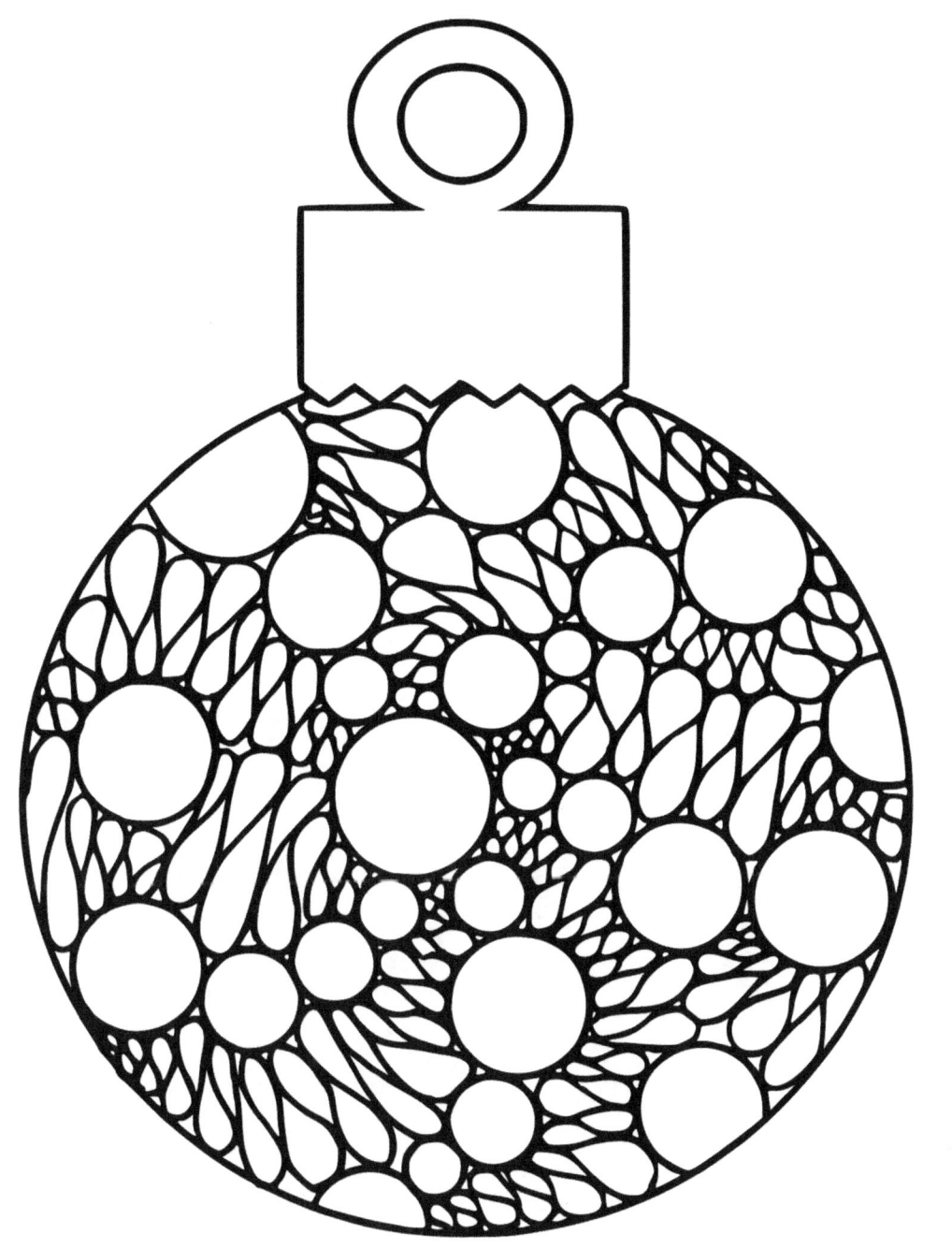

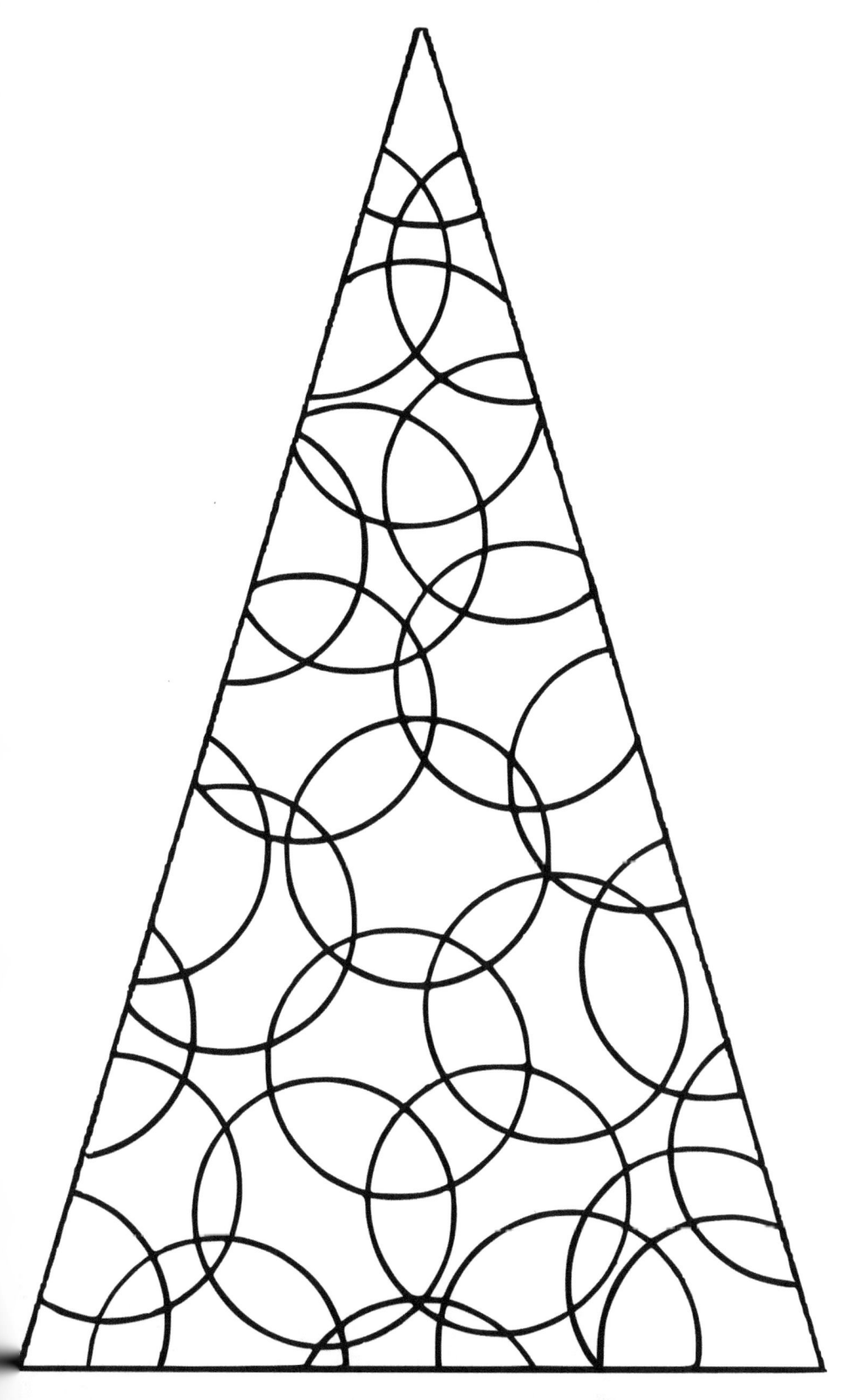

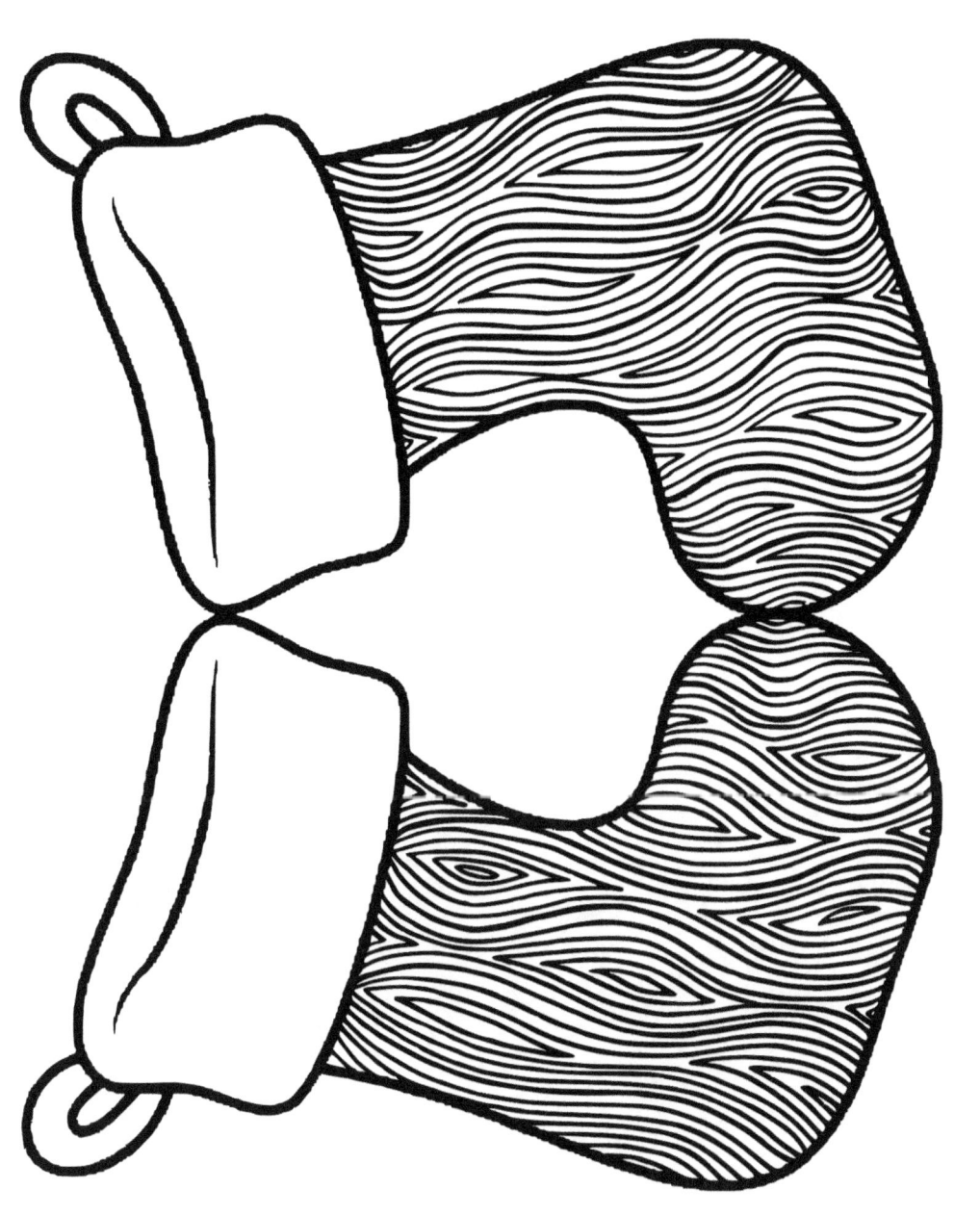

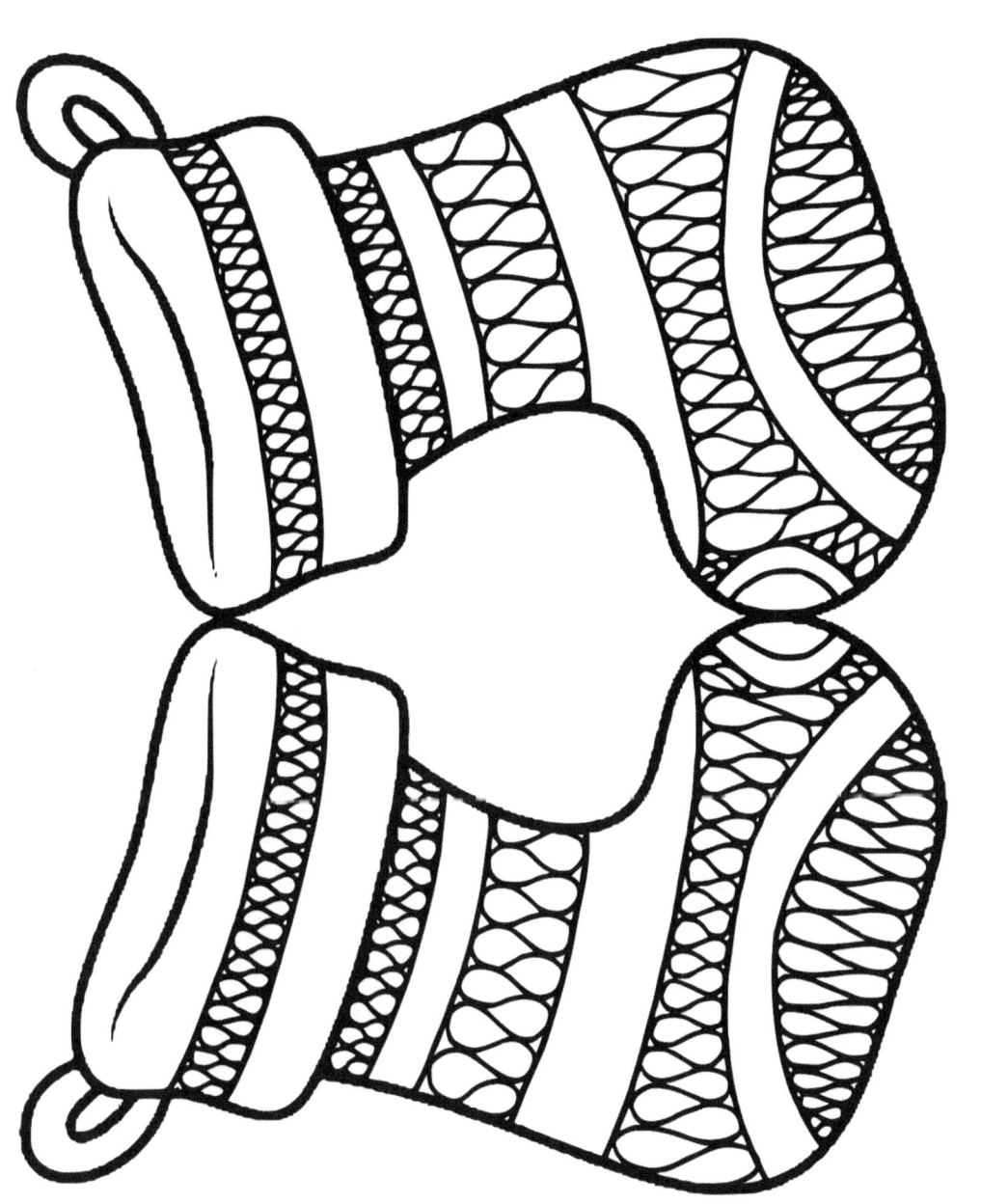

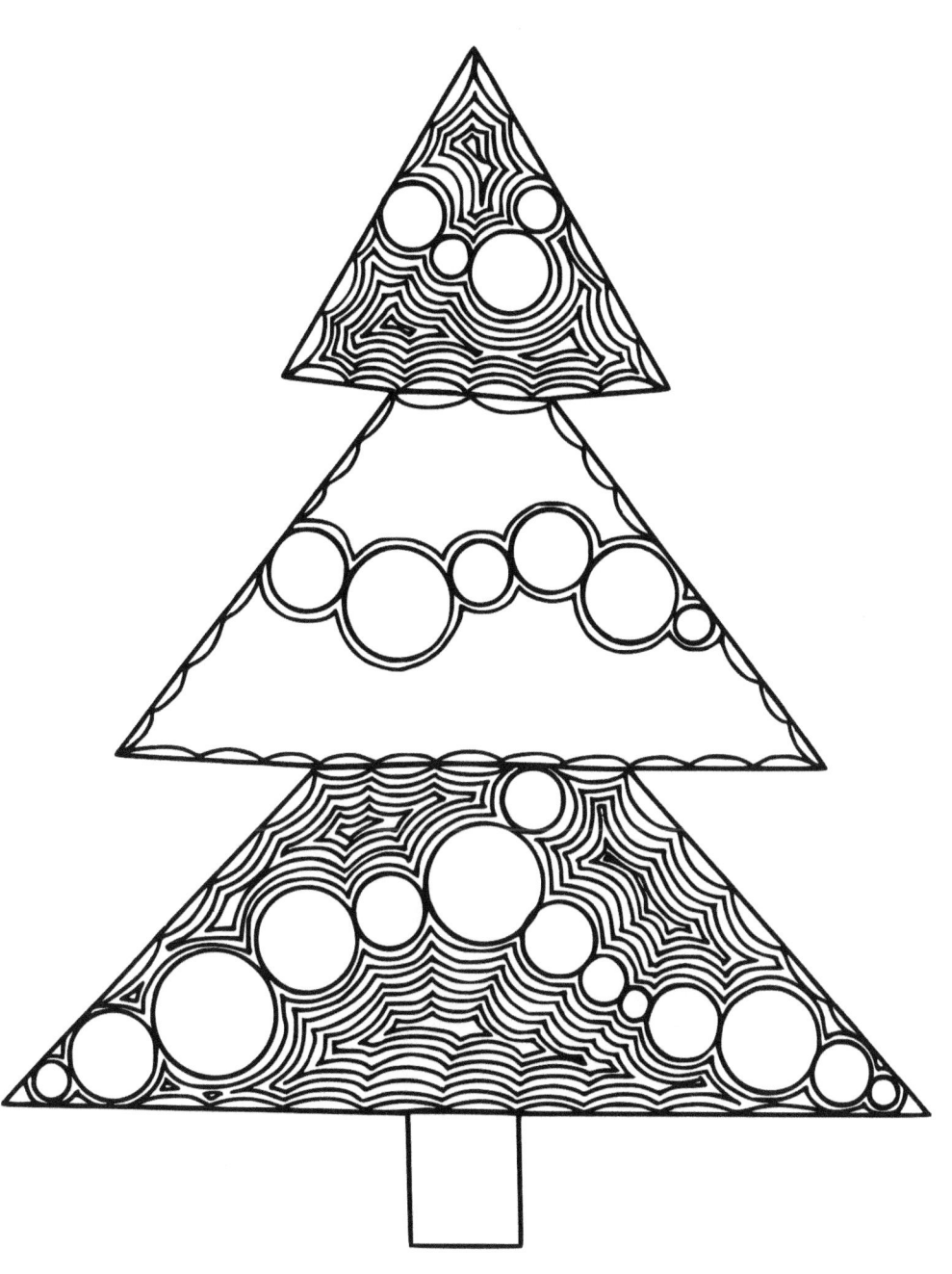

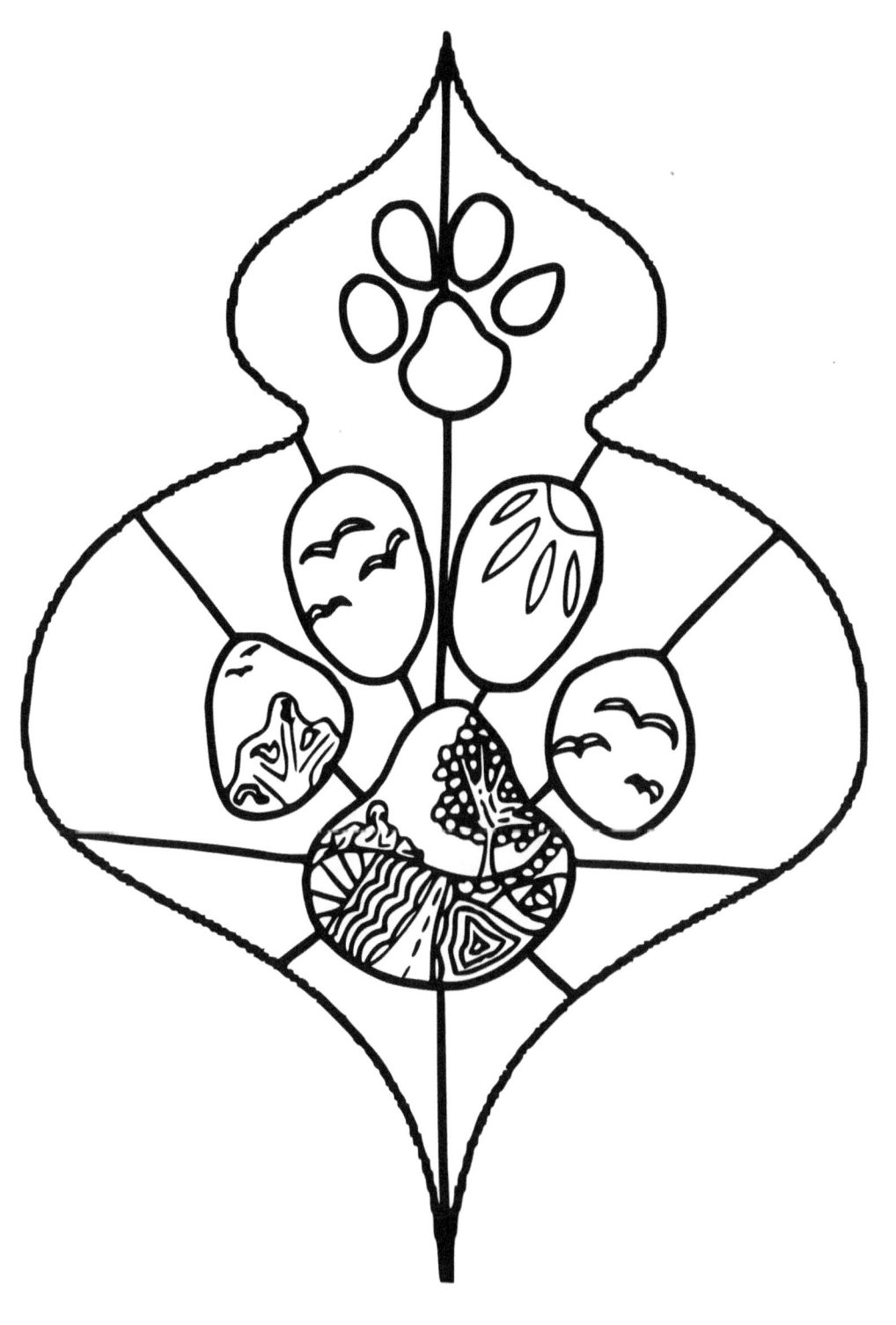

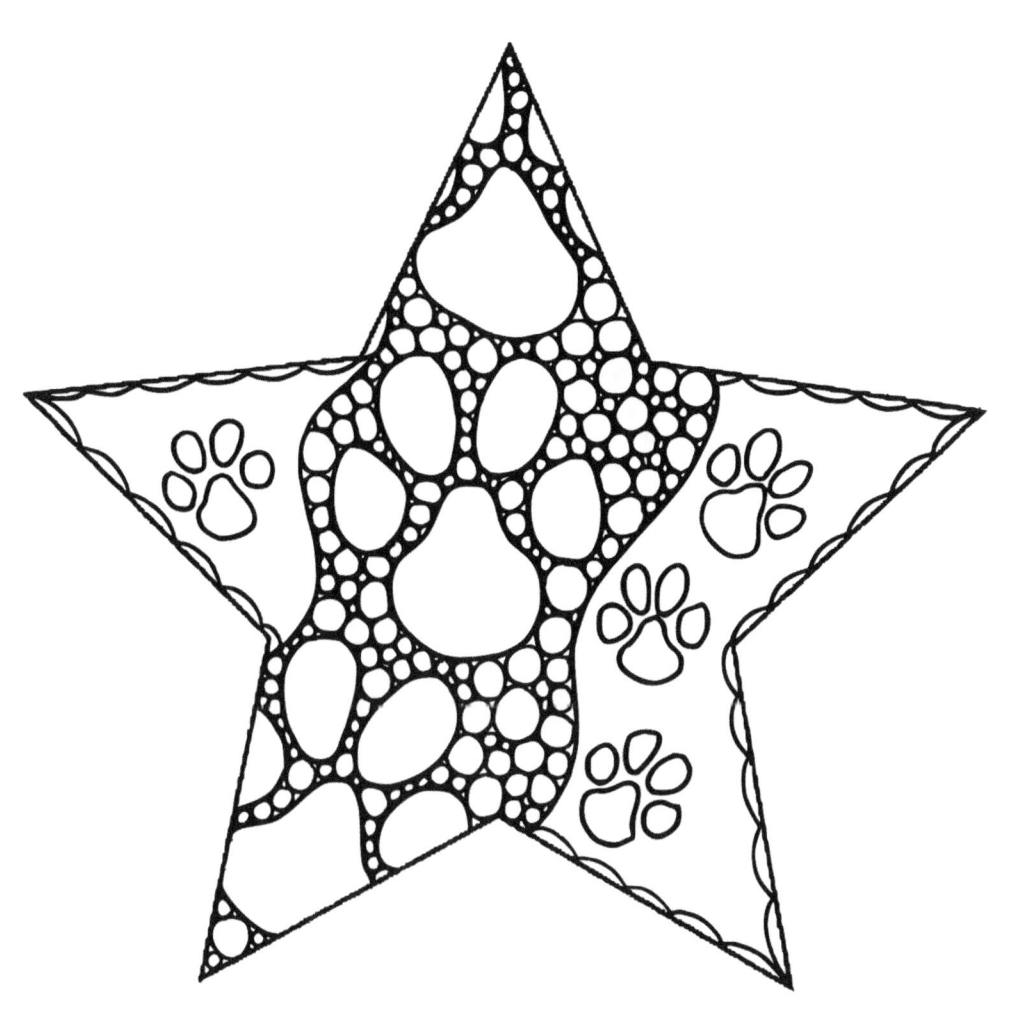

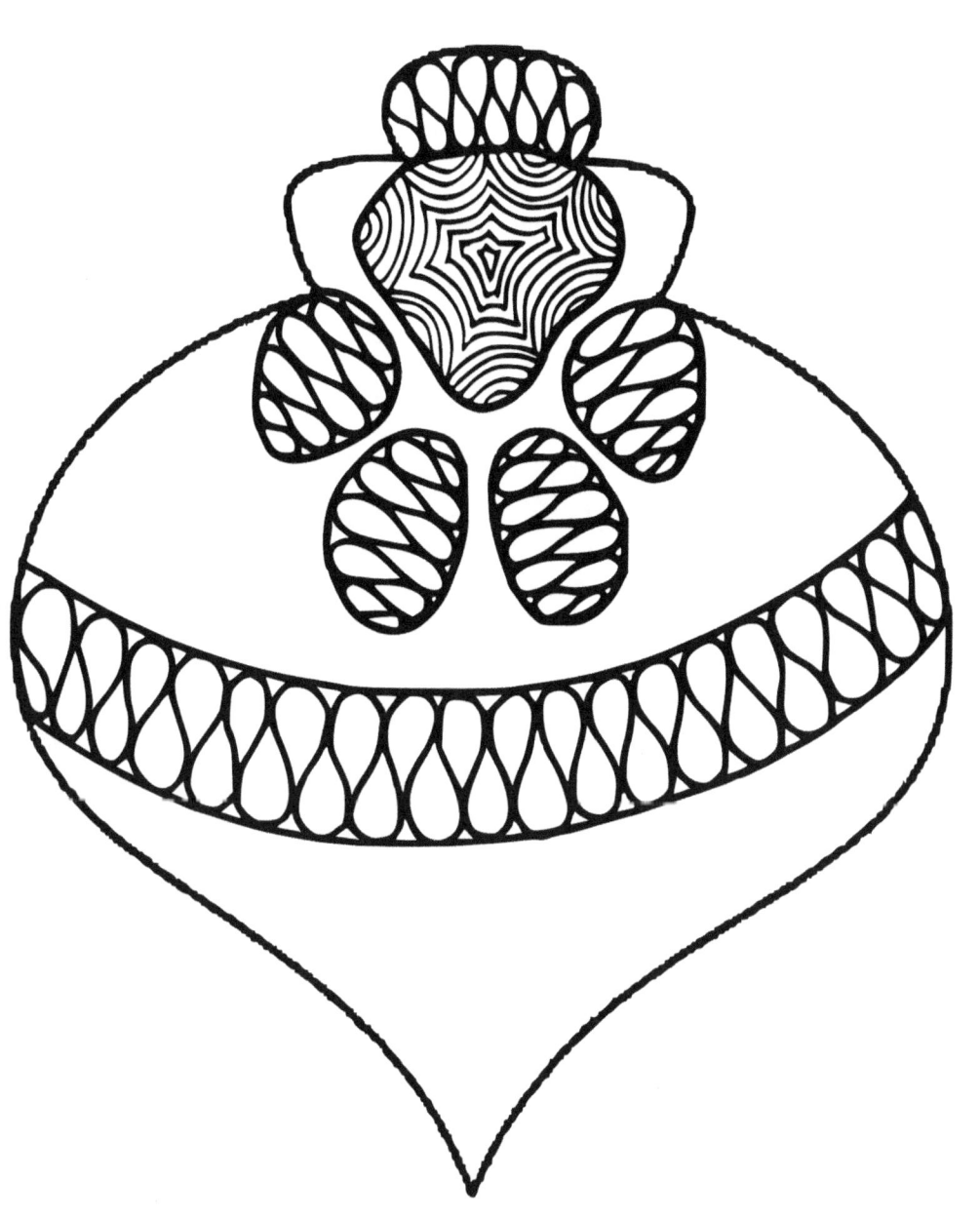

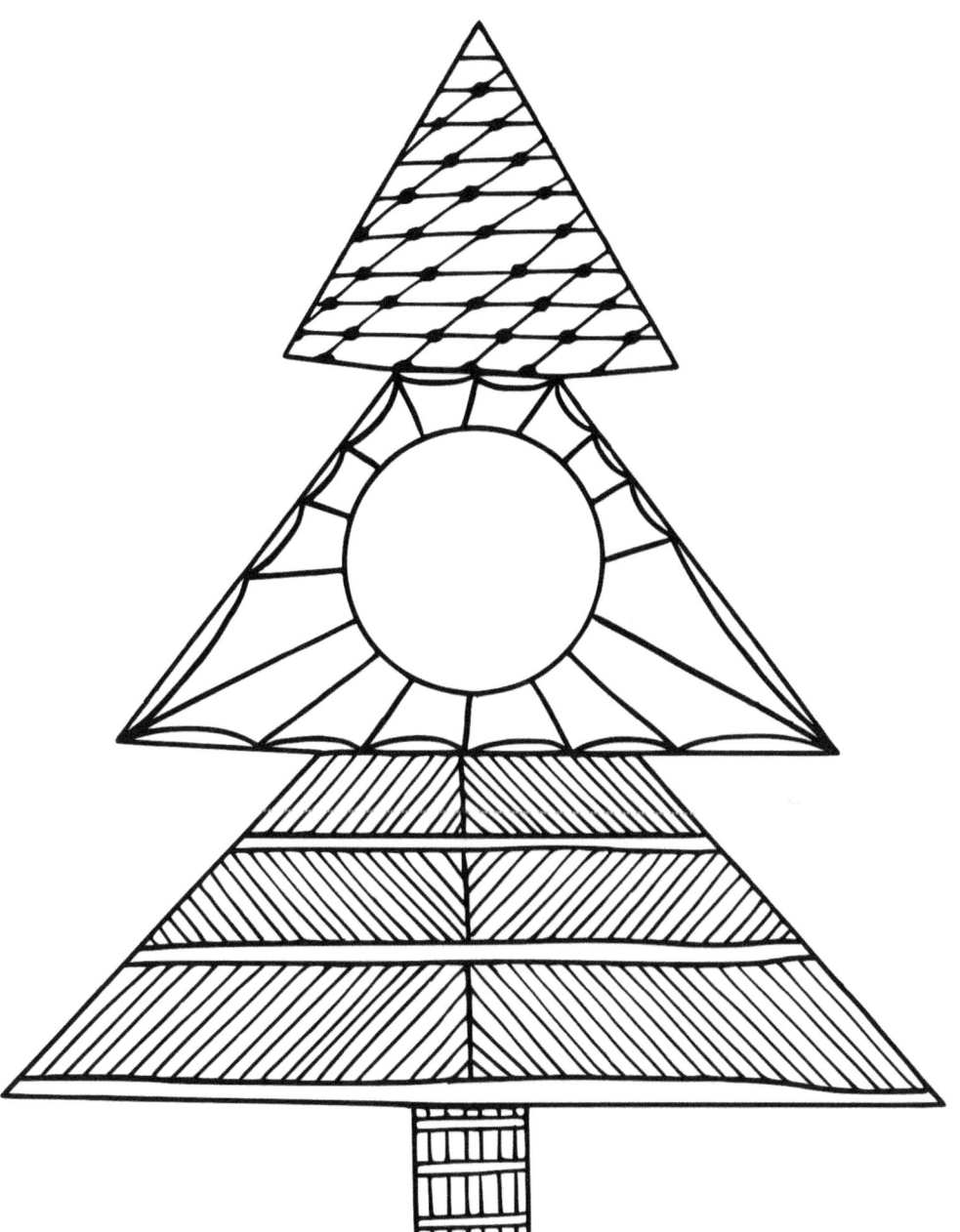

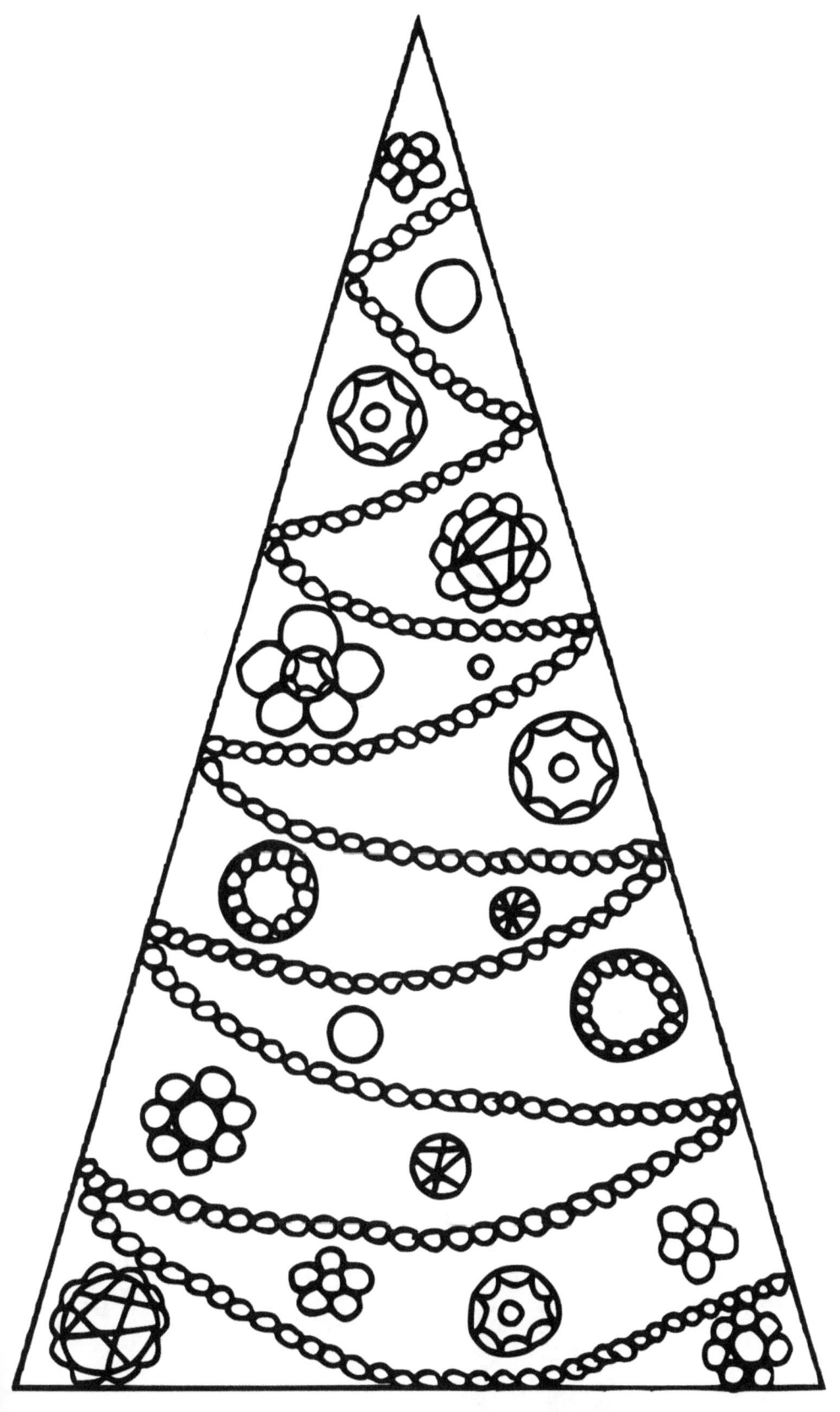

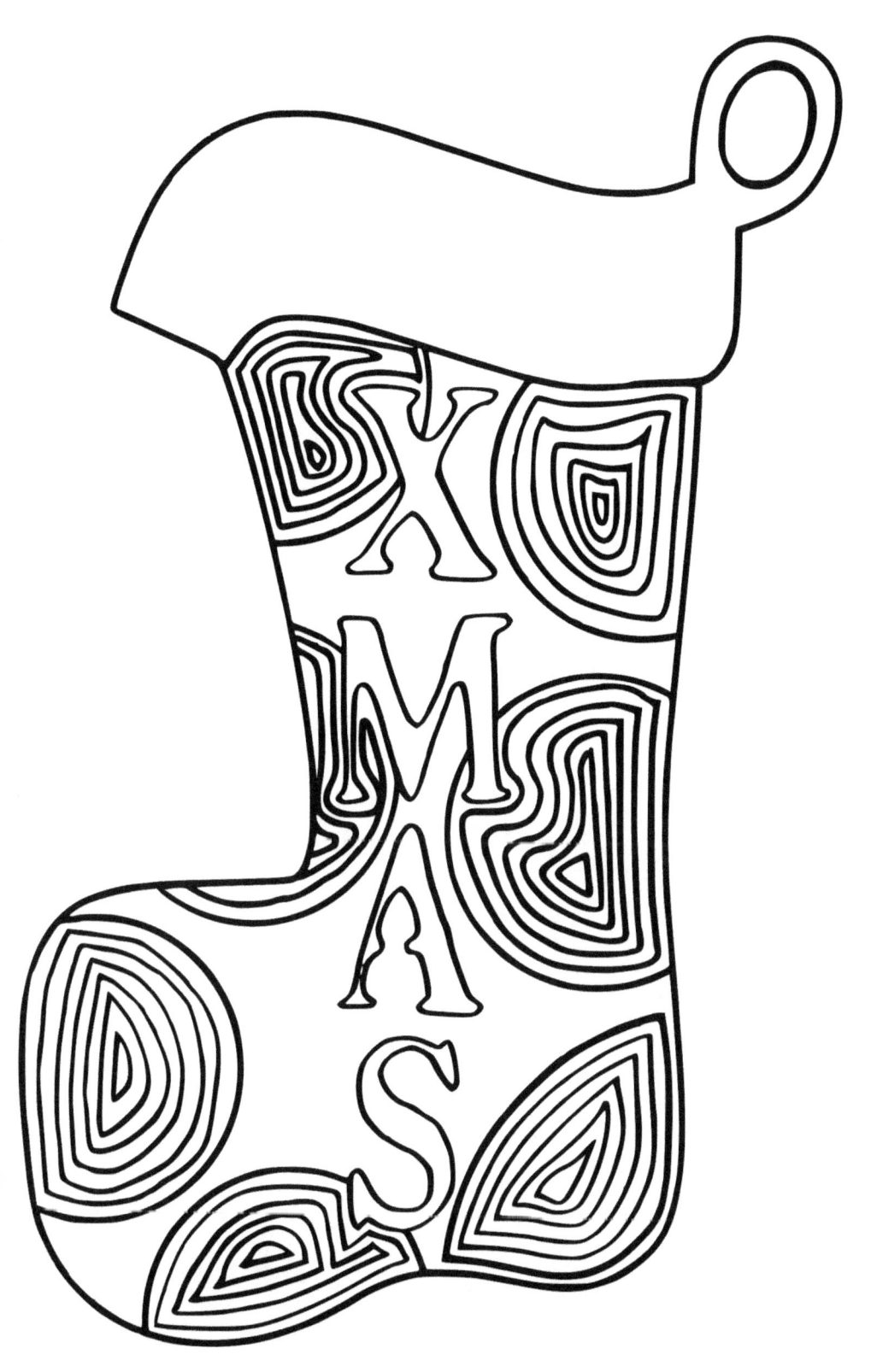

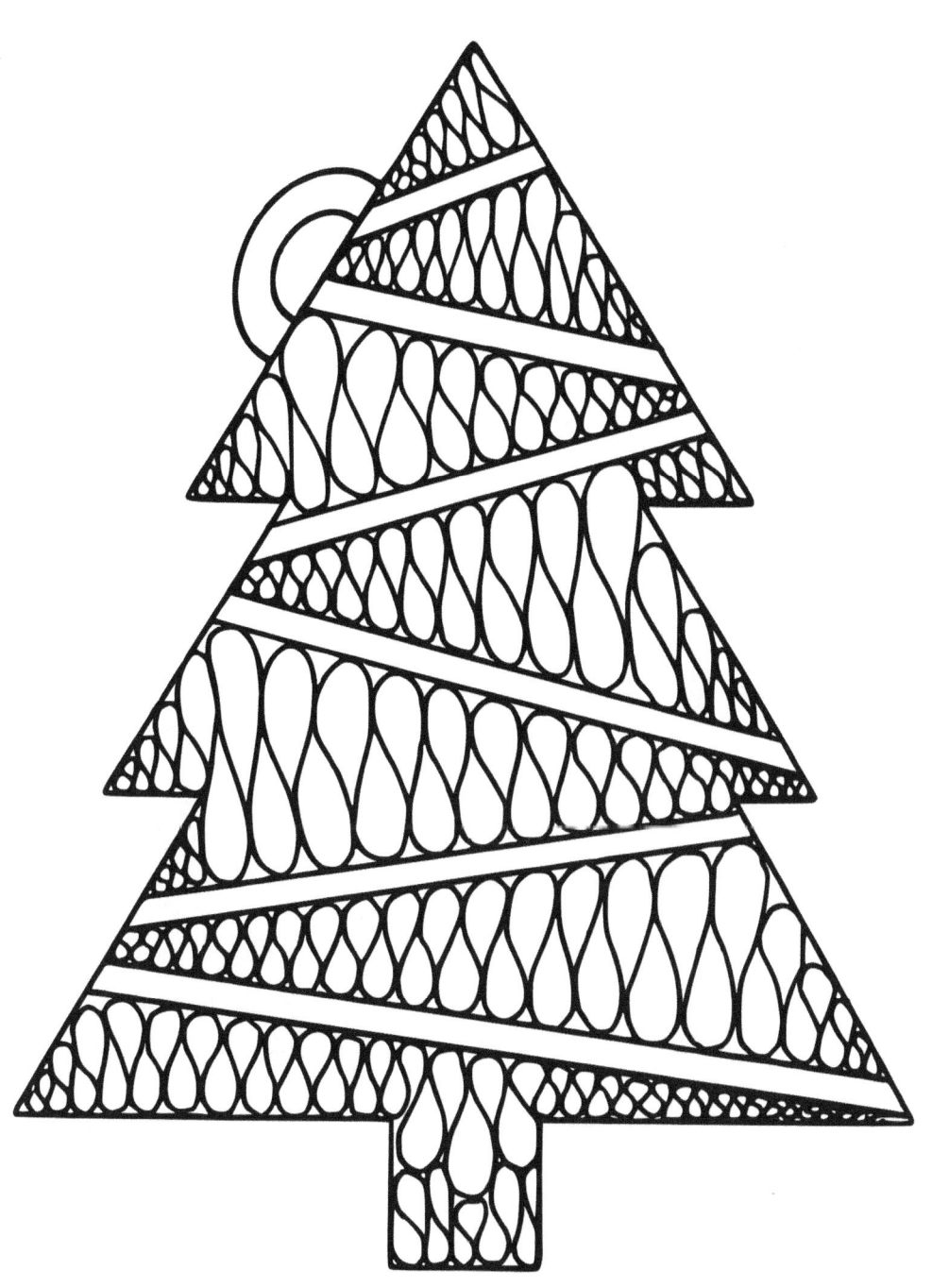

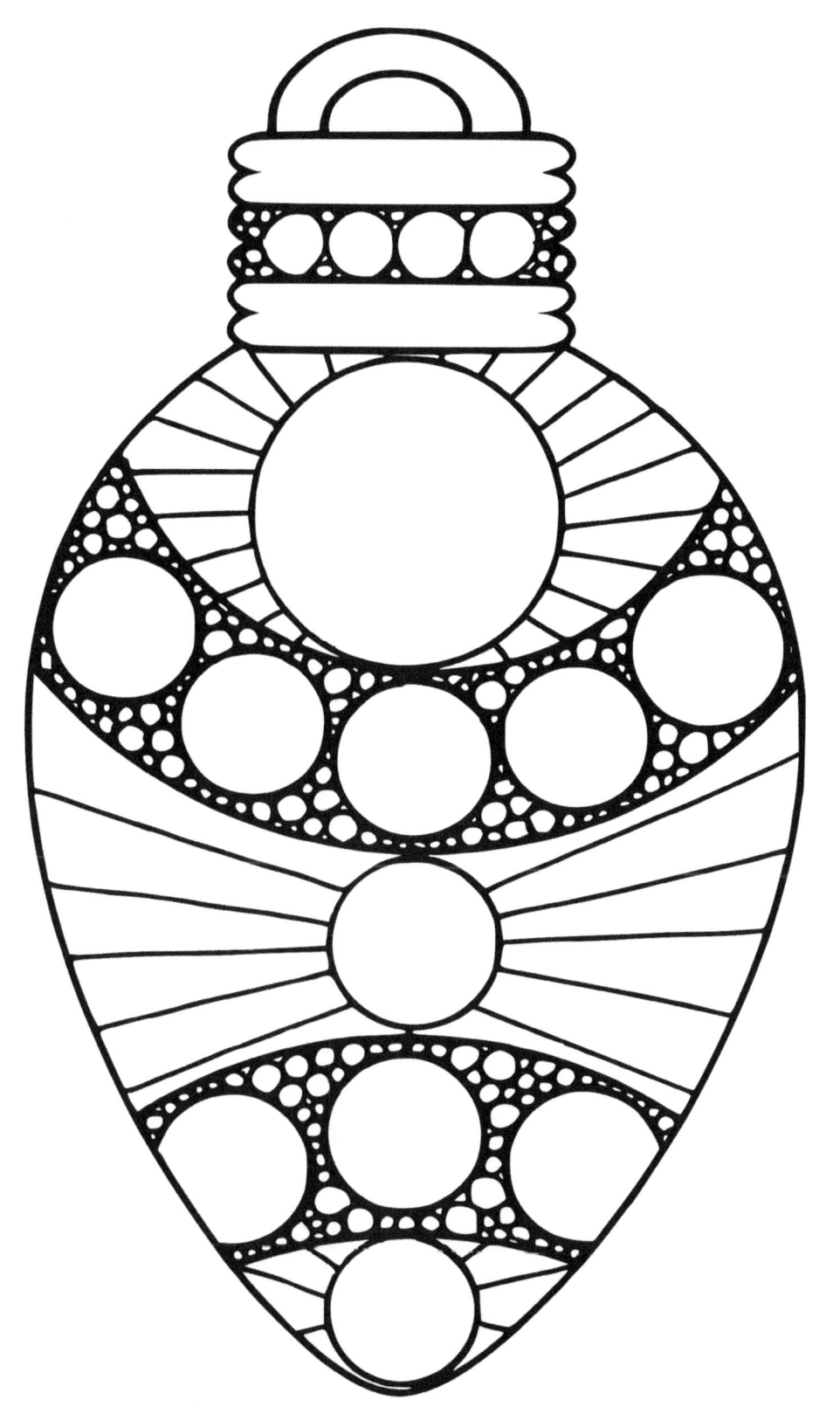

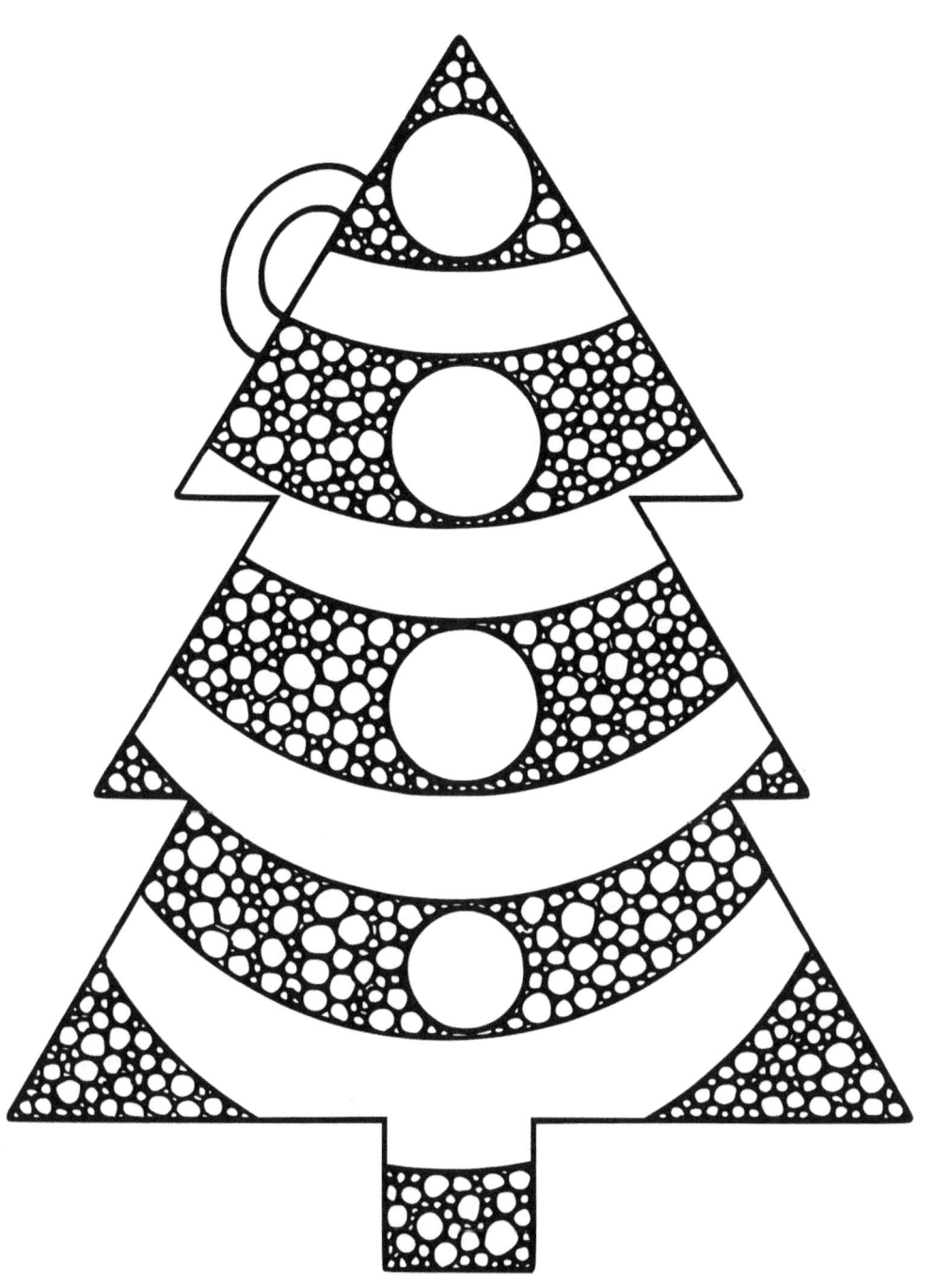

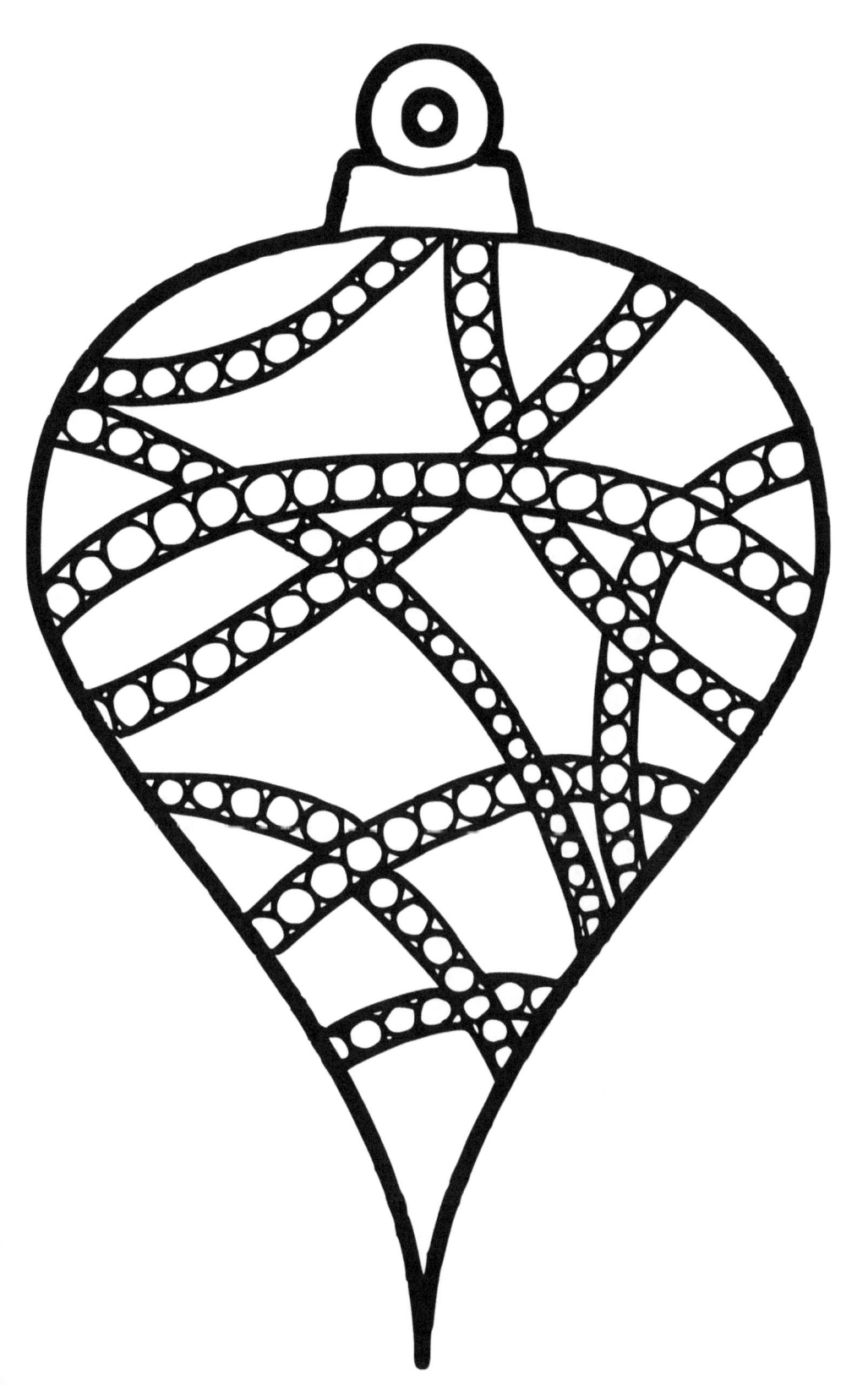

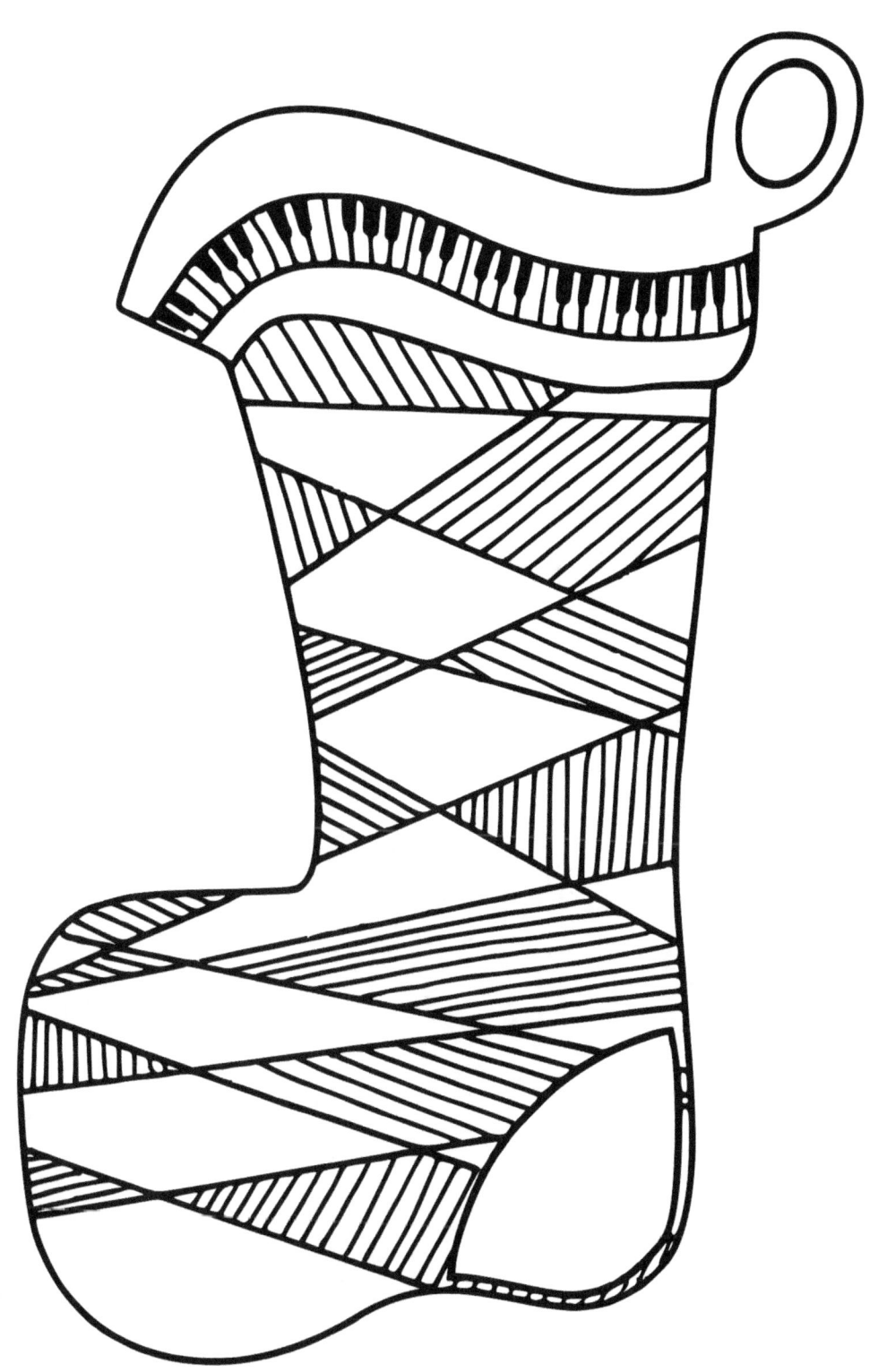

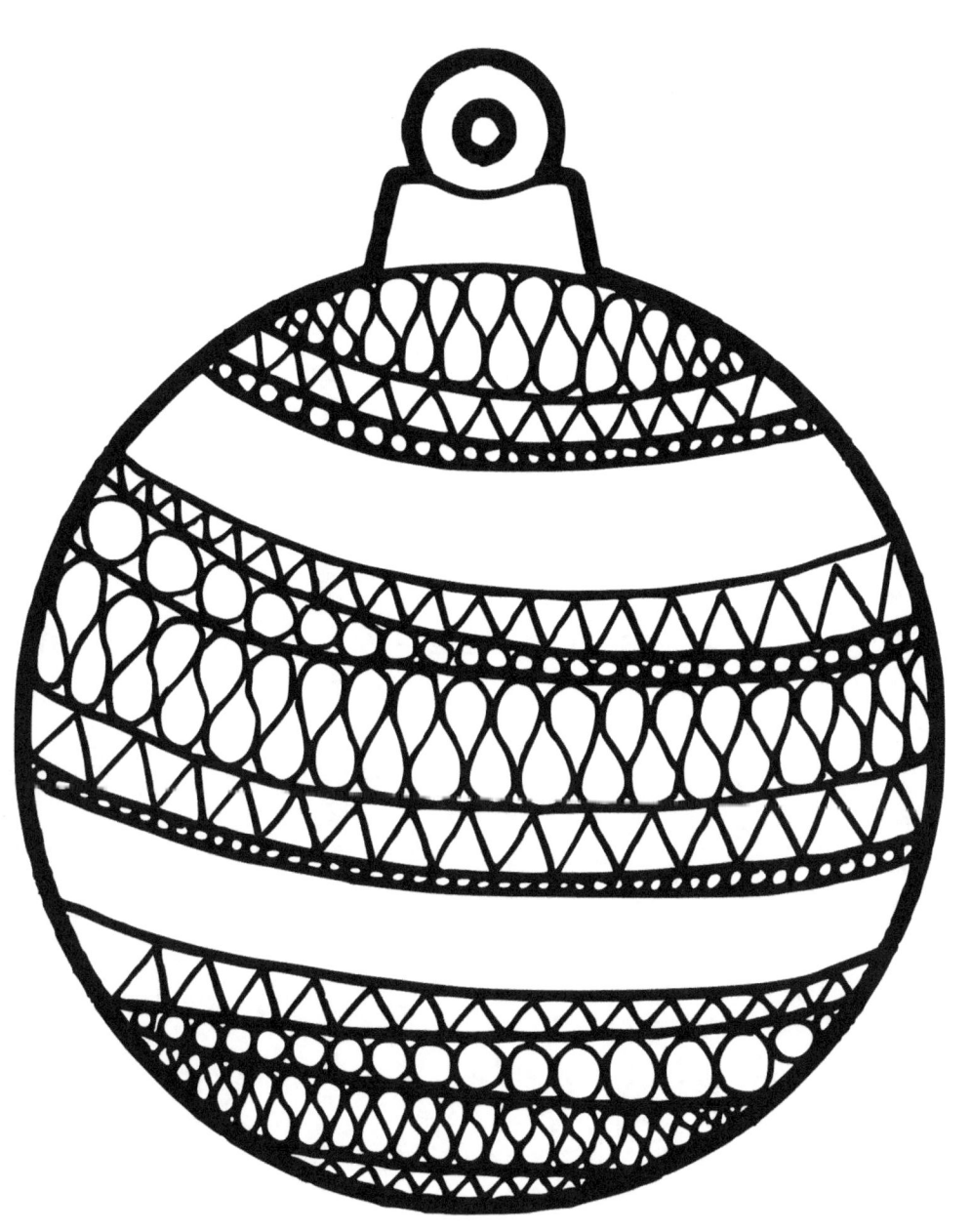

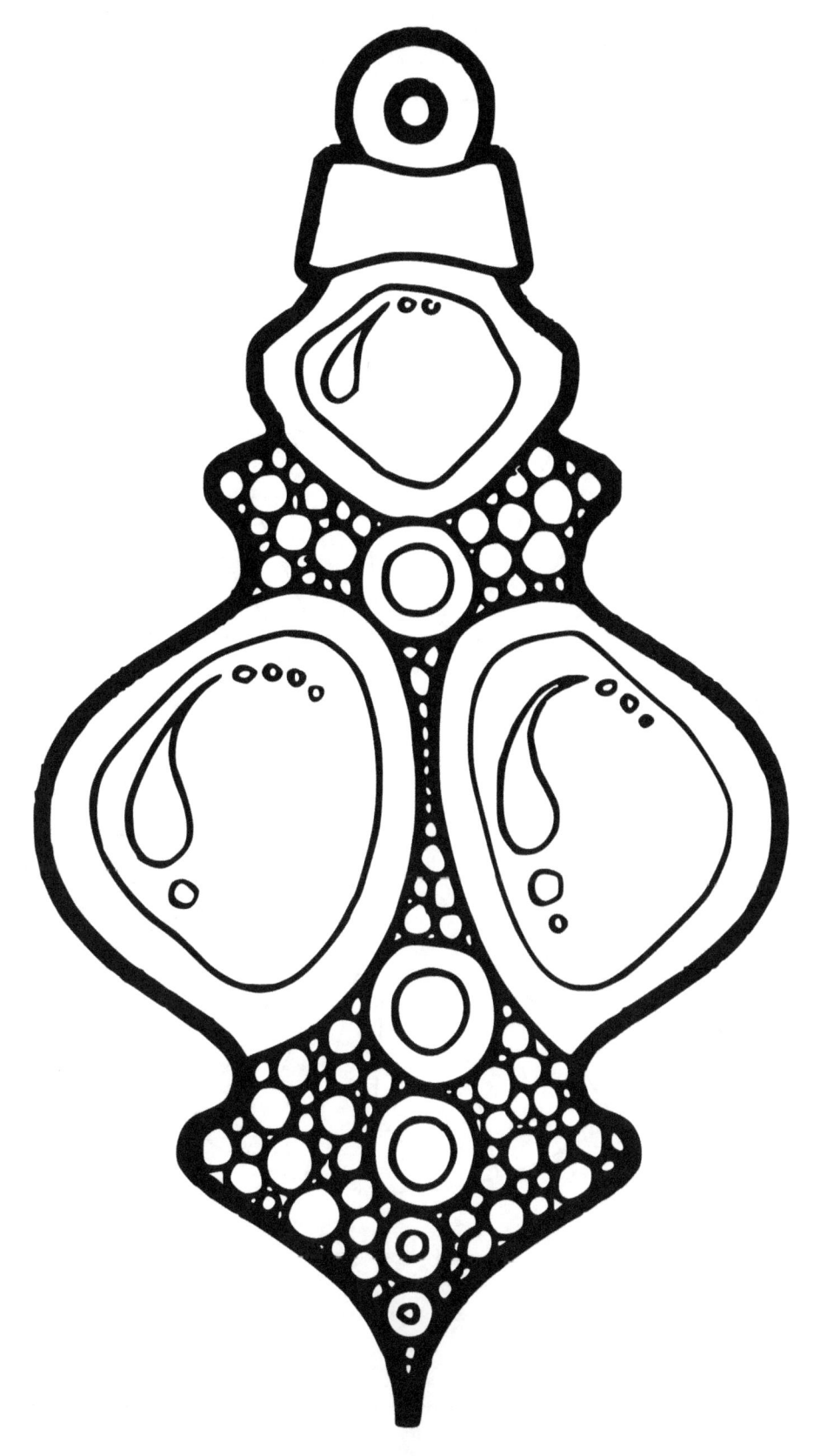

Test your colors here on the templates from

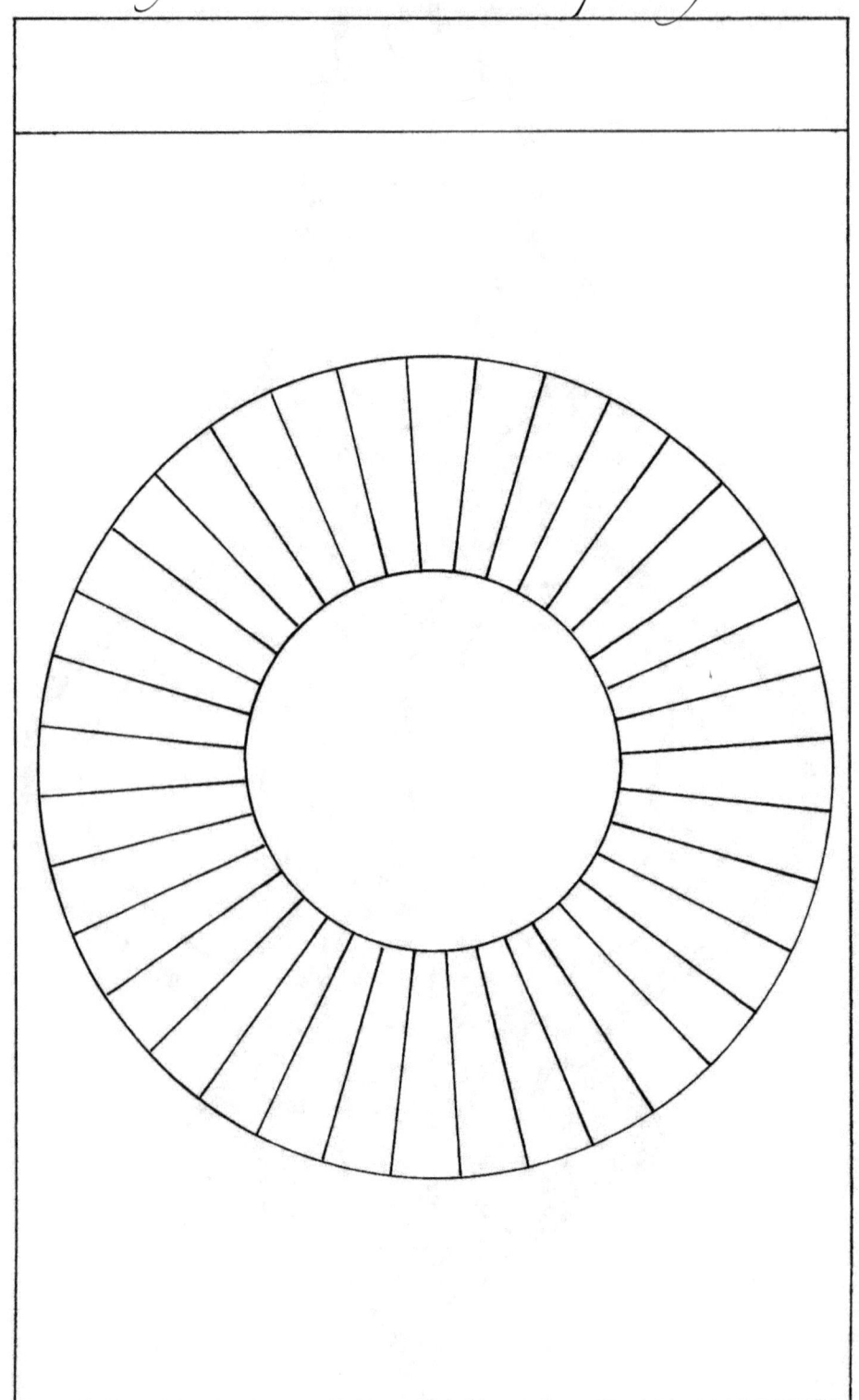

"My Pocket Coloring Companion"

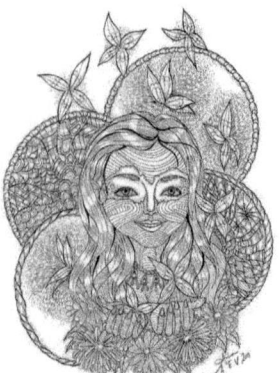 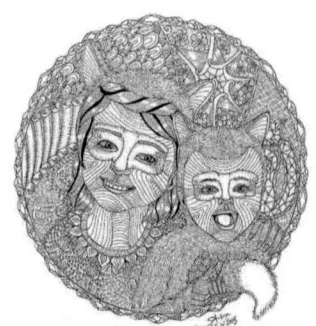 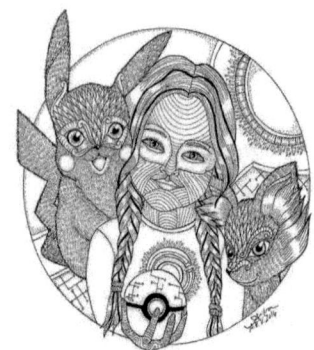

Interested in getting your own personal Coloring page?

Digital Portrait commission by alfred
Size: 12"x18" in size
Format: high quality printable PDF files
Final pieces will be:
1 Black and white
1 colored piece in PDF formats
Both signed by the artist
Price: 40 dollars
Maximum 3 subjects on one commision piece
Inquiries just message on his Facebook page

Alfred E. Villanueva
Philippines
Facebook : viworksart2015

www.ingramcontent.com/pod-product-compliance
Lightning Source LLC
Chambersburg PA
CBHW050209230526
45470CB00001B/308